A Special Issue of
Cognition & Emotion

How Distinctive is Affective Processing?

Guest Editors

Andreas B. Eder
University of Jena, Germany

Bernhard Hommel
*Leiden University Institute for Psychological
Research & Leiden Institute for Brain and Cognition,
The Netherlands*

and

Jan de Houwer
Ghent University, Belgium

T0347259

Psychology Press
Taylor & Francis Group
LONDON AND NEW YORK

First published 2008 by Psychology Press
27 Church Road, Hove, East Sussex BN3 2FA

Simultaneously published in the USA and Canada
by Psychology Press
711 Third Avenue, New York, NY 10017

First issued in paperback 2015

Psychology Press is an imprint of the Taylor & Francis Group, an informa business

© 2008 by Psychology Press

All rights reserved. No part of this book may be reprinted or
reproduced or utilised in any form or by any electronic,
mechanical, or other means, now known or hereafter invented,
including photocopying and recording, or in any information
storage or retrieval system, without permission in writing from
the publishers.

British Library Cataloguing in Publication Data
A catalogue record for this book is available from the British Library

ISBN 13: 978-1-138-88317-8 (pbk)
ISBN 13: 978-1-84169-814-4 (hbk)

ISSN: 0269-9931

Cover design by Hybert Design
Typeset in Ireland by Datapage International, Dublin

Contents*

COGNITION AND EMOTION
2007, 21 (6), 1137–1154

How distinctive is affective processing?
On the implications of using cognitive paradigms
to study affect and emotion

Andreas B. Eder

University of Jena, Jena, Germany

Bernhard Hommel

University of Leiden, Leiden, The Netherlands

Jan De Houwer

Ghent University, Ghent, Belgium

Influential theories on affect and emotion propose a fundamental differentiation between emotion and cognition, and research paradigms designed to test them focus on differences rather than similarities between affective and cognitive processes. This research orientation is increasingly challenged by the widespread and successful use of cognitive research paradigms in the study of affect and emotion—a challenge with far-reaching implications. Where and on what basis should theorists draw the line between cognition and emotion, and when is it useful to do so? Should researchers build more global, integrative models of cognition and emotion, or should they rely on local, content-specific models that draw attention to a differentiation between affective and cognitive processes? This special issue compiles different viewpoints on fundamental issues in the relationship between affect and cognition.

INTRODUCTION

Many researchers have argued that affective processing is fundamentally different from cognitive processing (e.g., LeDoux, 1998; Zajonc, 1980). However, recent research on affect and emotion relies heavily on cognitive methods and cognitive or cognitively inspired theorising: sequential priming (e.g., Fazio, Sanbonmatsu, Powell, & Kardess, 1986; Klauer & Musch, 2003)

Correspondence should be addressed to: Andreas B. Eder, Department of Psychology, University of Jena, Am Steiger 3/Haus 1, D-07743 Jena, Germany.
E-mail: Andreas.Eder@uni-jena.de

© 2007 Psychology Press, an imprint of the Taylor & Francis Group, an Informa business
www.psypress.com/cogemotion   DOI: 10.1080/02699930701437386

and task-switching (e.g., Dreisbach & Goschke, 2004), Simon tasks (e.g., De Houwer & Eelen, 1998) and Stroop tasks (e.g., De Houwer & Hermans, 1994; Williams, Mathews, & MacLeod, 1996), visual search tasks (e.g., Harris & Pashler, 2004; Öhman, Lundqvist, & Esteves, 2001), memory recall and recognition tasks (e.g., Bradley, Greenwald, Petry, & Lang, 1992; Eich & Metcalfe, 1989; Hamann, Ely, Grafton, & Kilts, 1999), attentional blink (e.g., Anderson, 2005; Keil & Ihssen, 2004), and startle-reflex paradigms (e.g., Bradley, Cuthbert, & Lang, 1990; Vrana, Spence, & Lang, 1988) are just a few of the many cognitive paradigms that were adapted in a strikingly successful manner to study human affect and emotion. In view of the apparent success of the cognitive approach in addressing affective phenomena one might ask how distinctive affective processing might be. Hence, how sure can we be that the mechanisms of affective processing are sufficiently unique to justify the claim of a specialised affective system on the psychological or neurophysiological level? Are cognitive paradigms appropriate for the identification of those affect-specific principles, or do they primarily uncover general information processing rules that are also applicable to affective information? How can research disentangle the possible complex blend of distinctive and general process contributions to affect and emotion? Is "hot cognition" what the term suggests: "hot" affective information processed by "cold" information principles? This special issue presents different viewpoints and state-of-the-art research addressing those questions, in an attempt to stimulate a broader discussion of the relationship between emotion and cognition.

In the following, we will briefly describe a number of reasons for why cognitive paradigms have become so popular in research on human emotion. Then we will critically examine some frequently encountered arguments for the affective distinctiveness, followed by a discussion of methodological possibilities for disentangling affect-specific and general processes.

THE RISE OF COGNITIVE PARADIGMS IN RESEARCH ON AFFECT AND EMOTION

The psychology of affect and emotion is challenged by particularly demanding complexities in its research methodologies. Affective and emotional states appear to be elusive and difficult to measure, and ethical considerations curtail the possibilities of experimental manipulation. Such difficulties have resulted in a long-time neglect of affect and emotion in psychological research during the twentieth century. In the last two decades, however, that picture has fundamentally changed. Modern research on affect and emotion is thriving with the availability of new psychophysiological and behavioural methods, and research paradigms originally developed for the investigation of cognitive processes have contributed much to this methodological advancement. What are the exact reasons for the current prevalence of cognitive paradigms in affect and emotion research?

In line with research into cognitive processes, early mainstream research into affect and emotion relied on introspective methods and self-report measures (e.g., James, 1884). Following the methodological advancements arising from Behaviourism, the reliance of emotion research on phenomenology was criticised on methodological and empirical grounds (e.g., Johnston, 1905; Rosenfeld & Baer, 1969), culminating in the tightly controlled behavioural methods that are now characteristic of modern cognitive psychology. Response latency and accuracy measurements increasingly replaced self-report and introspective observation with a consequent increase in conceptual clarification on the common ground of paradigmatic definitions. It did not take long before these new experimental procedures were applied in emotion research, and this was done for several reasons besides those arising from the standard objections against self-report and introspection (for which see Nisbett & Wilson, 1977; Schwarz, 1999).

First, self-report measures were amenable only to conscious, reportable feelings and ignored a range of affective states that are difficult to express verbally. Second, and more important for current theories of affect and emotion, self-report is not very suited to tapping automatic affective processes. This problem became particularly acute as theories on affect and emotion increasingly emphasised the importance of automatic affective processes (e.g., Robinson, 1998; Zajonc, 1980). In their search for appropriate methods, emotion researchers adapted paradigms that were developed for research into automatic cognitive processes. Third, the importance of cognitive theories of emotion evoked a need for cognitive research paradigms as a method of first choice. In *appraisal-based emotion theories*, for instance, cognitive processing stages are essential and determinative elements of emotions, and thus are of primary research interest. Moreover, every influential theory of emotion allows for some sort of interaction between emotion and cognition in its explanation of emotional behaviour. Such theoretical considerations undoubtedly influenced the move towards the use of cognitive paradigms in emotion research.

A fourth reason for the strong reliance on cognitive paradigms in affective research was the apparent success of cognitive methods in the explanation of human reasoning and behaviour. The experimental analysis of information processing enriched not only cognitive perspectives but also emotion theories (e.g., Bower, 1981; Lang, 1979; Lazarus, Averill, & Opton, 1970; Mandler, 1980). The productive cognitive approach to behaviour research occurred at a time when appropriate alternative methods for emotion psychology were lacking. The limitations of traditional methods such as self-report, and animal research were already obvious and under debate (e.g., Nisbett

& Wilson, 1977; Ristau, 1983). Similarly, the application of existing biophysiological methods was costly and inappropriate to phenomenologically oriented emotion research. The existence of successful cognitive research paradigms and concomitant lack of specific alternatives for emotion research caused many researchers in this field to resort to cognitive paradigms.

ARGUMENTS FOR AFFECTIVE DISTINCTIVENESS

Despite the growing use of cognitive paradigms in research on affect and emotion, this research was most often driven by the underlying assumption that affective processing is to a large extent qualitatively different from cognitive processing. This is, for instance, evidenced by the fact that in many studies on affective processing, not only affective but also nonaffective stimuli are used in an attempt to demonstrate that the observed effect occurred only for the affective stimuli (e.g., Murphy & Zajonc, 1993). In this section, we will review some of the arguments that have been raised in support of the idea that affective processing is distinct from cognitive processing.

Phenomenological arguments

The assumption of affective distinctiveness often rests on qualitative differences in the phenomenological surface of affect and cognition: Emotion and feelings are typically experienced very differently than thinking or reasoning, to name just a couple of "prototypical" cognitive processes. But such phenomenological arguments do not stand closer scrutiny, because different psychological "surfaces" in no way implicate differences in the operating system below the surface. For instance, reading a written word produces a very different experience than hearing that word pronounced— and, yet, the underlying mechanisms are very similar (e.g., Levelt, Roelofs, & Meyer, 1999). Moreover, affect and emotions are characterised by a wide diversity of phenomenological states, just think of a depression on the one hand and a state of elation on the other, yet, most researchers will group them together as emotional states. Based on a purely phenomenological criterion it is hard to see why sadness should be preferentially grouped with joy and not with creativity or mental effort to a single class of phenomena (i.e., emotions). Hence, unless one is equipped to argue that two of the most dissimilar affective states still feel more similar than the most similar pair of an affective and a cognitive state, phenomenology does not help us any further.

Content-related arguments

One may also consider that the type of information (affective vs. nonaffective) can serve as the key difference between affective and cognitive processing. However, there is little a priori reason why processing should differ more with respect to this than to any other distinction, such as living–nonliving, male–female, rich–poor, bright–dark, visual–auditory, etc. The variety of information that is "affectively processed" is huge and in no way bound to a simple dichotomy of emotional versus cognitive processing (Ekman, 2004). For example, some people might talk about the atrocities of the Nazi regime on some occasions in an affectionless manner, but on another occasions in an emphatically and terrified state. The engagement of affective processing is not purely stimulus driven but depends on an intricate complex of informational, contextual, and personal variables (e.g., Rusting & Larsen, 1998).

Embodiment arguments

Since its early days, research on affect and emotion has been distinguished by a strong interest in bodily influences on the generation of affective experiences (e.g., James, 1884; Schachter & Singer, 1962). In modern cognitive psychology, however, the mainstream of which was dominated by the computer metaphor with its distinction between "software" (mind) and "hardware" (body), the rediscovery of the mind was accompanied by the widespread neglect of the body, that is, of the fact that the mind is implemented in and coexists with a particular body. With those diverging research orientations emotion researchers accumulated some interesting findings on bodily influences that were particularly challenging for disembodied cognitive accounts. One such line of evidence is the demonstration that facial feedback impacts affective experiences and judgements (see McIntosh, 1996, for a review). For instance, in the well-known study of Strack, Martin, and Stepper (1988) participants rated a cartoon for funniness while holding a pen in their mouths. One group of participants was asked to hold the pen with their puckered lips, thus tacitly inhibiting muscles involved in smiling, while another group was instructed to hold the pen between their teeth, enforcing a subtle smile. The results showed that participants with a smile-facilitating pen position felt more amused with the cartoon than participants holding the pen in a smile-inhibiting position. The unobtrusive character of the smile manipulation rendered cognitive explanations in terms of self-perception processes unlikely.

Additional evidence for unique embodied affective processing appears to come from emotional states induced or altered by psychotropic substances. Drug and body effects on affective processing seriously question a simple transfer of principles derived from disembodied information-processing models. Instead, they call for distinctive affective processing rules und structures. Note, however, that the theoretical disembodiment of information processing also delimited the power of cognitive theories to account for purely cognitive phenomena. This motivated recent theories of embodied cognition that are better suited to explain body–affect interactions (e.g., Barsalou, 1999; Glenberg, 1999; Niedenthal, Barsalou, Winkielman, Krauth-Gruber, & Ric, 2005; Rumelhart, 1997). Hence, if there is a gap between cognitive theories and affective phenomena, it is, at least, strongly reduced by the emergence of theories that focus on the embodiment of cognitive psychological processes.

Functional arguments

In view of the tremendous variety of emotion elicitors and the huge variety of affective experiences, some researchers have advocated a functional differentiation between emotion and cognition. Emotional states might recruit and direct attentional resources differently, perhaps more effectively than cognition. They might highlight opportunities and dangers in the present environmental context, which may directly interrupt ongoing behaviour whenever appropriate and rapidly mobilise adaptive approach or avoidance behaviour (e.g., Lang, Bradley, & Cuthbert, 1997; Wentura & Rothermund, 2003). Note, however, that the objections to a phenomenological differentiation also apply to a functional distinction between affect and cognition. Different emotions frequently serve different functions on the psychological and behavioural level (e.g., sadness and anger), and the same emotion might be linked to different behaviours serving different purposes. A rat frightened by painful electric shocks might either show fight behaviour (e.g., Ulrich & Azrin, 1962), flight behaviour (e.g., Blanchard & Blanchard, 1968), or no activity at all (i.e., freeze behaviour; e.g., Fanselow, 1980). Accordingly, behavioural tactics like fight-or-flight-behaviour are not uniformly and rigidly linked to emotional states, and the same affective state might instigate different behavioural tendencies depending on contextual and situational variations (cf. Frijda, 2004; Scherer, 1984), perhaps reflecting the direct interplay between cognitive interpretation and affect-based motivation.

A corollary of the assumption of adaptive functionality and the existence of evolutionary old affective systems (e.g., MacLean, 1993; see next section) is the argument that evaluative processes emerge phylogenetically and ontogenetically prior to cognitive appraisal processes (Zajonc, 1980). In fear-conditioning studies, for example, rats exhibit defensive reactions that show remarkable similarities to reactions of humans on both the behavioural and physiological level (Debiec & LeDoux, 2004). The same argument is supported by observations of alleged emotional behaviour in newborns who presumably possess only rudimentary cognitive abilities (Meltzoff & Moore, 1977). The remarkable continuity between adult emotional responses and behaviours of infants and animals suggests the involvement of simple, perhaps "pre-cognitive" processing principles. Note, however, that the inference of affective processing in animals and babies relies exclusively on observable behaviour (e.g., Camras et al., 2002), so that we do not know whether those subjects do indeed experience states that human adults would consider "emotions". Moreover, even the successful demonstration of affective and emotional behaviour in animals and toddlers in no way rules out contributions from cognitive processes. For example, a recent study of Désiré, Veissier, Despré, and Boissy (2004) showed that the occurrence of a startle or orientation reaction in lambs (*Ovis aries*) depends critically on their appraisal of the suddenness and novelty of the relevant event. Empirical studies argue against an arbitrary exclusion of cognitive processes in animals and toddlers on theoretical grounds that draw too heavily on a modelling of cognition in terms of conscious and rational thinking (cf. Clore & Ortony, 2000; Lazarus, 1982).

In an attempt to attach the functional argument closer to evolutionary theory some emotion theorists have pointed out that even the most diverse emotional behaviours are serving the paramount goals of survival and general well-being (e.g., Tooby & Cosmides, 1990). However, the same adaptivity reasoning applies to cognitive processes. Perception–action systems are tuned to significant environmental affordances in the service of the selection of (adaptive) actions, but they are still considered to subserve cognitive functioning (e.g., Gibson, 1979; Milner & Goodale, 1995; Tucker & Ellis, 1998). Indeed, it is difficult to see why automatic response preparation triggered by the valence of masked or unmasked stimuli (e.g., Chen & Bargh, 1999; Murphy & Zajonc, 1993; but see also Rotteveel & Phaf, 2004) is taken to support the assumption of particularly adaptive, precognitive functions of affective processing even though nonaffective stimulus dimensions like spatial location or shape have exactly the same effect on behaviour (e.g., Eimer, 1995; Eimer & Schlaghecken, 1998; Neumann & Klotz, 1994). Likewise, the enhanced localisation of an angry or threatening face intermixed with an array of neutral facial expressions (e.g., Hansen & Hansen, 1988; Öhman et al., 2001; but see also Lipp, Derakshan, Waters, & Logies, 2004; Purcell, Steward, & Skov, 1996) is functionally very similar to the preferred attentional orientation to novel, unexpected nonaffective items within a visual array of familiar items (e.g., Johnston, Hawley, Plewe, & Elliott, 1990). On closer inspection many functional analogies can be drawn between "specific" emotional and general cognitive processing effects, which render isolated demonstrations of the "adaptive" functions of affective processing uninformative. Moreover, functional diversity not only divides cognition and emotion (if it does at all) but it also characterises the relationship between functions within cognition (e.g., Milner & Goodale, 1995) and within emotion (e.g., Frijda, 2004). In other words, the functional difference between some cognitive processes may be no smaller than between some cognitive and affective functions. Accordingly, unless it can be demonstrated that some basic characteristics are still shared by *all* affective but *no* cognitive functions, the functional argument does not support the distinction between cognition and emotion but, if anything, tends to eliminate it.

Neuroanatomical arguments

As mentioned above, some researchers have suggested the existence of a phylogenetically old neural system underlying affective and emotional behaviour. In the pioneering work of Papez (1937) and MacLean (1949) this neural network was identified as a *limbic system* that comprised a set of subcortical structures. Although some key structures turned out to be less involved than originally thought (e.g., the hippocampus), the limbic-system theory survived and became popular as the neural circuit mediating emotions (LeDoux, 2000). The last two decades have seen an explosion of research on emotional brain circuits, many studies showing the amygdala to be an important hub in the processing of danger- and fear-related stimuli (see Davis & Whalen, 2001, for a review). For instance, functional imaging studies have shown that the amygdaloid complex is more sensitive to fearful and angry faces than to happy ones (Breiter et al., 1996), and damage to the amygdala is known to impair recognition of fear expressions (Vuilleumier, 2005).

Important for the present discussion is the finding that the amygdala is not only activated by projections from the sensory areas in the neocortex but also by a more direct pathway from the thalamus, a subcortical region that was previously assumed to relay crude sensory information to neocortical sensory areas only (LeDoux, 1998). As a result, the direct thalamo–amygdala pathway might enable full-blown affective reactions, even though it bypasses the neocortex, which is supposed to be necessary for cognitive appraisals. Based on those findings LeDoux (1998) concluded that "emotion and cognition are best thought of as separate but interacting mental functions mediated by separate but interacting brain systems" (p. 69). He specifies this belief with the proposal of several dissociations between emotional and cognitive functions. For instance, the evaluative significance of an object is assumed to be processed separately from, and potentially faster than, its perceptual and semantic attributes (but see Mandler & Shebo, 1983). Furthermore, LeDoux proposed that emotional appraisals performed in the amygdala system are intimately connected to response control networks that narrow down the possible response options. Certain emotional appraisals are thereby connected to particular, evolutionarily functional, response patterns that involve specific bodily adaptations, explaining, for example, a quick withdrawal response in a fear reaction to a snake. Cognitive processing, on the contrary, allows for flexibility of action, and LeDoux assumed that mere thoughts were typically not associated with bodily sensations.

This sketch of a self-contained, highly specialised emotional brain system suggests a comparable degree of specialisation and self-containment on the psychological level. Although emotional and cognitive processes ordinarily go hand in hand, they may thus be fundamentally different because they arise in different brain networks and may frequently serve different and even conflicting goals. Note, however, that the compartmentalisation of the brain in emotional and cognitive networks depends critically on the localisation of clearly defined mental functions in the brain. If new neuroscientific evidence questions the exclusiveness of the functional localisation, the derived distinctiveness will also be in question. Moreover, even though the available data from neuroscientific studies are consistent with the claim that *particular* emotions (fear, in the case of LeDoux's work) are associated with brain areas that are not shared by *particular* cognitive processes, they in no way justify the claim that emotion-related processes are more similar to each other than are emotion-related and cognition-related processes. In other words, the dissimilarities between some affective mechanisms may be greater than between some affective and some cognitive processes—which would undermine, rather than support, a general distinction between cognition and emotion.

DISENTANGLING AFFECTIVE AND COGNITIVE MECHANISMS

The question of whether affective and cognitive processing are distinctive can be reduced to the question of whether evidence can be found for effects that are driven exclusively by the affective properties of stimuli or participants and that cannot be reduced to the operation of more general cognitive processes. Such evidence conclusive to the status of distinctiveness requires a special experimental setup that goes beyond the typical research designs employed in affect and emotion research. In the latter paradigms task performance in critical trials with affectively charged stimuli (e.g., threat words) is most commonly contrasted to a comparison performance in trials with affectively neutral, but in all other aspects matched stimuli (e.g., transport-related words). An emotional effect will be inferred if the task performance under affective stimulus conditions differs significantly from the task performance in the nonaffective comparison condition. Note, however, that emotional effects obtained in this way do not reveal anything about the distinctiveness of the processes driving them, because such paradigms do not test the possibility that the effects are driven by the specific stimulus configuration or by the processing goals implemented through the task setting. For example, there is the possibility that a faster detection of threat stimuli embedded in an array of affectively neutral stimuli depends more on the input configuration in the specific task setting (e.g., the popping out of distinct information as a figure before the background of an otherwise homogenous stimulus array) rather than on the informational value of the input itself (e.g., the threatening information). Consequently, additional experimental controls are needed if one wants to make the point that a selective orienting response to threatening information is independent of the specific stimulus configuration in the task setting.

One way to implement those additional controls involves a cross-referencing of affective and nonaffective stimulus conditions to affect-sensitive and affect-insensitive measures. In the case of affective distinctiveness the processing of affective information should impact only affect-sensitive but not affect-insensitive measures, whereas the processing of comparable neutral information should have exclusive impact (if any) on affect-insensitive measures. Consequently, this experimental design establishes a nonaffective task setting as a control task that is comparable to the affective processing task. Klauer and Musch (2002) fully realised such an experimental design in a series of experiments that examined the distinctiveness of processing principles underlying affective priming effects. In four experiments, participants were asked to classify evaluatively polarised target words that systematically varied on a second, nonaffective dimension (e.g., target colour). Each participant performed an additional control task comprising blocked gender decisions on first names, which also varied on the second dimension. In consequence, the gender-decision task paralleled the evaluative-decision task in all procedural details.

The results of all four experiments were unequivocal. Priming of only task-relevant dimensions was found, with no significant priming of task-irrelevant dimensions. For instance, when the task was to evaluate the targets as good or bad, responses were faster when the prime and target had the same valence than when this differed whereas the match between the colour of the prime and target had no effect. When the task was to name the colour of the target, the match between the valence of the prime and target had no effect but the match with regard to colour did. Most important for the present discussion was the fact that task-relevant priming was evidenced for all different types of classification tasks in comparable strength. In a sequential priming paradigm, an evaluative feature overlap had no different implications for classification performance than for a gender or location match and mismatch. The authors concluded that affective priming mechanisms involved the same general response competition principles suggested from previous work on sequential priming (e.g., Eriksen & Eriksen, 1974).

In a further series of experiments, Klauer and Musch (2002) examined the distinctiveness of another type of affective-priming mechanism, which was assumed to operate independently of response competition. This mechanism is called the affective-matching mechanism and is assumed to bias affirmative responses like "yes" decisions through feelings of plausibility engendered by a valence match, and "no" decisions through implausibility feelings produced by a valence mismatch. In this second set of studies, the evaluative decision task was replaced by a same–different judgement task (i.e., are prime and target similar with regard to a certain feature), and the same two-dimensional stimuli served as stimuli as in the experiments described above. The results of all four experiments pointed out a distinctiveness of the affective-matching mechanism. First, an evaluative stimulus match biased the same–different judgements regardless of the task-relevance of the evaluative dimension. Second, a biasing influence of the consistency relation was absent in the gender task, which lacked affectively charged stimuli. Taking all experiments together, Klauer and Musch's results pointed to the joint operation of a distinctive affective-matching mechanism and a general response-competition mechanism in affective priming (see also De Houwer, Hermans, Rothermund, & Wentura, 2002; Wentura, 2000).

The systematic cross-referencing of affective states and measures is a method of choice for a variety of behavioural paradigms, but not the only type of arrangement that allows for discrimination between distinctive and common processing mechanisms. Another research approach, which potentiates conclusions as to the distinctiveness of affective processing principles, employs psychophysiological methods. These methods revealed several physiological "markers" distinctive of affective and emotional processing, which ranged from peripheral measures such as the activation of smile muscles (zygomaticus major) and frown muscles (corrugator supercilium) up to the activation of central cerebral measures like the amygdaloid structures (see Cacioppo, Berntson, Larsen, Poehlmann, & Ito, 2000, for a recent overview). Such physiological markers will allow inferences about affective states, if their presence is systematically and meaningfully related to performance variations in a well-designed experimental task. Winkielman and Cacioppo (2001), for example, tested the hypothesis that processing ease is linked to positive affect, by means of facial EMG measurements. They recorded higher activity over the zygomaticus region during the viewing of easy-to-process stimuli even in an evaluatively ambiguous judgement situation (see also Harmon-Jones & Allen, 2001). This finding strongly argues for the involvement of positive affect in mere exposure effects (Zajonc, 1968), and challenges cognitive accounts that assign affective states no special status in the attribution of fluency differences (e.g., Bornstein & D'Agostino, 1994). Note, however, that the inference of hedonicity on the basis of a temporal covariation between smile muscle activation and processing ease still depends on certain theoretical assumptions, and does not imply causality. Moreover, the conclusiveness of psychophysiological evidence is fully determined by the soundness of the experimental design, in which the psychophysiological measurement is embedded (Cacioppo et al. 2003). In consequence, psychophysiological measurements combined with a systematic manipulation of affective states and measures are particularly conclusive to the experimental isolation of affective operating characteristics on the psychological and physiological level.

Another method frequently used in identifying emotional processes involves a differential approach to strong affective states such as emotional disturbances. In those paradigms the task performance of emotionally disturbed participants is compared to a baseline performance of normal participants within the very same task. Observed performance differences between both groups are then attributed to the operation of processing principles attributable to the emotional disturbance. Studies employing emotional Stroop tasks were particularly successful in the implementation of such research designs because of their strong clinical interest in attentional operating characteristics of panic and depression disorders (Williams et al., 1996). In the pioneering study of Mathews and MacLeod (1985), for example, participants with an anxiety disorder and a normal control group were asked to name the colour of threatening and nonthreatening words. Colour naming of threatening words was delayed only in the patient group, and there was a relationship between the type of threat word that most disrupted colour naming and the type of worries that predominated in the patient. Converging findings from many other studies corroborated the claim that emotional processes distinguish certain clinical populations.

Note, however, that such evidence is typically not conclusive of affective distinctiveness. The differential approach to the study of emotional states does not ensure tight control of other (possibly nonaffective) variables which might be associated with specific emotional disturbances. In consequence, the looming danger of confounding prevents unequivocal claims of affective distinctiveness. Furthermore, a simple generalisation of the processing principles derived from clinical studies of emotional disorders to everyday emotional processing is inherently problematic. The very nature of the interacting effect between emotionally disturbed and normal populations militates against a one-to-one transfer of the principles to the latter group. Despite the fact that processing characteristics observed in clinical populations are heuristically invaluable to emotion psychology, with the emotional Stroop effect serving as a prime example (e.g., Pratto & John, 1991), the mere demonstration of their existence is no solid argument for the application of these same principles to everyday emotional behaviour.

In conclusion, the experimental search for distinctive and general principles operating on affect and emotion is important but methodologically demanding. Available methods for the disentanglement of distinctive and general processes are critically reliant on experimental manipulations of the stimulus conditions and the dependent measures. An experimental design that systematically relates affective and nonaffective stimulus conditions and measures to each other is proposed as a promising approach for the disentanglement of affective and cognitive processes. Such an experimental approach could be enriched by psychophysiological measures capable of providing converging evidence on the physiological level. Clinical studies of emotional disorders frequently ascribe emotion psychology to the possible distinctive contributions of emotional processes; taken in isolation, however, they do not provide unequivocal evidence for affective distinctiveness. Such positive proof hinges critically on the active manipulation of affective states and measures.

THIS SPECIAL ISSUE

Cognitive psychologists have successfully applied an information-processing analysis to human reasoning and behaviour. The tracking of information processing through the system from stimuli to response (or vice versa, see Hommel, Müsseler, Aschersleben, & Prinz, 2001), and the segmentation of the processing stream have furthered our insight into the most diverse phenomena, ranging from sensory processes involved in shape perception to elaborate attributional processes in moral judgements (Massaro & Cowan, 1993; Neisser, 1967; Palmer & Kimchi, 1986). Though neglected for a long time, the analysis of emotional and affective phenomena is no exception to this success story. The formal concept of *information* treats different types of environmental inputs equivalently, much as a computer represents information derived from different peripheral input devices in equally meaningless bits and bytes (Shannon, 1948). From such a computational perspective it is not obvious why the processing of affective information should differ in a fundamental manner from the processing of nonaffective information (but see Simon, 1967). Should it really make a difference, in the processing principles engaged, whether someone recalls the death of a significant other or the shopping list in the mall? Might the snake lurking in the grass elicit a motor response in a substantially different way than the red stop signal at the crossroad? Many researchers seem to think so. As we have pointed out above, some of the reasons for this belief do not stand deeper analysis, suggesting that the necessity or use of separating affective from cognitive processes is questionable. How should we deal with this situation? Consider novel arguments pro or against the distinction? Give it up and build more integrative models? Or give it up to build more local, content-specific models that emphasise distinctions among cognitive processes and among affective processes? The present special issue intends to raise, or at least emphasise, these questions and stimulate their discussion, rather than closing the case in one way or another. Accordingly, we have compiled a broad selection of diverging viewpoints that covers the possible range of answers as widely as possible.

REFERENCES

Anderson, A. K. (2005). Affective influences on the attentional dynamics supporting awareness. *Journal of Experimental Psychology: General, 134,* 258–281.

Barsalou, L. W. (1999). Perceptual symbol systems. *Behavioral and Brain Sciences, 22,* 577–660.

Blanchard, R. J., & Blanchard, C. (1968). Escape and avoidance responses to a fear eliciting situation. *Psychonomic Sciences, 13,* 19–20.

Bornstein, R. F., & D'Agostino, P. R. (1994). The attribution and discounting of perceptual fluency: Preliminary tests of a perceptual fluency/attributional model of the mere exposure effect. *Social Cognition, 12,* 103–128.

Bower, G. H. (1981). Mood and memory. *American Psychologist, 36,* 129–148.

Bradley, M. M., Cuthbert, B. N., & Lang, P. J. (1990). Startle reflex modification: Emotion or attention? *Psychophysiology, 27,* 513–522.

Bradley, M. M., Greenwald, M. K., Petry, M. C., & Lang, P. J. (1992). Remembering pictures: Pleasure and arousal in memory. *Journal of Experimental Psychology: Learning, Memory, and Cognition, 18,* 379–390.

Breiter, H. C., Etcoff, N. L., Whalen, P. J., Kennedy, W. A., Rauch, S. L., Buckner, R. L., et al. (1996). Response and habituation of the human amygdala during visual processing of facial expression. *Neuron, 17,* 875–887.

Cacioppo, J. T., Berntson, G. G., Larsen, J. T., Poehlmann, K. M., & Ito, T. A. (2000). The psychophysiology of emotion. In R. Lewis & J. M. Haviland-Jones (Eds.), *The handbook of emotion* (2nd ed., pp. 173–191). New York: Guilford Press.

Cacioppo, J. T., Berntson, G. G., Lorig, T. S., Norris, C. J., Rickett, E., & Nusbaum, H. (2003). Just because you're imaging the brain doesn't mean you can stop using your head: A primer and set of first principles. *Journal of Personality and Social Psychology, 85,* 650–661.

Camras, L. A., Zhaolan, M., Ujiie, T., Dharamsi, S., Miyake, K., Oster, H., et al. (2002). Observing emotion in infants: Facial expression, body behavior, and rater judgments of responses to an expectancy-violating event. *Emotion, 2,* 179–193.

Chen, M., & Bargh, J. A. (1999). Consequences of automatic evaluation: Immediate behavioral predispositions to approach or avoid the stimulus. *Personality and Social Psychology Bulletin, 25,* 215–224.

Clore, G. L., & Ortony, A. (2000). Cognition in emotion: Always, sometimes, or never? In R. D. Lane & L. Nadel (Eds.), *Cognitive neuroscience of emotion* (pp. 24–61). New York: Oxford University Press.

Davis, M., & Whalen, P. J. (2001). The amygdala: Vigilance and emotion. *Molecular Psychiatry, 6,* 13–34.

De Houwer, J., & Eelen, P. (1998). An affective variant of the Simon paradigm. *Cognition and Emotion, 8,* 45–61.

De Houwer, J., & Hermans, D. (1994). Differences in the affective processing of words and pictures. *Cognition and Emotion*, *8*, 1–20.

De Houwer, Hermans, D., Rothermund, K., & Wentura, D. (2002). Affective priming of semantic categorisation responses. *Cognition and Emotion*, *16*, 643–666.

Debiec, J., & LeDoux, J. (2004). Fear and the brain. *Social Research*, *71*, 807–818.

Désiré, L., Veissier, I., Despré, G., & Boissy, A. (2004). On the way to assess emotions in animals: Do lambs (*Ovis aries*) evaluate an event through its suddenness, novelty, or unpredictability? *Journal of Comparative Psychology*, *118*, 363–374.

Dreisbach, G., & Goschke, T. (2004). How positive affect modulates cognitive control: Reduced perseveration at the cost of increased distractibility. *Journal of Experimental Psychology: Learning, Memory, and Cognition*, *30*, 343–353.

Eich, E., & Metcalfe, J. (1989). Mood dependent memory for internal versus external events. *Journal of Experimental Psychology: Learning, Memory, and Cognition*, *15*, 443–455.

Eimer, M. (1995). Stimulus–response compatibility and automatic response activation: Evidence from psychophysiological studies. *Journal of Experimental Psychology: Human Perception and Performance*, *21*, 837–845.

Eimer, M., & Schlaghecken, F. (1998). Effects of masked stimuli on motor activation: Behavioral and electrophysiological evidence. *Journal of Experimental Psychology: Human Perception and Performance*, *24*, 1737–1747.

Ekman, P. (2004). What we become emotional about. In A. S. R. Manstead, N. Frijda, & A. Fischer (Eds.), *Feelings and emotions: The Amsterdam symposium* (pp. 119–135). Cambridge, UK: Cambridge University Press.

Eriksen, B. A., & Eriksen, C. W (1974). Effects of noise letters upon the identification of a target letter in a nonsearch task. *Perception and Psychophysics*, *16*, 143–149.

Fanselow, M. S. (1980). Conditional and unconditional components of postshock freezing. *Pavlovian Journal of Biological Sciences*, *15*, 177–182.

Fazio, R. H., Sanbonmatsu, D. M., Powell, M. C., & Kardes, F. R. (1986). On the automatic activation of attitudes. *Journal of Personality and Social Psychology*, *50*, 229–238.

Frijda, N. H. (2004). Emotions and action. In A. S. R. Manstead, N. Frijda, & A. Fischer (Eds.), *Feelings and emotions: The Amsterdam symposium* (pp. 158–173). Cambridge, UK: Cambridge University Press.

Gibson, J. J. (1979). *The ecological approach to visual perception*. Boston: Houghton Mifflin.

Glenberg, A. (1999). Why mental models must be embodied. In G. Rickheit & C. Habel (Eds.), *Mental models in discourse processing and reasoning* (pp. 77–90). Amsterdam, The Netherlands: North-Holland/Elsevier Science.

Hamann, S. B., Ely, T. D., Grafton, S. T., & Kilts, C. D. (1999). Amygdala activity related to enhanced memory for pleasant and aversive stimuli. *Nature Neuroscience*, *2*, 289–294.

Hansen, C., & Hansen, R. (1988). Finding the face in the crowd: An anger superiority effect. *Journal of Personality and Social Psychology*, *54*, 917–924.

Harmon-Jones, E., & Allen, J. J. (2001). The role of affect in the mere exposure effect: Evidence from psychophysiological and individual differences approaches. *Personality and Social Psychology Bulletin*, *27*, 889–898.

Harris, C. R., & Pashler, H. (2004). Attention and the processing of emotional words and names: Not so special after all. *Psychological Science*, *15*, 171–178.

Hommel, B., Müsseler, J., Aschersleben, G., & Prinz, W. (2001). The theory of event coding (TEC): A framework for perception and action. *Behavioral and Brain Sciences*, *24*, 849–937.

James, W. (1884). What is an emotion? *Mind*, *9*, 188–205.

Johnston, C. H. (1905). The present state of the psychology of feeling. *Psychological Bulletin*, *2*, 161–171.

Johnston, W. A., Hawley, K. J., Plewe, S. H., & Elliott, J. M. (1990). Attention capture by novel stimuli. *Journal of Experimental Psychology: General*, *119*, 397–411.

Keil, A., & Ihssen, N. (2004). Identification facilitation for emotionally arousing verbs during the attentional blink. *Emotion, 4*, 23–35.

Klauer, K. C., & Musch, J. (2002). Goal-dependent and goal-independent effects of irrelevant evaluations. *Personality and Social Psychology Bulletin, 28*, 802–814.

Klauer, K. C., & Musch, J. (2003). Affective priming: Findings and theories. In J. Musch & K. C. Klauer (Eds.), *The psychology of evaluation: Affective processes in cognition and emotion* (pp. 7–49). Mahwah, NJ: Lawrence Erlbaum Associates, Inc.

Lang, P. J. (1979). A bio-informational theory of emotional imagery. *Psychophysiology, 16*, 495–512.

Lang, P. J., Bradley, M. M., & Cuthbert, B. N. (1997). Motivated attention: Affect, activation, and action. In P. J. Lang, R. F. Simons, & M. T. Balaban (Eds.), *Attention and orienting: Sensory and motivational processes* (pp. 97–135). Mahwah, NJ: Lawrence Erlbaum Associates, Inc.

Lazarus, R. S. (1982). Thoughts on the relations between emotion and cognition. *American Psychologist, 37*, 1019–1024.

Lazarus, R. S., Averill, J. R., & Opton, E. M., Jr. (1970). Toward a cognitive theory of emotion. In M. Arnold (Ed.), *Feelings and emotions* (pp. 207–231). New York: Academic Press.

LeDoux, J. E. (1998). *The emotional brain: The mysterious underpinnings of emotional life.* New York: Touchstone.

LeDoux, J. E. (2000). Emotion circuits in the brain. *Annual Review of Neuroscience, 23*, 155–184.

Levelt, W. J. M., Roelofs, A., & Meyer, A. S. (1999). A theory of lexical access in speech production. *Behavioral and Brain Sciences, 22*, 1–75.

Lipp, O. V., Derakshan, N., Waters, A. M., & Logies, S. (2004). Snakes and cats in the flower bed: Fast detection is not specific to pictures of fear-relevant animals. *Emotion, 4*, 233–250.

MacLean, P. D. (1949). Psychosomatic disease and the "visceral brain": Recent developments bearing on the Papez theory of emotion. *Psychosomatic Medicine, 11*, 338–353.

MacLean, P. D. (1993). Cerebral evolution of emotion. In M. Lewis & J. M. Haviland (Eds.), *Handbook of emotions* (pp. 67–83). New York: Guilford Press.

Mandler, G. (1980). The generation of emotion: A psychological theory. In R. Plutchik & H. Kellerman (Eds.), *Emotion: Theory, research, and experience: Vol. 1. Theories of emotion* (pp. 219–243). New York: Academic Press.

Mandler, G., & Shebo, B. J. (1983). Knowing and liking. *Motivation and Emotion, 7*, 125–144.

Massaro, D. W., & Cowan, N. (1993). Information processing models: Microscopes of the mind. *Annual Review of Psychology, 44*, 383–425.

Mathews, A., & MacLeod, C. (1985). Selective processing of threat cues in anxiety states. *Behaviour Research and Therapy, 23*, 563–569.

McIntosh, D. N. (1996). Facial feedback hypotheses: Evidence, implications and directions. *Motivation and Emotion, 20*, 121–147.

Meltzoff, A. N., & Moore, M. K. (1977). Imitation of facial and manual gestures by human neonates. *Science, 198*, 75–78.

Milner, A. D., & Goodale, M. A. (1995). *The visual brain in action.* London: Oxford University Press.

Murphy, S. T., & Zajonc, R. B. (1993). Affect, cognition, and awareness: Affective priming with optimal and suboptimal stimulus exposures. *Journal of Personality and Social Psychology, 64*, 723–739.

Neisser, U. (1967). *Cognitive psychology.* New York: Appleton-Century-Crofts.

Neumann, O., & Klotz, W. (1994). Motor responses to nonreportable, masked stimuli: Where is the limit of direct parameter specification? In C. Umiltà & M. Moscovitch (Eds.), *Attention and performance: 15. Conscious and nonconscious information processing* (pp. 123–150). Cambridge, MA: MIT Press.

Niedenthal, P. M., Barsalou, L. W., Winkielman, P., Krauth-Gruber, S., & Ric, F. (2005). Embodiment in attitudes, social perception, and emotion. *Personality and Social Psychology Review, 9*, 184–211.

Nisbett, R. E., & Wilson, T. D. (1977). Telling more than we can know: Verbal reports on mental processes. *Psychological Review, 84*, 231–259.

Öhman, A., Lundqvist, D., & Esteves, F. (2001). The face in the crowd revisited: A threat advantage with schematic stimuli. *Journal of Personality and Social Psychology, 80*, 381–396.

Palmer, S. E., & Kimchi, R. (1986). The information processing approach to cognition. In T. J. Knapp & L. C. Robertson (Eds.), *Approaches to cognition: Contrasts and controversies* (pp. 37–77). Hillsdale, NJ: Lawrence Erlbaum Associates, Inc.

Papez, J. W. (1937). A proposed mechanism of emotion. *Archives of Neurology and Psychiatry, 79*, 217–224.

Pratto, F., & John, O. (1991). Automatic vigilance: The attention-grabbing power of negative social information. *Journal of Personality and Social Psychology, 61*, 380–391.

Purcell, D. G., Steward, A. L., & Skov, R. B. (1996). It takes a confounded face to pop out of the crowd. *Perception, 25*, 1091–1108.

Ristau, C. A. (1983). Language, cognition, and awareness in animals? *Annals of the New York Academy of Sciences, 408*, 170–186.

Robinson, M. D. (1998). Running from William James' bear: A review of preattentive mechanisms and their contributions to emotional experience. *Cognition and Emotion, 12*, 667–696.

Rosenfeld, H. M., & Baer, D. M. (1969). Unnoticed verbal conditioning of an aware experimenter by a more aware subject: The double-agent effect. *Psychological Review, 76*, 425–532.

Rotteveel, M., & Phaf, R. H. (2004). Automatic affective evaluation does not automatically predispose for arm flexion and extension. *Emotion, 4*, 156–172.

Rumelhart, D. E. (1997). Affect and neuromodulation: A connectionist approach. In J. D. Cohen & J. W. Schooler (Eds.), *Scientific approaches to consciousness* (pp. 469–477). Hillsdale, NJ: Lawrence Erlbaum Associates, Inc.

Rusting, C. L., & Larsen, R. J. (1998). Personality and cognitive processing of affective information. *Personality and Social Psychology Bulletin, 24*, 200–213.

Schachter, S., & Singer, J. E. (1962). Cognitive, social, and physiological determinants of emotional state. *Psychological Review, 69*, 379–399.

Scherer, K. R. (1984). On the nature and function of emotion: A component process approach. In K. R. Scherer & P. Ekman (Eds.), *Approaches to emotion* (pp. 293–317). Hillsdale, NJ: Lawrence Erlbaum Associates, Inc.

Schwarz, N. (1999). Self-reports: How the questions shape the answers. *American Psychologist, 54*, 93–105.

Shannon, C. E. (1948). A mathematical theory of communication. *Bell System Technical Journal, 27*, 379–423, 623–658.

Simon, H. A. (1967). Motivational and emotional controls of cognition. *Psychological Review, 74*, 29–39.

Strack, F., Martin, L. L., & Stepper, S. (1988). Inhibiting and facilitating conditions of the human smile: A nonobtrusive test of the facial feedback hypothesis. *Journal of Personality and Social Psychology, 54*, 768–777.

Tooby, J., & Cosmides, L. (1990). The past explains the present: Emotional adaptations and the structure of ancestral environments. *Ethological Sociobiology, 11*, 375–424.

Tucker, M., & Ellis, R. (1998). On the relations between seen objects and components of potential actions. *Journal of Experimental Psychology: Human Perception and Performance, 24*, 830–846.

Ulrich, R. E., & Azrin, N. H. (1962). Reflexive fighting in response to aversive stimulation. *Journal of the Experimental Analysis of Behavior, 5*, 511–520.

Vrana, S. R., Spence, E. L., & Lang, P. J. (1988). The startle probe response: A new measure of emotion? *Journal of Abnormal Psychology, 97*, 487–491.

Vuilleumier, P. (2005). Staring fear in the face. *Nature, 433*, 22–23.

Wentura, D. (2000). Dissociative affective and associative priming effects in the lexical decision task: Yes vs. no responses to word targets reveal evaluative judgment tendencies. *Journal of Experimental Psychology: Learning, Memory, and Cognition, 26*, 456–469.

Wentura, D., & Rothermund, K. (2003). The "meddling-in" of affective information: A general model of automatic evaluation. In J. Musch & K. C. Klauer (Eds.), *The psychology of evaluation: Affective processes in cognition and emotion* (pp. 51–86). Mahwah, NJ: Lawrence Erlbaum Associates, Inc.

Williams, J. M., Mathews, A., & MacLeod, C. (1996). The emotional Stroop task and psychopathology. *Psychological Bulletin, 120*, 3–24.

Winkielman, P., & Cacioppo, J. T. (2001). Mind at ease puts a smile on the face: Psychophysiological evidence that processing facilitation increases positive affect. *Journal of Personality and Social Psychology, 81*, 989–1000.

Zajonc, R. B. (1968). Attitudinal effects of mere exposure. *Journal of Personality and Social Psychology* [Monograph], *9*, 1–27.

Zajonc, R. B. (1980). Feeling and thinking: Preferences need no inferences. *American Psychologist, 35*, 151–175.

COGNITION AND EMOTION
2007, 21 (6), 1155–1183

Differentiation in cognitive and emotional meanings: An evolutionary analysis

Philip J. Barnard

MRC Cognition and Brain Sciences Unit, Cambridge, Cambridgeshire, UK

David J. Duke

University of Leeds, Leeds, Yorkshire, UK

Richard W. Byrne

University of St Andrews, St Andrews, Fife, UK

Iain Davidson

University of New England, Armidale, New South Wales, Australia

It is often argued that human emotions, and the cognitions that accompany them, involve refinements of, and extensions to, more basic functionality shared with other species. Such refinements may rely on common or on distinct processes and representations. Multi-level theories of cognition and affect make distinctions between qualitatively different types of representations often dealing with bodily, affective and cognitive attributes of self-related meanings. This paper will adopt a particular multi-level perspective on mental architecture and show how a mechanism of subsystem differentiation could have allowed an evolutionarily "old" role for emotion in the control of action to have altered into one more closely coupled to meaning systems. We conclude by outlining some illustrative consequences of our analysis that might usefully be addressed in research in comparative psychology, cognitive archaeology, and in laboratory research on memory for emotional material.

Correspondence should be addressed to: Philip J. Barnard, MRC Cognition & Brain Sciences Unit, 15 Chaucer Road, Cambridge CB2 2EF, UK.
E-mail: philip.barnard@mrc-cbu.cam.ac.uk

The contribution of DJD was supported by an EPSRC Advanced Research Fellowship.

Much of the material for this article was initially developed in an interdisciplinary focus group involving P. Barnard, R. Byrne, I. Davidson, V. Janik, A. Miklósi, W. McGrew and P. Wiessner that took place at Collegium Budapest in the Autumn of 2003. The support of the Rector of the Collegium and its staff is gratefully acknowledged. The first author also acknowledges the mentorship of John Morton and, in particular, one of his papers on specifying mental architectures that inspired the approach taken here (Morton, 1968).

© 2007 Psychology Press, an imprint of the Taylor & Francis Group, an Informa business
www.psypress.com/cogemotion   DOI: 10.1080/02699930701437477

INTRODUCTION

Most theories of emotion posit interactions with cognition. Yet, finding an acceptable answer to the question of whether or not affective processes are distinct from cognitive ones poses real challenges. Eder, Hommel, and De Houwer (this issue) point out that arguments for the distinctiveness of affective processes characteristically draw our attention to very different issues, such as the role of embodiment (e.g., Niedenthal, Barsalou, Winkielman Krauth-Gruber, & Ric, 2005), the functional role of emotions (e.g., Lang, Bradley, & Cuthbert, 1997), the content of representations (e.g., Moors, this issue), or domain specificity in underlying brain systems (e.g., LeDoux, 1996).

The picture is made more intricate by the diverse range of cognitive paradigms used to study interactions between emotions, and cognitive "processes" that are themselves often defined in different ways. Paradigms frequently referenced include recognition of emotional states from facial expressions or tone of voice, through attending and responding to affectively significant words or pictures and affective priming (e.g., see Eder & Klauer, this issue; Storbeck & Clore, this issue), to the effects of affective state on memory, semantic interpretation and decision making (for representative coverage of many of these topics see chapters in Dalgleish & Power, 1999). Studies of patients with significant mood disorders such as depression and anxiety (e.g., see Williams, Watts, MacLeod, & Mathews, 1997) or damage to specific brain areas (again see LeDoux, 1996) also reveal an extensive range of deficits in performance on cognitive-affective tasks that vary in their specificity and this evidence directly informs wider debates concerning the extent to which cognitive and emotional processes and representations can usefully be considered as separable or "modularised".

There are also important comparative and evolutionary dimensions to the debate concerning the distinctiveness of affective processes (e.g., Lavender & Hommel, this issue; LeDoux, 1996; Öhman, Flykt, & Lundqvist, 2000; Zajonc, 1984). It is well known that there are homologies across species in the brain areas involved in emotion processing (e.g., Lawrence & Calder, 2004), notably the limbic system. Whatever the homologies, a large gulf exists between humans and other species. On the broadest cognitive canvas, our culture involves language, art, religion, music, education, advanced technologies and more (e.g., Mithen, 1996; Noble & Davidson, 1996). We are thought to have more advanced cognitive capabilities than other species, be they extant or extinct. A substantial literature on this topic includes many candidate theories for what makes humans special and how that came about (see Amati & Shallice, 2007, for a recent concise list). Among these, our use of spoken language implies that we have a larger number of processing modules and a larger variety of distinct and more "abstract" levels of representation than other animals and with that the potential for richer interactions between cognitive and affective influences on our experience and behaviour.

There is also an equally extensive debate concerning how emotion modules or programmes originally evolved to support the adaptive control of action and subsequently developed the qualities of human affect (e.g., see Frijda, 2004; Oatley & Johnson-Laird, 1987; Tooby & Cosmides, 2000) and several theorists argue from different perspectives for greater differentiation in human emotion representation than in animals. Plutchik (1980) and Turner (2000) both argue that humans have extra differentiation via the blending of more basic emotions and quite detailed arguments are emerging concerning specific emotions. Rozin, Haidt, and McCauley (1999), for example, propose that the basic emotion of disgust is more elaborated in humans, being augmented to encompass interpersonal and socio-moral dimensions in addition to its "old" evolutionary origins in oral rejection responses across mammalian species. There are also arguments that the rather more "refined" emotions may well differentiate in a developmental sequence akin to Piaget's stages of cognitive development (Lane, Quinlan, Schwartz, Walker, & Zeitlin, 1990).

A number of multi-level theories of human cognition and emotion (see Teasdale, 1999a, for an overview), such as the multiple entry memory model (MEM; Johnson, 1983), Interacting Cognitive Subsystems (ICS; Barnard & Teasdale, 1991), the SPAARS model (Power & Dalgleish, 1997), and the Dual Memory Model (DMM; Philippot, Baeyens, Douilliez, & Francart, 2004) incorporate process components in the human mind that are hard to justify in all mammalian species. For example, the MEM model links more intricate and emotional states such as nostalgia to the later evolutionary emergence of additional processes and levels within perceptual and reflective subsystems, while the ICS, SPAARS and DMM architectures distinguish two levels of meaning (propositional and schematic) that would seem rather less than parsimonious were the distinction to be applied to many mammalian species. Where additional types of mental representation are invoked, there is obviously a theoretical requirement to justify why they are needed. It also follows that any numerically larger number of components will generally require more "mappings" to be specified among component processes and representations.

In this paper, we trace a hypothetical evolutionary trajectory in which the cognitive and affective capabilities of the human mental architecture are argued to have co-evolved in a principled way from far simpler mental architectures with fewer processes and types of mental representations. Evidence for the evolution of more differentiated mental capability and behaviours can only be inferred indirectly from what little hard evidence is preserved in the archaeological record, coupled with inferences from comparative evidence from different species alive today. This inevitably means that support for key aspects of our argument is of a qualitatively different nature from the support more usually invoked with laboratory paradigms. In this respect, we rely rather more than is typical on the systematic application of computational principles. Our specific focus will be on how a particular multi-level theory, interacting cognitive subsystems (ICS), and the two levels of meaning it claims to underpin human performance in cognitive-affective paradigms, could also be systematically grounded in evolutionary argumentation.

A BRIEF OVERVIEW OF THE ICS MENTAL ARCHITECTURE

The ICS mental architecture was originally developed to provide an account of a range of phenomena in memory tasks and selective attention based upon resources that would be required in the comprehension and production of spoken and written language (Barnard, 1985). It was subsequently augmented to account for mood effects on memory, the processing of dysfunctional models of the self in depression across a range of cognitive affective tasks and to develop new interventions to bring dysfunctional thinking and its affective correlates back within the normal range (Barnard & Teasdale, 1991; Teasdale, 1999b; Teasdale & Barnard, 1993). The model has been described as a "macro-theory" in that it enabled accounts of a wide range of normal and dysfunctional cognitive-affective phenomena to be developed on the basis of a common set of component processes and representations (Barnard, 2004). The full ICS architecture is presented in Figure 1.

The first key characteristic of this mental architecture is that it is composed of *nine* subsystems. Each subsystem is specialised to process information in a particular type of representation constructed in a mental "code". Three of the subsystems (Visual, Acoustic, and Body State) process sensory codes the characteristics of which are determined by constraints on sense receptors—such as colour and luminance, pitch and timbre, or warmth and pain. Two others are specialised to control outputs to skeletal and vocal musculatures. The four remaining "central subsystems" are specialised to process more abstract mental codes. Two represent structures in the auditory–verbal (Morphonolexical) domain and in the domain of spatial praxis. The remaining subsystems process two qualitatively different ways of encoding meaning—"Propositional" meaning and "Implicational" meaning. The former kind of meaning is that most usually thought of as the kind of meanings that are expressed in sentences while implicational meaning encodes more holistic and abstract schematic models of cognitive-affective experience. Information flow among subsystems is depicted in this figure by the arrows linking outputs of one subsystem to the input of

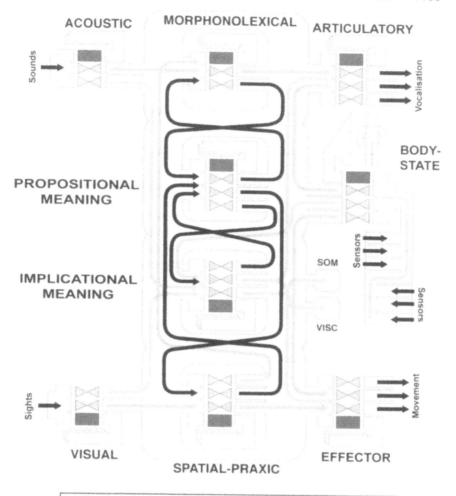

Figure 1. The 9-subsystem ICS architecture proposed by Barnard and Teasdale (1991). The names Spatial–praxic and Effector subsystems replace the names Object and Limb subsystems used in earlier publications to be consistent with usage in the current paper. Reciprocal flows of information among the four central subsystems are depicted in black while other routes for information flow are depicted in grey.

another. From these flow patterns it can be seen that the Implicational subsystem combines inputs from the Propositional subsystem with direct flows from the Body State, Acoustic, and Visual subsystems. It is postulated to be the level of mental representation at which derivatives of states of the

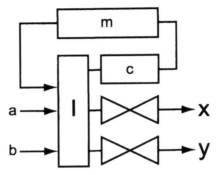

Figure 2. The basic organisation of processes within all subsystems.

body, the external world and propositional meanings about the self, the world and others are all brought together and integrated. Implicational synthesis underlies both generic senses of meaning, including "intuitions", and any associated affect linked to those meanings. This level is also the mental hub from which new propositional content is generated and from which Somatic (SOM) and Visceral (VISC) responses are initiated along with some residual pre-wired vocal and effector responses. While the processing of emotional "information" is distributed over multiple subsystems, the key intersections are focused within implicationally encoded schematic models (see Teasdale & Barnard, 1993, for further details).

The second key feature of the architecture is that all of these subsystems share a common internal structure in which functionally independent processes are organised in parallel. The model assumes that these processes either abstract and reconstruct representations in a particular code, or map information in one coding space into another via a transformation. The common internal structure replicated across all the subsystems in Figure 1 is shown in Figure 2 in a notated form that will be used later in our proposal for an evolutionary mechanism of subsystem differentiation. Inputs (denoted by a & b) arrive at a subsystem from either external or internal sources and are mapped into an "input array" (I) which can be thought of as a vector with a large number of constituent elements organised into types such as "a" and "b". From this array, a process "copies" (c) all arriving information into an image record (m). This holds a temporally organised record of recent input from which regularities underlying recurring patterns are abstracted, and from which information can be re-mapped from the memory (m) back onto the input array. This creates a copy–memory–recover loop. In parallel with this, a set of transformation processes, depicted in both Figures 1 and 2 as horizontal dumbbells, acts either on immediate inputs or on current input patterns augmented by material reconstructed from the image record m on to the array I. These transformation processes generate the flows to other subsystems specified in Figure 1 and are simply denoted as outputs "x and y" in Figure 2. These arrangements have other significant properties as well as principles governing information flow, such as the proposal that transformation processes can only deal with a single stream of information from the more complex patterns that can exist on the input array and these are described elsewhere (e.g., Barnard, 1985, 1999; Teasdale & Barnard, 1993).

This general arrangement of processes and subsystems in ICS was initially justified on the basis of both evidence and parsimony. A wide range of evidence in early cognitive research on memory (e.g., see Baddeley, 1986, 1990) was consistent with the existence of independent storage components for very short-term visual or "iconic" information and auditory or "echoic" information. Other evidence suggested that short-term memory for lexical material relied on acoustic coding and longer-term retention was dependent on semantic coding while the manipulation and retention of the visual domain made use of spatial imagery. Neuropsychological evidence concerning constraints on mental architecture was reviewed by Shallice (1988). Quite severe neuropsychological deficits in short-term memory did not seem to prevent information entering long-term memory. Deficits in both short- and long-term memory also occurred in patients whose on-line language comprehension and production could be largely intact. While other evidence from priming research and work with "blindsight" patients indicated that transformations from one level of representation to another could be carried out without conscious access to images of their content. Taken together these strands of evidence supported the parallel arrangement of transformation processes and the copy-memory component of Figure 2 and proposed in the earliest formulation of ICS (Barnard, 1985).

The parallel arrangement of processes in Figure 1 and the specific coding spaces it proposes is also parsimonious. Within the central subsystems, on-line reciprocal mappings among representational levels could be supported without proliferation of process components of the kind that could readily occur if we were to approach the problem of arriving at a mental architecture by "bolting together" different theories of perception, attention, language, memory, thinking, emotion and the control of action—each bringing with it multiple components and with that the potential for a combinatorial explosion in process mappings. Importantly, as a candidate macro-theory with constrained resources, ICS can address performance across task domains *without* invoking a qualitatively distinct set of central executive mechanisms with homunculus-like properties (Barnard, 1999).

The third key feature of the ICS architecture is its account of emotion. Teasdale and Barnard (1993, pp. 86–96) argue that the new-born human arrives in the world with a set of innately prepared emotional responses to states such as a protest–frustration reaction to the withdrawal of a sweet fluid, alarm in response to a rapidly looming shape whereas rocking, cuddling, fondling or grooming would invoke a positive response. Over the course of development, emotional differentiation occurs as the range of co-occurrences of sensory information experienced increases and its properties are modelled in the Implicational record of Figure 1. These are subsequently augmented as the other subsystems are populated with information patterns concerning more abstract auditory–verbal, spatial–praxic and propositional knowledge similar to the Piaget-based stages argued for by Lane et al. (1990).

COGNITION AND EMOTION IN THE CONTROL OF ACTION

It was noted earlier that a widespread view is that emotion programmes or modules originally evolved to support the control of action, and that human mechanisms have in some way modified these evolutionarily old capabilities, but the detailed evolutionary trajectory followed across these modifications is typically left less than fully specified. The fact that all subsystems in ICS share a common internal architecture has particular attractions in this context, since it provides a vehicle around which more detailed specification of an evolutionary pathway for such modifications can be built. It can be argued that most animals have mental architectures far simpler than that shown in Figure 1 with fewer subsystems, and in which the role of emotional information involves a direct coupling to action selection. Figure 3 depicts one such hypothetical mental architecture with five rather than nine subsystems. It involves resources that we conjecture would be sufficient to explain the "cognition" and behaviour of a mammal, such as a monkey, that exhibits intricate concurrent co-ordination and control of its skeletal musculatures.

Within an architecture with only one multi-modal central subsystem there would be strictly limited capability for abstraction. As indicated by the flow patterns this central subsystem transforms patterns of inputs that are derivatives of distal (acoustic, visual) and bodily sensation. As with the Implicational subsystem of Figure 1, the Multi-modal subsystem directly controls Somatic and Visceral response mechanisms as well as generating outputs to a single Effector subsystem specialised for co-ordinating the actions of interdependent skeletal musculatures. There is also strictly limited potential for the concurrent processing of different streams of information. Here, the architecture allows only direct transformations from sensory to an Effector subsystem and the capability to modify action selection based on patterns of information in the Multi-modal subsystem. These patterns would be in part constrained by moment-to-moment changes in bodily states and states of the physical environment and in part by the option to augment

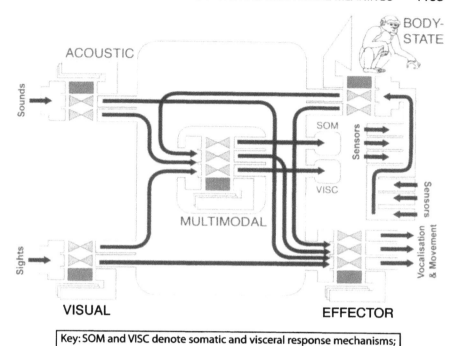

Figure 3. A 5-subsystem mental architecture including Somatic (SOM) and Visceral (VISC) response mechanisms. The image and memory record of the Body State subsystem is assumed to reflect the flexible body morphology shared by, for example, the clade of Haplorhine primates. Multiple arrows below this subsystem indicate paths for sensory inputs from body organs of all types.

those inputs by recovering (via the copy–memory–recover loop of Figure 2) recent states or wider regularities underlying past temporally extended multi-modal contingencies. As with the human infant, were such an architecture to have innately prepared emotional responses, then this 5-subsystem architecture would be entirely consistent with the view that affective states are synthesised multi-modally and function directly to guide action selection.

The 5-subsystem architecture, while computationally powerful, does not allow for processing exchanges among different levels of central representation of the form that would allow human auditory–verbal, spatial–praxic and propositional imagery to occur at the same time as acting in the world under the guidance of positive, neutral or negative affective markers. The 5-subsystem architecture cannot "think or reflect" while acting. Clearly, more processes are concurrently active in the 9-subsystem architecture (Figure 1) than in the 5-subsystem architecture (Figure 3). Another crucial difference between the two architectures concerns the ways in which multi-modal integration occurs, and the levels of abstraction involved. The Implicational subsystem of the full 9-subsystem (human) version of ICS receives an *additional* input derived from the processing of propositional representations and is hence a system in which affective processing and emotional experience are continually modulated by meaning. For the 5-subsystem architecture to be held as an antecedent to the 9-subsystem architecture there must be a mechanism, an "information-processing" analogue of cell division in biology, that enabled a small set of "core" processes to differentiate in the normal course of natural selection into a larger set of processes with more specialised "cognitive" functions. That mechanism must accommodate the development of higher levels of abstraction and our ability to think and reflect while acting in the world.

A MECHANISM FOR SUBSYSTEM DIFFERENTIATION

The original ICS model held that the memory records associated with each subsystem functioned in the support of learning by extracting statistical regularities underlying experience of co-occurrences of information in a particular mental code. The domain of cognitive modelling has been dominated for decades by rule-based production system models (e.g., Newell, 1990) or connectionism (Rummelhart, McClelland, & PDP Group, 1986). However, recent mathematical and computational developments have shown that statistical methods, in the form of dimension reduction, have considerable power and potential. These methods, when combined with the specification of an ICS subsystem (Figure 2), allow us to derive a mechanism for subsystem differentiation in which a daughter subsystem can emerge from a parent subsystem.

Principal components analysis (PCA) has, among many other applications, been beneficially applied to modelling identity and emotional dimensions of facial expressions (Calder, Burton, Miller, Young, & Akamatsu, 2001). Another mathematical technique for dimension reduction, singular value decomposition (SVD), has been used to develop latent semantic analysis, which is capable of modelling the meanings expressed by a vocabulary size typical of a college student, and the analysis relates well to key laboratory phenomena (e.g., see Landauer & Dumais, 1997). Recent evidence also indicates that PCA can be applied to dynamic changes in facial expression *over time* (Bettinger & Cootes, 2004). This indicates that statistical methods are, at least in principle, capable of modelling regularities over time of the sort proposed to underlie learning in ICS by Teasdale and Barnard (1993). Given a PCA characterisation of variation in some data, it is possible to invert it and reconstruct the original input to some reasonable degree of approximation. This property allows dimension reduction not only to serve as a model of learning, but also to serve as a way of thinking about how information is recovered from an image record of the kind proposed in ICS. In ICS, the transformation processes were originally conceptualised as extracting the invariants underlying information patterns and passing these on to the next subsystem in line—as when information in an acoustic pattern is transformed into a Morphonolexical representation, when this is in turn transformed into Propositional meaning, or when the latter is transformed for input to the Implicational subsystem. Each code in the central subsystems of ICS is derived in part from the invariants passed to them from other subsystems. In these respects PCA can act as a way of thinking about *both* the copy–memory–recover cycle and the transformation processes shown in Figure 2.

In the argument we develop here, we assume the existence of a system for computing PCAs and their inverses, though the argument could well apply with other mathematical forms of dimension reduction. We also assume that the mechanism underlying dimension reduction can be characterised in terms of connections between "nodes" representing the content of mental codes. We believe this assumption to be reasonable as, for example, PCAs are known to be computable within connectionist models (O'Reilly & Munakata, 2000). Figure 4 presents a schematic diagram to support our basic argument for the differentiation of one system into two interacting ones.

Figure 4(i) simply replicates Figure 2, while Figure 4(vi) shows two interacting subsystems of identical form. The figures in between assist, in manner not unlike arguments in geometry, presentation of key aspects of our proposal concerning subsystem differentiation. The essence of this argument is that the copy–memory–recover loop of Figure 4(i) contains the seeds of additional process components and that in some underlying neural implementation process components can be separated. Here, we focus our argument not on the neural level of implementation but on how that can be expressed in terms of a PCA system that could characterise the workings of that neural apparatus mathematically. In this respect, process components mediating inputs and outputs can be viewed as functionally distinct when the patterns of information processed from inputs to outputs are statistically independent of each other. At the level of neural implementation this can be equated with there being minimal cross-talk between the nodes mediating the dependence of subsets of output patterns on input patterns.

Figure 4(ii) simply rearranges the components of Figure 4(i) by subdividing the input array I. It marks the idea that there would be elements of the input array that are used to generate the output x and a statistically separate set of dimensions that are used to generate output y—as for example might apply in the ICS model when the processing of the identity of spoken words is passed from the Acoustic subsystem to the

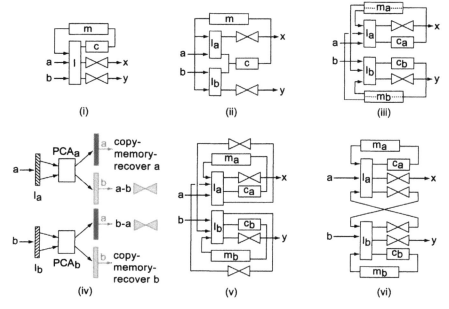

Figure 4.   The differentiation of one subsystem into two interacting ones.

Morphonolexical subsystem while the emotional tone of voice in which they are expressed is passed directly to the Implicational subsystem (see Figure 1).

Figure 4(iii) is more intricate. Here the single copy process of Figure 4(ii) has itself been subdivided into two, as has the memory component m— again reflecting the idea that separable subsets of the coding space (here denoted by a in the upper part of the figure and b in the lower part) are copied into a temporally extended memory.[1] Crucially, note that the re-mapping of information from the memory component "a" back on to the input array substitutes two component arrows where there was only one before—and a horizontal dotted line within each of the two memory components marks their potential fractionation. The two arrows now distinguish two aspects of the flow from memory back to the input array I that were undifferentiated in Figure 4(ii). In each case one return arrow now leads to the "a" component of the input array and the other leads to the "b" component of the input array. The importance of these subdivisions can be illustrated more concretely by reference to the Calder et al. (2001) PCA analysis of facial expressions. They found a subset of PCA dimensions that

---

[1] For the present purposes, we do not deal directly with temporal extent—we merely assume that it can be treated as a source of variation over which PCA systems can be applied (Bettinger & Cootes, 2004).

captured facial identity, a statistically independent set that captured facial expression of emotional states and yet other dimensions that captured aspects of both. As with the example of words and tone of voice, this means that any *output* transformations carrying only facial identity or only emotional state can simply be treated as independent processes. However, if one were to *invert* the PCA process to reconstruct an approximation of the original input, i.e., a recovered representation of a face—the function of memory retrieval, it would be necessary to take into account those dimensions that related to aspects of *both*, i.e., the influence of a (e.g., emotion) in reconstructing b (e.g., identity) and the influence of b in reconstructing a. Such considerations would apply not just to attributes of faces but to any mental coding space, and it is these relationships that are now explicitly captured in Figure 4(iii) by the two arrows leading from each of the two memory components a and b, onto the fractionated input arrays Ia and Ib. This relates directly to the point that the copy–memory–recover component contains the seeds of extra component processes.

This crucial point is reinforced in Figure 4(iv). This separately depicts what is functionally being computed in the copy–memory–recover loop for "a" (upper panel) and in the copy memory loop for "b" (lower panel). In each case a part of the PCA relates to copying and recovering elements of "a" or "b" while the other component either maps from a to b (upper panel), reflecting the influence of a in the reconstruction of elements of b, or maps from b to a (lower panel) representing the influence of b on the reconstruction of elements of a. At a functional level these can be equated with "proto-transformations" from a coding space confined to elements of "a" to the coding space confined to elements of "b" and vice versa. On the basis of this argument, at that point where full statistical independence is achieved, we can fractionate the copy–memory–recover cycles in Figure 5(iii). In effect this fractionates each m into components above and below the horizontal dotted lines, with one processing pathway that is still a copy–memory–recover loop, and one that is a transformation, for which we substitute in a dumbbell symbol. This is depicted in Figure 4(v) in a way that preserves the overall structure of Figure 4(iii). A simple spatial rearrangement of these elements yields Figure 4(vi) with two interacting subsystems.

Our mechanism of subsystem differentiation depends only on the reconfiguration of elements in an underlying PCA system. This has the attraction that it could have come about as more or less capacity or connectivity in the same wetware is reallocated among dimensions in a single PCA space. These changes can occur in the kind of small incremental steps required by acceptable evolutionary arguments. The end result of a particular progression would entail the coding spaces of a daughter subsystem eventually becoming wholly distinct from those of its parent subsystem. If we follow the principle that any one process can only transform a single coherent stream of information at a given time (see Barnard, 1985; Duke, Barnard, Duce, & May, 1998), then direct consequences follow for the capability of the resulting architecture. In Figure 4(vi) there are four processes transforming inputs to outputs that can be active concurrently as opposed to the two present in Figure 4(i).

The interaction of two "central" subsystems adds considerable computational power relative to an architecture with only one central subsystem. The new components provide conditions under which higher order invariants can contribute to the control of action. With a single central subsystem, limited potential exists for the reordering of elements within a stream of information. This can only be achieved by recovering elements from the memory record and reinstating them at a later point in time. The "dialogue" that can occur between two interacting subsystems enables more extensive reordering of elements within streams of information and hence more combinatorial power.

In what follows, we first present a brief overview of how this mechanism could have led to a direct evolutionary sequence from a mammalian mental architecture with a single central subsystem outlined earlier to the full ICS model. At each step in this sequence a single subsystem will be added. We then use this brief outline to focus attention on how meaning systems can be thought of as grounded in the control of action and how the addition of successive subsystems would have modified the nature of the relationship between cognition and emotion.

THE EVOLUTIONARY TRAJECTORY FROM A 5-SUBSYSTEM ARCHITECTURE TO A 9-SUBSYSTEM ARCHITECTURE

In the 5-subsystem architecture (Figure 3), considered earlier to apply with some species of monkey, visuo-spatial processing in the control of action involved two routes. One route directly connected their Visual subsystem to an Effector subsystem co-ordinating their limbs, hands, heads and eyes. The former instantiates a PCA of visually derived information while the latter instantiates a PCA to support muscular control. The second route was via the Multi-modal subsystem, which performs a third, more abstract PCA of all sensory inputs and modulates action control on the basis of higher order contingencies. Were a monkey to twist a fruit to pull it from a tree while foraging, changes in the visual arrangement of surface features would be temporally correlated with properties of the dynamics of muscular control as the action is executed. Were the multi-modal PCA to extract a set of dimensions capturing the commonalities, then that would be something akin to the concept of rotation in a spatial frame of reference. If this were to be extended to a collection of such correlations then a fraction of the multi-modal PCA would be developing the elements of a spatial–praxic coding system. Were that fraction to become fully statistically independent from other multi-modal dimensions, then conditions exist for our proposed mechanism (Figure 4) to allow a separate spatial subsystem to emerge, which functions to augment praxis. A vital element of this argument is that the emergence of a new *central* subsystem seems to require *complexity to be present in two different subsystems* (here vision and effector/manual dexterity). Additionally, what is represented in both needs to be dynamically *correlated over time* within the temporal extent of the memory record (m in Figure 2). These are both enabling conditions for a higher order PCA of shared invariants to emerge and hence to allow a daughter subsystem to be born from the original Multi-modal subsystem by the mechanism elaborated in Figure 4. An architecture with a 6th subsystem specialised for spatial–praxis is shown in Figure 5.

Precisely the same argument can be applied in the auditory–verbal domain. There is, of course, a huge debate in various literatures concerning the evolutionary emergence of speech and language (e.g., see Christiansen & Kirby, 2003; Noble & Davidson, 1996). Since our intention here is to concentrate on emotional meanings, we simply outline a sequence in the auditory–verbal domain that directly parallels that outlined above for the emergence of a specialised Spatial–praxic subsystem. Figure 6 shows two different architectures, one with seven subsystems and one with eight. The line of argument supporting this is straightforward. Great apes cannot independently control breathing and this restricts their articulation to relatively simple vocal patterns such as the "pant hoot". Fossilised vertebrae of different species indicate greater innervation of the thoracic region in later than in earlier hominins, that would be compatible with independent control of breathing and, by inference, more differentiated vocalisation (MacLarnon & Hewitt, 1999; see also Davidson, 2003, for other evidence in the archaeological record). Differentiated vocalisations create new patterns and control of the speech musculature would be expected to become independent of patterning in other, uncorrelated areas of motor control, notably of the limbs. Conditions now exist for the separation of the control of vocal articulation from other effectors and hence the emergence of that independent subsystem[2] specialised for vocal articulation (Figure 6a). The evolutionary emergence of complex vocal articulation would have created conditions exactly like those in the visual co-ordination of flexible movement that enabled the emergence of a Spatial–praxic subsystem. There are now

---

[2] The precise mechanism for the emergence of a separate effector subsystem requires only a subset of the full argument for two interacting ones presented in Figure 4 but relies on exactly the same logic.

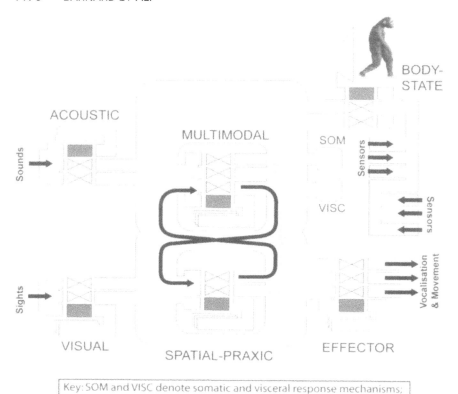

Figure 5. A 6-subsystem mental architecture. The reciprocal interaction between the new Spatial–praxic subsystem and the Multi-modal subsystem is now highlighted in black.

two complex sources of variation whose dynamics over time are correlated (heard speech and vocal articulation). Hence, when the Multi-modal subsystem has extracted a significant subset of invariants for the control of that output, and that subset becomes statistically independent from other fractions of the multi-modal domain then, by the argument we are following, the eighth, "Morphonolexical" subsystem would emerge (Figure 6b).

The presence of complex variation *both* in the spatial–praxic domain *and* in the auditory–verbal domain creates exactly those conditions where there are once again two correlated sources of variation over time. In the simplest case, verbal phrases may have "represented" states in the spatial–praxic domain including a wide range of actions and/or communicative gestures such as pointing. By extension of our earlier argument, conditions are now present for the emergence of a ninth subsystem encapsulating new

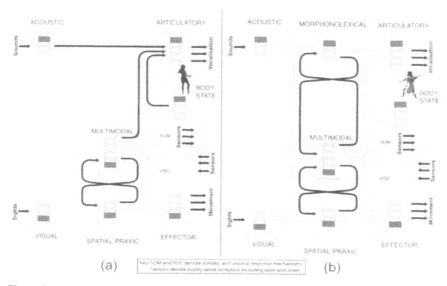

Figure 6. (a) Seven-subsystem mental architecture with new routes for control of vocalisation also highlighted in black. (b) Eight-subsystem mental architecture with reciprocal interactions between the Multi-modal subsystem and both Spatial–praxic and Morphonolexical subsystems highlighted in black.

underlying invariants. Of course, what spatial–praxis and auditory–verbal communication have in common is an abstraction with exactly the properties we assign to "propositional" meaning: abstract semantic reference to entities, their properties and interrelationships. This would result in an evolutionary transition to the full 9-subsytem architecture we started out with in Figure 1.

This outline of the evolution of 6-, 7-, 8- and 9-subsystem architectures has numerous ramifications that will be addressed in more detail in other publications. Here, we simply note those features most relevant to the debate concerning the distinctiveness of cognitive and emotional processes. The 6-subsystem architecture now includes additional, more differentiated, cognitive processes that allow a form of internal mental imagery to occur concurrently with the control of action. The arrangement is very similar to that which applies to a visuo-spatial scratchpad interacting with a central executive in Baddeley's (1986) cognitive model of working memory. This architecture we attribute at least to the great apes and therefore by inference to the last common ancestor of both apes and the human lineage (see Byrne, 1995, pp. 27–30). We conjecture that it could well account for the more advanced forms of learning proposed for great apes (e.g., see Byrne, 2002) as well as for the ability of some apes to communicate generatively using visual symbols (e.g., Savage-Rumbaugh, 1986). We know of no extant species for which a clear case can be made for 7- and 8-subsystem mental architectures, though the logic of our analysis predicts that *there must have been* hominins in the direct human lineage that had such architectures. A case can be made that one or more species developed a 7-subsystem architecture perhaps even in the era of *Homo erectus*, while later, archaic species of *Homo* such as *Homo heidelbergensis* and *Homo neanderthalensis* are obvious candidates for 8-subsystem architectures. A mental architecture with eight subsystems would bear a striking similarity to Baddeley's (1986) full working memory model in which a central executive (equated here with the Multi-modal subsystem) controls both a visuo-spatial scratch-pad (here mediated by reciprocal exchanges between the Multi-modal subsystem and the Spatial–praxic subsystem) as well as a phonological loop (mediated here by exchanges between the Multi-modal subsystem and the Morphonolexical system). Hence, empirical evidence collected in support of that model could be recruited to infer key aspects of the likely mental capabilities of precursor species as well as our own (for one application of arguments based on the WM model to cognitive evolution see Coolidge & Wynn, 2005).

The addition of successive "cognitive" resources in the trajectory from a 5- to a 9-subsystem architecture allows successive architectures to do more things concurrently, to base their computations on increased levels of abstraction, and to accomplish increasingly sophisticated "reorganisation" of elements in streams of information flowing round the full system. The 5-subsystem architecture would have devoted all its resources to the control of action. The 6-subsystem successor has the capability to mentally manipulate information in the spatial–praxic domain while acting in the world. The PCA that mediates spatial–praxis is also a *second order* abstraction whose properties are now passed to the Multi-modal subsystem—in addition to the first-order products flowing on the direct pathways from the three sensory subsystems to the Multi-modal subsystem (Figure 5). The 7-subsystem architectures would have allowed an enlarged suite of concurrent streams. The 8-subsystem architecture has the capability to reorganise information in both spatial–praxic and auditory–verbal domains and hence could well have exhibited a form of "generative" spoken communication. The transition from eight to nine adds another layer of "semantic" abstraction and with that a capability for generative use of meaning in thought and language. A behaviourally modern human with this architecture has reciprocal processing exchanges between two levels of meaning. This enables us to manipulate meanings, i.e., "think", at the same time as processing all of the contingencies handled within the eight-subsystem arrangement. Teasdale and Barnard (1993) referred to these exchanges between two levels of meaning as "the central engine" of human ideation.

EMOTION, COGNITION AND MEANING

The hypothetical evolutionary trajectory we have outlined has direct consequences for the cognition–emotion debate. At the very least, it provides a basis for understanding how an evolutionarily old role for affective markers in action selection came to relate to more differentiated forms of emotional meanings. Throughout the trajectory from 5- to 9-subsystem architectures, each new subsystem that emerges fulfils a function that is essentially "cognitive" in nature with the kinds of properties outlined in the previous paragraph. Even so, each step in our trajectory altered the nature of the inputs to the Multi-modal subsystem and, with that, the kinds of cognitive-affective syntheses computed in the PCAs of all those Multi-modal subsystems than preceded the 9-subsystem architecture. Along this trajectory pre-prepared emotional responses would enter into very different combinations with "cognitive" components. The direct link to immediate constraints on action selection in the 5-subsystem architecture is augmented in the 6-, 7-, and 8-subsystem architectures by second-order abstractions and then by inputs from third-order (propositional) abstractions in the 9-subsystem architecture. The PCA computed in the Implicational subsystem of this architecture would have coding dimensions capable of capturing fourth-order invariants over the fraction of its coding space that applied to inputs from the Propositional subsystem. In this architecture affect can be allied with meanings in addition to the direct products of perception. As discussed by Teasdale and Barnard (1993), propositional meaning enables the concept of an emotion to be invoked without the experience of it—a feature that proved particularly problematic for earlier "associative network" models with spreading activation such as that proposed by Bower (1981).

While evolutionary arguments are of a necessarily speculative nature, we can at least use them to provide some concrete illustrations for otherwise abstract conjectures. This can be approached by considering some hypothetical effects of the manufacture and use of tools by those early precursor species to *Homo sapiens* that we argue had a 6-subsystem mental architecture comparable to those of extant species of great ape. Tool use creates new opportunities for variation and pattern in behaviours (e.g., see Davidson & McGrew, 2005). There are several lines of argument for enhanced cognitive capabilities. Stone knapping requires well-timed and carefully aimed blows of some force, and the use of stone flakes in cutting meat or plant material, such as wood, would have required a significant degree of manipulative skill (see Byrne, 2004, for a fuller list). It also requires the ability to discriminate properties of physical materials, like their hardness, or environments in which materials of that type could be found. The literature is replete with discussions of cognitive dimensions of tool use, the implications for dietary advantage, and even the possible impact of being a toolmaker on sexual selection (e.g., see collection in Gibson & Ingold, 1993, or Wynn, 2002), but it has so far largely neglected affective dimensions.

Stone flakes can be as sharp as a surgeon's scalpel and there are very obvious risks of harm not only to a "target" but also to the tool users themselves. There would undoubtedly have been periodic accidental bruising, cutting, piercing or grazing in the course of skill acquisition or in routine tool use. The same observation would apply to pointed wooden implements that could also have been used far earlier than their appearance in the archaeological record.[3] The behaviours enabled by cognitive advance massively raise the stakes in terms of the number of different ways harm and benefit can come about. Harm inflicted either by self-as-agent of the action, or potentially by others as the agent of the action would imply that negative markers of affect in the Multi-modal subsystem of a 6-subsytem architecture could now attach to entities with more abstract properties (e.g., sharpness) than were possible in the 5-subsystem architecture. Affect could also attach to at least some invariants underlying the organisation of action sequences—though we should be very careful not to assign these the status of fully fledged "cognitive plans". Exchanges between the two central subsystems in this architecture allows for affect to be attached to entities or abstractions over spatial–praxic sequences even when they were not being currently processed in sensory subsystems.

It is easy to imagine a whole range of behavioural scenarios in which other basic emotions might have been generated. Would early hominins with 6-subsystem architectures have experienced positive affect as they completed the manufacture of a tool that was of the "right form" to be fit for purpose? Would they have experienced surprise at a physical object when the stone core being shaped into a tool fractured in the wrong way? Were they frustrated or angry when attempting to cut a tough ligament using a blunted edge? What kind of affective states may have occurred while observing another hominin obtain food via the use of a tool that they themselves did not have access to, or fear when approached by an opponent with a pointed stick? If excrement were to attach to a blade during the processing of a carcass would they have felt disgust? Clearly, any detail in answers to these or other related questions would be mere speculation. However, the general idea that tool use would have led to new combinatorial states for abstract properties of objects, agents, praxis and affect seems a much less controversial proposal when abstracted away from the detail of specific

---

[3] Thieme (1997) reports the appearance of spears at Schoeningen in Germany dated to some 400,000 years ago. Stone flakes from far earlier carry the traces of wood material (Dominguez-Rodrigo, Serrallonga, Juan-Tresserras, Alcala, & Luque, 2001). Since wood is inedible and this is well prior to clear evidence of the control of fire, this is at least consistent with tool manufacture.

instances. If so, it would follow that emotion processing would have been more differentiated than in precursor species with 5-subsystem architectures.

The presence of some higher order ingredients in the multi-modal PCA space has wider implications for differentiation in cognitive processing. These ingredients can be thought of as bringing into being spatial–praxic dimensions underpinning later developments that ultimately culminated in human meaning. Suppose, prior to the development of tools, that material could only be "partitioned" into parts by tearing or biting and that this could be achieved by a simple mapping of perceptual patterns onto actions. Once tools emerged there would be *far more variation* in how partition could be achieved (cutting, slicing, using a hammer stone to separate a flake from a core or to fragment a nutshell to obtain its contents, or using a chopper to open an oyster shell). The "instruments" now used to partition other things need to be distinguished on the basis of their properties (shape, sharpness, mass, etc.), as do the things that are best partitioned in each manner. Likewise, there may be other subsets of similarities in patterns of actions carried out by hominins—grinding actions, probing actions, digging actions, carrying actions or throwing actions—all of which arose from the use of tools. Yet other examples of variation and underlying pattern in the behaviour of social agents not directly related to tool use could equally well have been developed—for example, gestural communication (e.g., see Noble & Davidson, 1996).

Variation of this type is a precursor for new invariants to emerge that capture underlying commonalities and roles. While simple categorisation is clearly part of this, our analysis embeds categorisation specifically within relationships that hold between self/other agents, objects and environments within multi-modal abstractions supporting *action selection*. This parallels the kinds of distinctions that are made in case grammars (e.g., Fillmore, 1968). These distinguish the semantic roles taken by animate and inanimate entities *in relation to the action* expressed by the verb. Byrne et al. (2004) noted that case roles realised in human language are also *implicit* in the behaviour of chimpanzees (see Table 1). We chose our example of tool use because it is easy to see how it could have contributed to the foundations for invariants underlying several of these roles, but not yet of a truly "propositional" nature.

The greatly elaborated behavioural repertoire permitted by a 6-subsystem architecture, therefore would have created conditions where new patterns occur in multi-modal dimensions and these need to be modelled for the augmentation of action selection. There must be a significant degree of variation in related states for the modelling of underlying invariants to be of value in guiding behaviour. At this point "meaning" is merely implicit within a single multi-modal system that synthesises over sensory, affective and

TABLE 1
Semantic roles in "propositions" and possible precursor spatial–praxic variation

Semantic role	Fillmore's definition	Linguistic example (propositional)	Chimpanzee behaviours as exemplars of spatial–praxic variation of the type likely to have been differentiating in the multi-modal space of any six-subsystem architecture
Agent	*Instigator* of an event	*John* opens the door	Chimpanzee, *"Mike"* twists off a *Strychnos* fruit
Counter-agent	Force or resistance **against which** the action is carried out	John hit **the desk**	A chimpanzee strikes a *Strychnos* fruit against a **stone** to break it open
Object	Entity that **moves or changes** or whose position or existence is **under consideration**	**Mary** is seven years old	Chimpanzee, "**Figan**" is alpha male
Result	Entity that comes **into existence** as a result of the action	Mary made **a cake**	Chimpanzee makes a **fishing probe** by stripping leaves from a grass stem
Instrument	Inanimate **stimulus** or immediate **physical cause** of an event	**The key** unlocked the door	**Spherical stone**, used as a hammer by a chimpanzee to crack nuts
Dative	Animate being **affected** by the action named by the verb	I gave my sweets to **Mary**	Female chimpanzee, "**Flora**", is being groomed by another
Experiencer	Animate being having a given **experience** or **mental state**	**Daddy** is cross	Piloerection, *waa* barks and stick waving show that chimpanzee "**Frodo**" is angry
Locative	**Location** or **spatial orientation** of the **state or action named** by the verb	Toby sits by **the fire**	Chimpanzees sit **under the tree around the anvil**

Note: Adapted from Byrne et al., 2004.

praxic dimensions to select among actions that can be beneficially applied to states of the world, body and "mind".

With the addition of the 7th (Articulatory) and 8th (Morphonolexical) subsystems, emotional states computed in the Multi-modal subsystem would now occur not just over properties of action sequences but also over properties of verbal communication. By extension of the arguments offered earlier, an owner of the 7-subsystem architecture could have felt happy, surprised, angry, frightened or disgusted as a function of similarity in vocal form. An owner of the 8-subsystem architecture could additionally generate similar emotional reactions to whole phrases, be they heard or "imagined", with similar content in abstract organisations. Each of these developments would encapsulate differentiation in emotion processing over and above that attained in a 6-subsystem mental architecture.

In the 6-, 7- and 8-subsystem architectures dimensions of "meaning" were implicit in the multi-modal component, in the sense addressed in Table 1, and these relate to a blend of first- and second-order abstractions. Meaning only becomes a separate coding space, and therefore explicit, in the 9-subsystem arrangement. The presence of a central engine, and the reciprocal exchanges it permits, provides the resources for its owner to walk and/or make tools while it is talking and thinking about what it is saying, doing or even its own mental state at one and the same time. It can think abstractly about what might be wrong with the tool it is making, how to design a better one or how to tell someone else to do it, with all that implies for cognitive creativity and cultural transmission.

In the final human architecture, affective dimensions would now attach within a coding space of holistic schematic meanings, and those meanings would be a cross product of immediate experience and "thought". Importantly, the PCA now constructed in this domain would encompass material about the self, other animate agents, objects and environments. It would be "modelling" a wide range of cognitive and affective contingencies within the human existential space. The modelling would cover knowledge in domains that we would consider primarily "cognitive" such as deep expertise in intellectual pursuits like art, literature, science or chess, as well as in interpersonal domains such as theory of mind, or conventions guiding actions in a social world. At the end of our evolutionary trajectory "affective processing" is retained within the Implicational subsystem. It still receives the same first-order derivatives from sensory inputs (vision, audition and body states) as the 5-subsystem architecture, along with its links to somatic and visceral response mechanisms and the release of other innately prepared effector actions. However, it now blends fast situational awareness carried by first-order derivates of immediate patterns of sensation—say, facial expressions, tones of voice and bodily correlates of, say, anxiety, with the products of propositional thought. This cognitive-affective coding space is now far removed from that used to augment action selection in the 5-subsystem architecture we started out with. It receives and generates qualitatively different inputs and outputs from the original Multi-modal subsystem taken as our basis for mental capabilities of monkeys. As additional cognitive processes differentiated across the evolutionary trajectory we have outlined, cognitive processing has developed via the unfolding of a one-stage multi-modal process modulating action selection into many stages that can interact reciprocally.

DISCUSSION

Our aim in this paper was to contribute to the theoretical foundations of the debate concerning the distinctiveness of affective processing. Our presentation of a mechanism for process and subsystem differentiation allowed us to specify a hypothetical trajectory in some detail as a basis for further discussion and debate. In terms of its substance, the analysis provides some explicit claims concerning the nature of the connective tissue whereby the role of basic emotions was successfully modified from a direct coupling to action selection to one in which affective markers blend with increasingly abstract mental codes until we achieve a mental architecture with the kind of subtle linkages between meaning and emotion we observe in the human mind.

The clearest implication of what we have proposed is that meaningful answers to questions concerning distinctions between cognitive and affective processes are all going to be a function of the mental architecture used to characterise the species in focus. In the argument we have presented, affect always attaches to a synthesis of multi-modal inputs and a general mechanism underlies it (dimension reduction and inversion). But what affect *attaches to* varies as a function of the particular way processes have evolved in the spatial–praxic, auditory–verbal and propositional domains—specialised functions that are all associated with the label "cognitive". As with some other perspectives (e.g., Storbeck & Clore, this issue) affect and cognition is thought of here as fundamentally interactive, and the interactions are closely dependent upon the content of information being processed throughout the mental architecture, its behavioural significance or meaning. Whereas the 5-subsystem architecture allowed a narrow range of "routes" to the generation of affect, the 9-subsystem architecture allows multiple routes, an attribute brought into focus not only in other multi-level models (e.g., Power & Dalgleish, 1997) but also in arguments based upon the intricate circuitry in brain architecture (e.g., LeDoux, 1996; Duncan & Barrett, this issue). Here the particular routes to the generation of affect in human mental architecture have been derived via the step-by-step application of a set of assumptions about process differentiation.

Evolutionary arguments of the form developed here also have direct consequences for ideas that might well be examined in future empirical research in comparative psychology on the relationship between emotion and cognition. For example, in our discussion of the use of stone tools, we noted that affect in a 6-subsystem architecture can attach to representations of abstract organisations of spatial–praxic information not possible with the 5-subsystem architecture. Hence it should be possible to test such an idea with extant species. Great apes should, for example, generate similar affective responses to similar organisations of spatial–praxis on the basis or higher order categorisations whereas monkeys should generate similar affective responses only to patterns that are similar in lower order derivatives of perceptual form. One of the current authors (Byrne) in field observation at Mahale, Tanzania, during 1984 watched a male chimpanzee eating the brain of a monkey while perching on a mass of lianas roughly 2 m above the ground. Instead of dropping the small, clean shards of brain case, the male carefully balanced each on a horizontal liana, so that when he left the shards were "organised" in a well-ordered row along the liana. In this case an abstract attribute of spatial–praxis, akin to "neatness", appeared to hold in the positive context of food intake where the behaviour and its resulting product apparently served no obvious goal-based function. If abstract properties such as proto-"neatness" are systematically linked to positive affect in this species but not others, perhaps the origins of doing something just for "fun", then the idea should be testable in laboratory research.

In the domain of cognitive archaeology, there are also significant implications for interpretation of evidence in the archaeological record. Our analysis suggests that only three fundamental reconfigurations of mental architecture were required in between us and our last common ancestor with great apes—although differing degrees of incremental representational differentiation are possible within each reconfiguration. In our earlier discussion we noted that a 7-subsystem architecture could well have been in place during the era of *Homo erectus*. At this point, "Acheulean" stone tools are present in the archaeological record, with a more sophisticated manufacture and symmetrical appearance than those of earlier "Oldowan" stone industries (e.g., see Noble & Davison, 1996). The Oldowan tools could well have been created by species with 6-subsystem architectures not unlike that we conjecture could hold with gorillas and chimpanzees who have the capability to make comparable tools (see Byrne, 2004; Toth, Schick, Savage-Rumbaugh, & Sevcik, 1993). Our analysis raises the possibility that the presence of Acheulean tools is consistent not only with advances in manual or spatial skill, allied in our analysis to the far earlier emergence of a 6-subsystem architecture, but with the emergence of vocalisation. The guidance of vocalisation, and a significant capability to blend positive and negative affect with more flexible vocal patterns that are not innately endowed, could well have facilitated a form of cultural transmission of skills from generation to generation that would have been far more problematic for species with a mental architecture lacking flexible articulation. The evolutionary trajectory we have proposed holds that flexible vocalisation emerged in the first major reconfiguration of mental architecture following the development of more sophisticated spatial–praxic skills and therefore offers some convergent scaffolding for other arguments for the emergence of speech. For example, empirically grounded work on the relationships that hold between brain size and grooming, a social behaviour linked to positive affect, has also been used to suggest that vocal communication may well have begun to serve a grooming-like function in the era of *Homo erectus* (e.g., Aiello & Dunbar, 1993; Dunbar, 2004).

An evolutionary analysis of the form presented here, and the ICS model on which it depends, could not make direct predictions into standard laboratory paradigm without more detailed consideration of the demands imposed, for example, by specific memory tasks (e.g., see Ramponi, Barnard, & Nimmo-Smith, 2004) or attention tasks (see Barnard, Ramponi, Battye, & Mackintosh, 2005). It can, however, serve to frame the way in which such predictions are derived as well as emphasising key contrasts with other current theories. Our analysis indicates that emotional differentiation is not a product of blending more basic emotions (Plutchik, 1980; Turner, 2000). Rather, it involves a blending of affective markers with derivatives of propositional thought. In this context, a good deal is known about the ways emotional material influences attention and memory. One of the more dominant theories in this domain is that evolutionarily old mechanisms of arousal and valence are the main determinants of such effects in, for example, recognition memory for pictures (Ochsner, 2000) or in the disruption of attention by emotional material in paradigms such as the attentional blink effect (Anderson, 2005). The current analysis strongly suggests that such effects should be determined at least in part by meaning. Hence, were emotional pictures to be matched for arousal and valence, there should still be significant variation in recognition memory as a function of schematic meaning. Indeed, Croucher (2007) has shown that recognition memory for negative emotional pictures matched for arousal and valence is considerably better for those pictures with high personal impact than those with low personal impact—a rating that is directly related to the schematic meanings of the content in the pictures. In contrast, when pictures are matched for impact, and distinctiveness is factored out, Croucher found that no significant effects of the arousal variable remained. This effect, while challenging for traditional dimensional models of emotions based on evolutionary old mechanisms, is wholly consistent with the view advocated here.

More widely, multi-level theories, by their very nature require specification of the levels involved as well as a specification of how component resources interact. Particularly with a macro-theory such as ICS, this leaves such approaches open to the criticism that such models are "unnecessarily" complex in comparison to simpler models that are paradigm specific. Here, we have established a clear audit trace for the particular configuration of cognitive-affective resources proposed by ICS. The evolutionary argument thus complements and reinforces other arguments for the utility of this architecture from empirical data (e.g., Barnard et al., 2005; Ramponi et al.,

2004) and those concerning our subjective experience of feelings (e.g., Teasdale & Barnard, 1993) as well as those from computational modelling (e.g., Barnard & Bowman, 2003; Barnard, May, Duke, & Duce, 2000).

REFERENCES

Aiello, L. C., & Dunbar, R. (1993). Neocortex size, group size, and the evolution of language. *Current Anthropology, 34,* 184–193.

Amati, D., & Shallice, T. (2007). On the emergence of modern humans. *Cognition, 103*(3), 358–385.

Anderson, A. K. (2005). Affective influences on the attentional dynamics supporting awareness. *Journal of Experimental Psychology General, 134*(2), 258–281.

Baddeley, A. (1986). *Working memory.* Oxford, UK: Clarendon Press.

Baddeley, A. (1990). *Human memory: Theory and practice.* Hove, UK: Lawrence Erlbaum Associates, Ltd.

Barnard, P. J. (1985). Interacting cognitive subsystems: A psycholinguistic approach to short-term memory. In A. Ellis (Ed.), *Progress in the psychology of language* (Vol. 2, pp. 197–258). London: Lawrence Erlbaum Associates, Ltd.

Barnard, P. J. (1999). Interacting cognitive subsystems: Modelling working memory phenomena within a multi-processor architecture. In A. Miyake & P. Shah (Eds.), *Models of working memory* (pp. 298–339). Cambridge, UK: Cambridge University Press.

Barnard, P. J. (2004). Bridging between basic theory and clinical practice. *Behaviour Research and Therapy, 42,* 977–1000.

Barnard, P. J., & Bowman, H. (2003). Rendering information processing models of cognition and affect computationally explicit: Distributed executive control and the deployment of attention. *Cognitive Science Quarterly, 3*(3), 297–328.

Barnard, P. J., May, J., Duke, D., & Duce, D. (2000). Systems, interactions and macrotheory. *ACM Transactions on Human-Computer Interaction, 7*(2), 222–262.

Barnard, P. J., Ramponi, C., Battye, G., & Mackintosh, B. (2005). Anxiety and the deployment of visual attention over time. *Visual Cognition, 12,* 181–211.

Barnard, P. J., & Teasdale, J. D. (1991). Interacting cognitive subsystems: A systemic approach to cognitive-affective interaction and change. *Cognition and Emotion, 5,* 1–39.

Bettinger, F., & Cootes, T. F. (2004, May). *A model of facial behaviour.* Paper presented at the Sixth IEEE International Conference on Automatic Face and Gesture Recognition, Seoul, South Korea.

Bower, G. H. (1981). Mood and memory. *The American Psychologist, 36,* 129–148.

Byrne, R. W. (1995). *The thinking ape: evolutionary origins of intelligence.* Oxford, UK: Oxford University Press.

Byrne, R. W. (2002). Imitation of novel complex actions: What does the evidence from animals mean? *Advances in the Study of Behaviour, 31,* 77–105.

Byrne, R. W. (2004). The manual skills behind hominid tool use. In A. E. Russon & D. R. Begun (Eds.), *Evolutionary origins of great ape intelligence* (pp. 31–44). Cambridge, UK: Cambridge University Press.

Byrne, R. W., Barnard, P. J., Davidson, I., Janik, V. M., McGrew, W., Miklósi, A., et al. (2004). Understanding culture across species. *Trends in Cognitive Sciences, 8,* 341–346.

Calder, A. J., Burton, A. M., Miller, P., Young, A. W., & Akamatsu, S. (2001). A principal component analysis of facial expressions. *Vision Research, 41*(9), 1179–1208.

Christiansen, M. H., & Kirby, S. (2003). *Language evolution.* Oxford, UK: Oxford University Press.

Coolidge, F. L., & Wynn, T. (2005). Working memory, its executive functions and the emergence of modern thinking. *Cambridge Archaeological Journal, 15*(1), 5–26.

Croucher, C. (2007). *Impact and the recollection of emotional images.* PhD Thesis, University of Cambridge, UK.

Dalgleish, T., & Power, M. J. (1999). *The handbook of cognition and emotion.* Chichester, UK: Wiley.

Davidson, I. (2003). The archaeological evidence of language origins: States of art. In M. H. Christiansen & S. Kirby (Eds.), *Language evolution* (pp. 452–464). Oxford, UK: Oxford University Press.

Davidson, I., & McGrew, W. C. (2005). Stone tools and the uniqueness of human culture. *Journal of the Royal Anthropological Institute, 11,* 793–817.

Dominguez-Rodrigo, M., Serrallonga, J., Juan-Tresserras, J., Alcala, L., & Luque, L. (2001). Woodworking activities by early humans. *Journal of Human Evolution, 40,* 289–299.

Duke, D. J., Barnard, P. J., Duce, D. A., & May, J. (1998). Syndetic modelling. *Human–Computer Interaction, 13*(4), 337–393.

Dunbar, R. (2004). *The human story.* London: Faber & Faber.

Fillmore, C. (1968). The case for case. In E. Bach & R. Harms (Eds.), *Universals in linguistic theory* (pp. 1–88). New York: Holt, Rinehart, & Winston.

Frijda, N. H. (2004). Emotions and action. In A. S. R. Manstead, N. Frijda, & A. Fischer (Eds.), *Feelings and emotions: The Amsterdam symposium* (pp. 158–173). Cambridge, UK: Cambridge University Press.

Gibson, K. R., & Ingold, T. (1993). *Tools, language and cognition in human evolution.* Cambridge, UK: Cambridge University Press.

Johnson, M. K. (1983). A multiple-entry, modular memory system. In G. H. Bower (Ed.), *The psychology of learning and motivation. Vol. 17: Advances in research and theory* (pp. 81–123). New York: Academic Press.

Landauer, T. K., & Dumais, S. T. (1997). A solution to Plato's problem: The latent semantic analysis theory of the acquisition, induction and representation of knowledge. *Psychological Review, 104,* 211–240.

Lane, R. D., Quinlan, D. M., Schwartz, G. E., Walker, P. A., & Zeitlin, S. B. (1990). The levels of emotional awareness scale: A cognitive developmental measure of emotion. *Journal of Personality Assessment, 55,* 124–134.

Lang, P. J., Bradley, M. M., & Cuthbert, B. N. (1997). Motivated attention: Affect activation, and action. In P. J. Lang, R. F. Simons, & M. T. Balaban (Eds.), *Attention and orienting: Sensory and motivational processes* (pp. 97–135). Mahwah, NJ: Lawrence Erlbaum Associates, Inc.

Lawrence, A., & Calder, A. (2004). Homologising human emotions. In D. Evans & P. Cruse (Eds.), *Emotion, evolution, and rationality* (pp. 15–47). Oxford, UK: Oxford University Press.

LeDoux, J. E. (1996). *The emotional brain: The mysterious underpinnings of emotional life.* New York: Touchstone.

MacLarnon, A., & Hewitt, G. (1999). The evolution of human speech: The role of enhanced breathing control. *American Journal of Physical Anthropology, 109,* 341–363.

Mithen, S. (1996). *The prehistory of the mind: The cognitive origins of art, religion, and science.* London: Thames & Hudson.

Morton, J. (1968). Considerations of grammar and computation in language behaviour. In J. C. Catford (Ed.), *Studies in language and language behavior* (CRLLB Progress Report No. VI). Ann Arbor, MI: University of Michigan.

Newell, A. (1990). *Unified theories of cognition.* Cambridge, MA: Harvard University Press.

Niedenthal, P. M., Barsalou, L. W., Winkielman, P., Krauth-Gruber, S., & Ric, F. (2005). Embodiment in attitudes, social perception, and emotion. *Personality and Social Psychology Bulletin, 9*(3), 184–211.

Noble, W., & Davidson, I. (1996). *Human evolution, language and mind.* Cambridge, UK: Cambridge University Press.

Oatley, K., & Johnson-Laird, P. N. (1987). Towards a cognitive theory of emotions. *Cognition and Emotion, 1,* 29–50.

Ochsner, K. N. (2000). Are affective events richly recollected or simply familiar? The experience and process of recognizing feelings past. *Journal of Experimental Psychology: General, 129*(2), 242–261.

Öhman, A., Flykt, A., & Lundqvist, D. (2000). Unconscious emotion: Evolutionary perspectives, psychophysiological data, and neuropsychological mechanisms. In R. D. Lane & L. Nadel (Eds.), *Cognitive neuroscience of emotion* (pp. 296–327). Oxford, UK: Oxford University Press.

O'Reilly, R. C., & Munakata, Y. (2000). *Computational explorations in cognitive neuroscience: Understanding the mind by simulating the brain.* Cambridge, MA: MIT Press.

Philippot, P., Baeyens, C., Douilliez, C., & Francart, B. (2004). Cognitive regulation of emotion: Application to clinical disorders. In P. Philippot & R. S. Feldman (Eds.), *The regulation of emotion* (pp. 71–97). Mahwah, NJ: Lawrence Erlbaum Associates, Inc.

Plutchik, R. (1980). *Emotion: A psychoevolutionary synthesis.* New York: Harper & Row.

Power, M., & Dalgleish, T. (1997). *Cognition and emotion: From order to disorder.* Hove, UK: Psychology Press.

Ramponi, C., Barnard, P., & Nimmo-Smith, M. I. (2004). Recollection deficits in dysphoric mood: An effect of schematic models and executive mode? *Memory, 12*(5), 655–670.

Rozin, P., Haidt, J., & McCauley, C. (1999). Disgust: The body and soul emotion. In T. Dalgleish & M. J. Power (Eds.), *Handbook of cognition and emotion* (pp. 429–445). Chichester, UK: Wiley.

Rumelhart, D. E., McClelland, J. L., & PDP, Group (1986). *Parallel distributed processing: Explorations in the microstructure of cognition. Vol. 1: Foundations and Vol. 2: Psychological and biological models.* Cambridge, MA: MIT Press.

Savage-Rumbaugh, S. (1986). *Ape language: From conditioned response to symbol.* New York: Columbia University Press.

Shallice, T. (1988). *From neuropsychology to mental structure.* Cambridge, UK: Cambridge University Press.

Teasdale, J. D. (1999a). Multi-level theories of cognition and emotion. In T. Dalgleish & M. J. Power (Eds.), *The handbook of cognition and emotion* (pp. 665–681). Chichester, UK: Wiley.

Teasdale, J. D. (1999b). Emotional processing, three modes of mind, and the prevention of relapse in depression. *Behaviour Research and Therapy, 37,* S53–S77.

Teasdale, J. D., & Barnard, P. J. (1993). *Affect, cognition and change.* Hove, UK: Lawrence Erlbaum Associates, Ltd.

Thieme, H. (1997). Lower Palaeolithic hunting spears from Germany. *Nature, 385,* 807–810.

Tooby, L., & Cosmides, J. (2000). Evolutionary psychology and the emotions. In M. Lewis & J. M. Haviland-Jones (Eds.), *Handbook of emotions* (2nd ed., pp. 91–115). New York: Guilford Press.

Toth, N., Schick, K. D., Savage-Rumbaugh, E. S., & Sevcik, R. A. (1993). *Pan* the tool-maker: Investigations into the stone tool-making and tool-using capabilities of a bonobo (*Pan paniscus*). *Journal of Archaeological Science, 20,* 81–91.

Turner, J. H. (2000). *On the origins of human emotions.* Stanford, CA: Stanford University Press.

Williams, J. M. G., Watts, F. N., MacLeod, C., & Mathews, A. (1997). *Cognitive psychology and emotional disorders* (2nd ed.). Chichester, UK: Wiley.

Wynn, T. (2002). Archaeology and cognitive evolution. *Behavioural and Brain Sciences, 25,* 389–438.

Zajonc, R. B. (1984). On the primacy of affect. *American Psychologist, 39,* 117–123.

COGNITION AND EMOTION
2007, 21 (6), 1184–1211

Affect is a form of cognition: A neurobiological analysis

Seth Duncan and Lisa Feldman Barrett

Boston College, Chestnut Hill, MA, USA

In this paper, we suggest that affect meets the traditional definition of "cognition" such that the affect–cognition distinction is phenomenological, rather than ontological. We review how the affect–cognition distinction is not respected in the human brain, and discuss the neural mechanisms by which affect influences sensory processing. As a result of this sensory modulation, affect performs several basic "cognitive" functions. Affect appears to be necessary for normal conscious experience, language fluency, and memory. Finally, we suggest that understanding the differences between affect and cognition will require systematic study of how the phenomenological distinction characterising the two comes about, and why such a distinction is functional.

Scholars have long assumed that cognition and affect are separable (and often opposing) mental processes (Aristotle, 1991; Plato, 1992). Modern psychological science no longer views them as opposing forces within the human mind, but continues to be grounded by the assumption that "thinking" (e.g., sensing and categorising an object, or deliberating on an object) is a fundamentally different sort of psychological activity than "affecting" (i.e., constructing a state to represent how the object affects you). Many psychologists believe that cognition and affect interact (cf. Storbeck & Clore, 2007 this issue). Cognitions might trigger affective feelings or behaviours, and affect might influence cognitive processes like memory and attention but the two are considered to be separate in some real and fundamental way (what philosophers would call "ontologically" distinct). The purpose of this special issue is to discuss the distinctiveness of affect and cognition, and in this paper we question whether the boundary between the two is given by nature, or whether it is a phenomenological distinction that

Correspondence should be addressed to: Lisa Feldman Barrett, Department of Psychology, Boston College, Chestnut Hill, MA 02467, USA. E-mail: barretli@bc.edu

Preparation of this manuscript was supported by NIMH grant K02 MH001981 and NIA grant ROI AG030311 to LFB.

During the preparation of this article the authors benefited from discussions with Elizabeth Kensinger, Ann Kring, and Luiz Pessoa.

© 2007 Psychology Press, an imprint of the Taylor & Francis Group, an Informa business
www.psypress.com/cogemotion   DOI: 10.1080/02699930701437931

can, at times, be functional. The psychologist's fallacy, Dewey (1894) wrote, "is to confuse the standpoint of the observer and explainer with that of the fact observed" (p. 555; see also James, 1890/1950, p. 196). There is a risk, he explains, of confusing functional distinctions with ontological ones. We might not go as far as to call the distinction between affect and cognition a fallacy, but it may be the case that the distinction between the two is rooted in function rather than in nature.

In his formative book on cognitive psychology, Neisser wrote, "The term 'cognition' refers to all processes by which ... sensory input is transformed, reduced, elaborated, stored, recovered, and used" (Neisser, 1967, p. 4). Following Neisser, we suggest that affect is a form of cognition. Neisser's definition of cognition was purposefully broad, and the field has moved beyond this broad definition. Even the distinction between sensation and cognition has been called into question, given the emerging evidence that that perceptual and conceptual processing have substantial overlap (Barsalou, in press; Barsalou, Simmons, Barbey, & Wilson, 2003b). In this paper, we focus on the idea that affect makes important contributions to both sensory and cognitive processing. Since all objects and events have somatovisceral consequences, cognitive and sensory experiences are necessarily affectively infused to some degree. There is no such thing as a "non-affective thought". Affect plays a role in perception and cognition, even when people cannot feel its influence.

We begin by offering a precise definition of affect, following which we pose the question of whether an affect–cognition distinction is respected by the human brain. We answer this question by outlining the neural reference space for what is traditionally called affective processing and then focus on accumulating findings that increasingly blur the affect–cognition boundary. Specifically, we discuss how affect modulates bottom-up contributions to sensory processing in both direct and indirect ways. We then suggest the consequences of this modulation for consciousness, language, and memory. In the end, we conclude that the affect–cognition divide is grounded in phenomenology, and offer some thoughts on how this phenomenological distinction arises.

CORE AFFECT

The word "affect" is generally used to refer to any state that represents how an object or situation impacts a person. The term "core affect" has been recently introduced to refer to a basic, psychologically primitive state that can be described by two psychological properties: hedonic valence (pleasure/displeasure) and arousal (activation/sleepy). Core affect has been characterised as the constant stream of transient alterations in an organism's neurophysiological and somatovisceral state that represent its immediate relationship to the flow of changing events (Barrett, 2006; Russell, 2003; Russell & Barrett, 1999); in a sense, core affect is a neurophysiologic barometer of the individual's relationship to an environment at a given point in time. To the extent that an object or event changes a person's "internal milieu" it can be said to have affective meaning—these changes are what we mean when we say that a person has an affective reaction to an object or stimulus. They are the means by which information about the external world is translated into an internal code or representations (Barnard, Duke, Byrne, & Davidson, 2007 this issue; Damasio, 1999; Nauta, 1971; Ongur & Price, 2000).

Core affect functions as "core knowledge" (see Spelke, 2000, on "core knowledge"), the hardwiring for which is present at birth (Bridges, 1932; Emde, Gaensbauer, & Harmon, 1976; Spitz, 1965; Sroufe, 1979) and is homologous in other mammalian species (Cardinal, Parkinson, Hall, & Everitt, 2002; Rolls, 1999; Schneirla, 1959). Core affect is universal to all humans (Mesquita, 2003; Russell, 1983; Scherer, 1997; Wierzbicka, 1992), is evident in all instrument-based measures of emotion (see Barrett, 2006, for a review), and forms the "core" of emotion experience (Barrett, 2006; Barrett, Mesquita, Ochsner, & Gross, 2007; Russell, 2003). Core affect (i.e., the neurophysiological state) is available to consciousness, and is experienced as feeling pleasant or unpleasant (valence) and to a lesser extent as activated or deactivated (arousal; see Russell & Barrett, 1999, for a review). If core affect is a neurophysiologic barometer that sums up the individual's relationship to the environment at a given point in time, then self-reported feelings are the barometer readings. Feelings of core affect provide a common metric for comparing qualitatively different events (Cabanac, 2002). As we discuss later, core affect is a precondition for first-person experiences of the world, and forms the core of conscious experience (Edelman & Tononi, 2000; Searle, 1992, 2004; Titchener, 1909; Wundt, 1897).

People experience core affective feelings as phenomenologically distinct from thoughts and memories, but, as we discuss in the next section, the circuitry that implements core affect serves as a core feature of cognitive processing in the human brain. By virtue of its broad, distributed connectivity, this circuitry modulates sensory processes both directly (via direct projections to sensory cortex) and indirectly (via projections to the thalamus and brainstem). Through this modulation, core affect plays a crucial role in all levels of cognitive processing, determining what people are conscious of, how they use and understand language, and what content is encoded and retrieved in memory.

THE BASIC CIRCUITRY OF CORE AFFECT

One way to address the question of whether cognition and affect are separable processes is to see if these psychological categories are respected by the human brain. The traditional view, depicted in Figure 1, and rooted in the works of Papez (1937) and MacLean (1949), and recently reinforced by LeDoux (1996), is that affect is cognitively impenetrable and implemented or entailed in subcortical regions of the brain (for a discussion see Barrett, Ochsner, & Gross, 2006). A simplified version of this traditional view is that negative and positive affect are computed in the amygdala and nucleus accumbens, respectively, both of which receive sensory input from thalamic nuclei and sensory cortex, and both of which send output to the brainstem. Cognitive processes are thought to regulate affective processing after the fact via inhibitory projections from the prefrontal cortex to these subcortical areas. Accordingly, the assumption has been that the brain respects the cognitive–affective divide.

Our review of the neuroanatomical and neuroimaging literature reveals, however, that no brain areas can be designated specifically as "cognitive" or "affective". Although it is the case that subcortical regions are regulated by prefrontal cortical regions, this state of affairs does not inevitably translate into the conclusion that cognitive parts of the brain regulate affective parts of the brain. Instead, it appears that affect is instantiated by a widely distributed, functional network that includes both subcortical regions (typically called "affective") and anterior frontal regions (traditionally called "cognitive"). As a result, parts of the brain that have traditionally

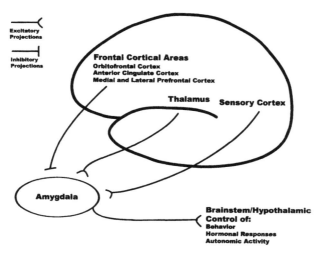

Figure 1.   A simplified version of the traditional view of the cognition/emotion distinction within the brain (adapted from LeDoux, 1996).

been called "cognitive" participate in instantiating an affective state, not merely regulating that state after it has been established. Furthermore, the parts of the brain that have traditionally been called "affective" participate in cognitive processes. The so-called "affective" brain areas (e.g., the amygdala and brainstem) participate in sensory processing and contribute to consciousness in a manner that meets most definitions of "cognition".

Affect is widely distributed throughout the brain

Core affect serves the primary function of translating sensory information from the external environment into an internal, meaningful representation that can be used to safely navigate the world. Widely distributed circuitry accomplishes this function, by binding sensory and somatovisceral information to create a valenced, mental representation of external objects (e.g., facial behaviours, foods, etc.). The function of this circuitry is to link sensory information about a stimulus with a representation of how the stimulus affects the person's internal (somatovisceral) state (Barbas, Saha, Rempel-Clower, & Ghashghaei, 2003; Ghashghaei & Barbas, 2002; Kringelbach & Rolls, 2004; Ongur, Ferry, & Price, 2003; Ongur & Price, 2000). This circuitry involves areas of the brain that are traditionally considered to be "affective" (e.g., amygdala and ventral striatum), along with anterior portions of the cortex that have traditionally been considered cognitive, including the lateral orbitofrontal cortex (OFC), the medial OFC, often called the ventromedial prefrontal cortex (vmPFC), and anterior cingulate cortex (ACC; see Figure 2). As we discuss here, these anterior cortical areas do not appear to simply regulate the amygdala, but rather they appear integral to computing the value of an object and guiding visceral and motor responses accordingly.

Although the details remain to be specified, the available evidence suggests that neural representations of sensory information about a stimulus and its somatovisceral impact are entailed by two related functional circuits that make up a ventral system for core affect (see Carmichael & Price, 1996; Elliott, Friston, & Dolan, 2000; Ongur & Price, 2000, for reviews). The first functional circuit involves connections between the basolateral complex (BL) of the amygdala (which, along with other amygdalar nuclei directs the organism to learn more about a stimulus so as to better determine its predictive value for well-being and survival; Davis & Whalen, 2001; Kim, Somerville, Johnstone, Alexander, & Whalen, 2003; Whalen, 1998) and the central and lateral aspects of the OFC, which are necessary to a flexible, experience- or context-dependent representation of an object's value (Dolan & Morris, 2000; Elliott et al., 2000; Kringelbach, 2005; Kringelbach & Rolls, 2004). Both the BL and lateral OFC (including the closely related anterior insula) have robust connections with cortical representations of every

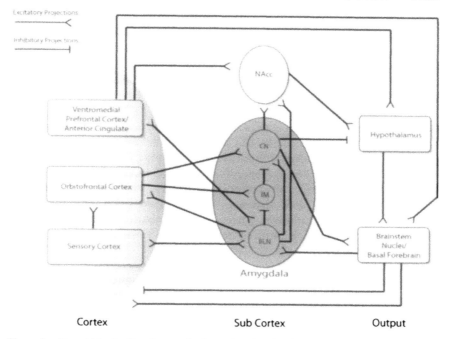

Figure 2.   The widely distributed network of neural regions involved in computing a core affective state. These regions include subcortical areas typically considered to be "affective" (e.g., the amygdala and nucleus accumbens), as well as portions of the cortex that are typically considered "cognitive", e.g., the ventromedial prefrontal cortex/anterior cingulate and orbitofrontal cortex (adapted from Barbas et al., 2003).

sensory modality and have strong reciprocal connections (Ghashghaei & Barbas, 2002; Kringelbach & Rolls, 2004; McDonald, 1998; Stefanacci & Amaral, 2002), so that they form a functional circuit that integrates sensory (including visceral) information. This information is needed to establish (at least initially) a value-based representation of an object that includes both external sensory features of the object, along with its impact on the homeostatic state of the body (Craig, 2002). One recent formulation argues that the BL complex formulates the predictive value of a stimulus, whereas the OFC participates in generating a response based on that prediction (Holland & Gallagher, 1999).

The second circuit, entailing a neural representation that guides visceromotor control, involves reciprocal connections between the vmPFC, including the closely related subgenual anterior cingulate cortex (ACC), and the amygdala. Together, these areas modulate the visceromotor (i.e., autonomic, chemical, and behavioural) responses that are part of the value-based representations of an object (Koski & Paus, 2000; Ongur &

Price, 2000). The vmPFC, in particular, may help to link sensory representations of stimuli and their associated visceromotor (i.e., core affective) outcomes and provides an "affective working memory" whose contents inform choices and judgments contingent upon an assessment of affective value (as computed by the BL and lateral OFC). This conclusion fits with the finding that vmPFC is important for altering simple stimulus-reinforcer associations via extinction (Milad et al., 2005; Phelps, Delgado, Nearing, & LeDoux, 2004; Quirk, Russo, Barron, & Lebron, 2000) or reversal learning (Fellows & Farah, 2003) and is preferentially activated by somatovisceral or interoceptive information (Hurliman, Nagode, & Pardo, 2005) more generally. The representations encoded in vmPFC may also be useful for decisions based on intuitions and feelings rather than on explicit rules (Goel & Dolan, 2003; Shamay-Tsoory, Tomer, Berger, Goldsher, & Aharon-Peretz, 2005), including guesses and familiarity-based discriminations (Elliott et al., 2000; Elliott, Rees, & Dolan, 1999; Schnider, Treyer, & Buck, 2000; Schnyer, Nicholls, & Verfaellie, 2005).

Conventional wisdom says that frontal areas regulate emotion, meaning that they offer a mechanism for control of the amygdala. Accumulating evidence, however, indicates that they are crucial components of a system that binds sensory information from inside the body with sensory information from outside the body. In doing so, the OFC and vmPFC (and adjacent ACC) guide appropriate responses to external objects. That is not to say that these frontal areas do not perform cognitive functions. These areas are heteromodal association areas and function to integrate sensory information from different sources. The main point of this paper, however, is that these areas (via the amygdala) project back to sensory cortices, influencing sensory processing in a fundamental way. The iterative nature of this process makes it difficult to derive simple cause and effect relationships between sensory and affective processing, although we will focus on one direction: how core affect influences how information about external objects is processed in the first place.

The cognitive functions of core affect

The amygdala's role in sensory processing has been clearly worked out, and so we focus our review on the amygdala for illustrative purposes. The amygdala modulates sensory processing in three ways. First, the amygdala can indirectly influence sensory processing through a top-down form of attention involving the dorsolateral prefrontal cortex (via connections with the OFC) in a goal-directed way (cf. Ochsner & Gross, 2005). Second, the amygdala can directly enhance stimulus-driven sensory processing via strong reciprocal connections with unimodal sensory areas, such as ventral visual cortex. Third, the amygdala engages in a bottom-up form of attention modulation, entraining all sensory cortical areas to select between competing sensory representations. In the next sections, we discuss the psychological consequences of these last two circuits. We are primarily interested in the latter two because they direct sensory processing based on the state of the organism.

The amygdala directly modulates sensory processing.   In this section, we focus our discussion on the manner in which the amygdala directly modulates visual processing, because the connectivity between the ventral stream and amygdala is well documented in primates. The amygdala, particularly the basal nucleus, influences visual processing in a very direct manner by modulating the intensity of neural firing in all portions of the ventral visual stream, from association visual cortex to primary visual cortex (Amaral, Behniea, & Kelly, 2003; Amaral & Price, 1984; Freese & Amaral, 2005). Here, we will review evidence to suggest that, through extensive feedback projections, the amygdala facilitates associative connections between affective value and basic visual features of the environment, even in V1. We also review evidence that the amygdala enhances the visual awareness of objects that have been deemed to have affective value (e.g., facial behaviours that depict emotions such as fear) by modulating activity in the more anterior aspects of the ventral stream. Given the amygdala's extensive connectivity to all sensory cortices, however, we expect that this discussion would hold true for the affective impact on other sensory modalities as well.

The amygdala appears to be important for developing associations between affective value and primitive features of the visual world. The primary visual cortex (V1) receives strong, excitatory projections from the basal nucleus of the amygdala. These excitatory neurons from the amygdala project to spiny, pyramidal cells in V1, which are commonly involved in associative learning (Freese & Amaral, 2006). Neuroimaging studies have reported increased activation around the V1/V2 boundary in response to affectively evocative (compared to neutral) stimuli (Moll et al., 2002). More specific evidence for affective modulation of V1 activity comes from a study using event-related potentials (ERPs) to classically conditioned images. Black and white gratings (CS+) previously paired with affectively evocative images (i.e., IAPS images) elicited higher amplitude ERPs recorded over primary visual cortex than did gratings (CS−) not paired with images (Stolarova, Keil, & Moratti, 2006). The increased CS+ event-related potential amplitude over V1 occurs roughly 50 ms post-stimulus onset, well before information could reach core affective circuitry and forward back to V1. As a result, we conjecture that, over time, this V1 activity becomes amygdala independent, suggesting that associative, affective learning occurs, not only in the amygdala, but in sensory cortex as well. As the activity in V1 eventually gains independence, the distinction between affective and non-affective processing in the brain becomes further blurred.

Correlational findings also support the conjecture that the amygdala modulates the extent of visual processing. Neuroimaging studies consistently demonstrate that aversive images produce greater activity (than do neutral images) in the amygdala and throughout the entire visual cortex (e.g., Breiter et al., 1996; Lane, Chua, & Dolan, 1999; Lang et al., 1998; Moll et al., 2002; Morris et al., 1998; Taylor, Liberzon, & Koeppe, 2000). This enhanced activity in the visual cortex appears to be related to enhanced awareness of objects. Objective awareness of valenced stimuli (i.e., greater perceptual sensitivity in signal-detection tasks, even when participants report no conscious awareness of the stimulus) is associated with increased amygdala activation, and the absence of objective awareness is associated with no increase in amygdala activation over baseline levels (Pessoa, Jappe, Sturman, & Ungerleider, 2006). Furthermore, increased amygdala activation co-occurs with increased activation in fusiform gyrus (FG; a portion of the brain involved in complex object recognition that is activated when objects reach visual awareness; Bar et al., 2001; Tong, Nakayama, Vaughan, & Kanwisher, 1998), but only when people are objectively aware of the stimuli (i.e., faces) presented to them (Pessoa et al., 2006).[1] Greater amygdala and FG co-activation is observed when participants are instructed to attend to faces as opposed to a concurrent distractor (e.g., houses; Anderson, Chistoff, Panitz, De Rosa, & Gabrieli, 2003; Pessoa, McKenna, Gutierrez, & Ungerleider, 2002; Vuilleumier, Armony, Driver, & Dolan, 2001); in binocular rivalry studies where a house is presented to one eye, and a facial depiction presented to the other, FG activity increases in the hemisphere corresponding to the dominant visual field (i.e., the eye whose sensory input reaches conscious awareness; Williams, Morris, McGlone, Abbott, & Mattingley, 2004). These correlational findings are consistent with neuropsychological evidence that patients with amygdala lesions show a decreased FG response

---

[1] Based upon neuroanatomical studies of rodents, it is typically assumed that the ability to detect a valenced stimulus under the threshold of awareness is mediated by the projections from the thalamus to the amygdala (i.e., the "low-road"; LeDoux, 1996). It has been argued, however, that the "low road" is impoverished in primates (for reviews, see Pessoa & Ungerleider, 2004; Rolls, 2000). It is possible that objective awareness of valenced stimuli is mediated by activity in the ventral stream that is directed by the amygdala. Subliminal presentations of valenced stimuli might be associated with increased activation in the amygdala and ventral visual stream, but such activation may not be sufficient (i.e., too few neurons fire, or neurons do not fire for a sufficient duration) for the neural activation to reach the threshold of conscious awareness. The degree of conscious awareness for a valenced stimulus is most likely modulated by the degree of activity in the ventral stream, such that conscious and non-conscious perceptions of valenced stimuli involve the same circuitry (rather than by two different circuits).

to facial depictions of fear (Vuilleumier, Richardson, Armony, Driver, & Dolan, 2004).

Preliminary evidence from our own lab suggests that affective experience can lead to the same enhanced awareness of objects that is associated with increased amygdala and FG activation. Using the signal-detection approach employed by Pessoa and colleagues (Pessoa et al., 2006), we have found that individuals who characterise themselves as introverted (and who report decreased levels of positive affect; Lucas & Baird, 2004) demonstrate greater perceptual sensitivity to briefly presented (16 ms) faces depicting fear than those who are lower in introversion (Duncan & Barrett, unpublished data). Taken together, these findings suggest the intriguing hypothesis that what people literally see in the world around them may in part be determined by their core affective state.

Not only do the anatomical and experimental evidence implicate the amygdala in sensory processing, but mood disorders, which are associated with amygdala hyperactivity, also involve sensory dysfunction. As discussed earlier, core affect involves a binding of sensory and somatovisceral information. In mood disorders this binding may be functionally compromised, resulting in hyperactive responses in the amygdala and visual cortex to affective stimuli. Serotonergic neurons that originate in the raphe nucleus project to the amygdala (Azmitia & Gannon, 1986; Bauman & Amaral, 2005; Brown, Crane, & Goldman, 1979; Sadikot & Parent, 1990) and inhibit its activity (Rainnie, 2003). An amygdala disinhibition effect is seen in depressed individuals because they have decreased levels of synaptic serotonin. As a result, individuals who suffer from depression have greater activation in the amygdala at rest than do non-clinical controls (Abercrombie et al., 1998; Drevets, Videen, MacLeod, Haller, & Raichle, 1992). The psychological consequence of this enhanced amygdala activation is that depressed and anxious individuals will be overly sensitive to valenced sensory information. Anxious and depressed individuals have greater amygdala activity in response to masked fearful faces than healthy controls (Sheline et al., 2001), and exhibit sustained amygdala responses to negative words (Siegle, Steinhauer, Thase, Stenger, & Carter, 2002). Along with an increase in amygdala activation in response to negative visual stimuli among depressed individuals there is an increase in activity throughout the ventral visual stream (Davidson, Irwin, Anderle, & Kalin, 2003), which increases the likelihood that the stimulus reaches awareness. Administering SSRIs (which increase the levels of synaptic serotonin) can decrease amygdala responses to faces depicting fear (Sheline et al., 2001) and aversive images (Davidson et al., 2003) to normal levels. Disrupted core affective circuitry, then, can have dramatic effects on sensory processing.

The amygdala indirectly modulates sensory processing by influencing bottom-up forms of attention. The circuitry that computes core affect plays an integral role in regulating sensory processing throughout the brain via its projections to the brainstem and basal forebrain, two parts of the brain that are necessary for consciousness. This modulation can occur in two ways (cf. Edelman & Tononi, 2000). First, brainstem and basal forebrain nuclei modulate the connections between thalamus and cortex (cortico-thalamic circuits) that are partly responsible for forming and selecting the groups of neurons that fire in synchrony (called neuronal assemblies) to form conscious percepts (the things people are aware of seeing). Brainstem and basal forebrain areas accomplish this modulation by projecting to two nuclei in the thalamus: the intralaminar nucleus and the reticular nucleus. The intralaminar nucleus controls cortical activity via strong recursive (or re-entrant) projections from thalamus to cortex. The reticular nucleus regulates activity within the thalamus, which in turn controls the degree of sensory transmission to cortex. Second, brainstem and basal forebrain nuclei have diffuse, unidirectional afferent projections throughout the cortical mantle, acting as a "leaky garden hose" (Edelman, 2004, p. 25) that controls the degree of neuronal firing.[2] Core affective circuitry (e.g., amygdala, vmPFC, and ventral striatum) offers the only path by which sensory information from the outside world reaches the brainstem and basal forebrain (Mesulam, 2000). In these ways, areas involved with establishing a core affective state can indirectly constrain ongoing processing throughout the rest of the cortex, selecting for neuronal assemblies that maximise reward or minimise threat, thereby influencing which contents are experienced in the moment, and which are more likely to be stored in long-term memory (Edelman, 2004; Edelman & Tononi, 2000).

There are important psychological and phenomenological consequences arising from core affective circuitry's indirect modulation of cortical activity via brainstem and basal forebrain nuclei. First, core affective circuitry helps to select the information that reaches conscious awareness by directing the formation and maintenance of the neuronal assemblies that underlie conscious experience. Therefore, along with more deliberate top-down forms of attention (from lateral prefrontal areas) and bottom-up forms of stimulation from the sensory world, core affect helps to orchestrate the

---

[2] For example, cholinergic projections from basal forebrain augment neural responses to motivationally relevant sensory events, and enhance their storage in long-term memory; noradrenergic innervations from locus coeruleus increase the signal-to-noise ratio and precision of neuronal firing to such events; dopaminergic projections from substantia nigra and ventral tegmental area mark the salience of an event and gate access to voluntary motor outputs; and serotonergic projections from the rostral raphe nucleus reduce distractibility and gate the processing of motivationally relevant sensory cues (Mesulam, 2000; Parvizi & Damasio, 2001).

binding of sensory information into a single, unified conscious field. Second, via multiple iterations of processing, the external sensory information that drives brainstem and basal forebrain activity becomes processed with and bound to somatovisceral information. As a result, conscious percepts of the external world are intrinsically infused with affective content. The idea that affect is a basic property of consciousness is not new (Titchener, 1909; Wundt, 1897) and it continues to be incorporated into contemporary perspectives, including Damasio's somatic marker hypothesis (Damasio, 1999), Edelman's theory of neural Darwinism (Edelman, 1987; Edelman & Tononi, 2000), Searle's theory of consciousness (Searle, 2004), and Humphrey's theory of conscious sensation (Humphrey, 2006). As we discuss below, core affect is a necessary component of normal conscious experience.

The fact that core affect intrinsically drives the neuronal circuitry that selects and instantiates conscious content leaves open the possibility that disruptions in consciousness may occur when there are extreme disturbances of core affect. First, it is possible to speculate that intense or disrupted core affect could lead to a "psychotic break", or disintegration of the unified conscious field where sensory information from separate modalities no longer seem integrated. This form of dysfunction in consciousness is most commonly associated with schizophrenia, but can also be observed in severe instances of major depressive episodes. Schizophrenia is often associated with abnormalities in the anatomy of core affective circuitry, particularly reduced amygdala volume (Pinkham, Penn, Perkins, & Lieberman, 2003; Wright et al., 2000). In cases of intense of disrupted core affect, core affective circuitry may relax its control over cortico-thalamic processing, leading to disorganised, fractured perception (Tononi & Edelman, 2000). On average schizophrenia is not associated with disruptions in affective experience (Kring & Germans, 2004; Kring & Werner, 2004), but it is still possible that certain endophenotypes may show an association between disorganised perception and disordered core affect. It is also possible that disorganised perception might result from large or unexpected changes in a person's core affective state even when pervasive negative affect is not a tonic feature of the disorder.

In a second form of disrupted consciousness, affective value is applied to objects and events indiscriminately, leading to delusions, or the belief that otherwise neutral objects have significant affective importance or value for well-being. In a recent study by Holt and colleagues (Holt et al., 2006b), schizophrenia patients suffering from delusions were more likely to rate neutral words as unpleasant and were slower to correctly classify neutral words as neutral than were non-delusional schizophrenia patients and healthy controls. Delusions seem to occur when the connections between core affective circuitry and sensory cortices become deregulated and overly active, infusing a persons' sensory experience with an unrealistically strong affective meaning. Delusional patients with schizophrenia, for example, have greater amygdala responses to neutral faces than do non-delusional patients (Holt et al., 2006a).

If delusions are the misattribution of affective value to neutral objects and events, Capgras syndrome can be thought of as an anti-delusion: the inability to attribute affective value to objects when doing so is necessary for normal conscious experience. In Capgras syndrome, the affective meaning in sensory experience is lost due to compromised connections between the amygdala and the inferior temporal cortex (a brain region involved in recognising facial identity; Ellis & Young, 1990; Hirstein & Ramachandran, 1997). As a result, patients suffering from Capgras syndrome do not experience a sense of familiarity when seeing friends and family and believe that impostors have replaced those individuals. Patients with Capgras also do not show an increased skin conductance response that is typically seen when people view familiar faces (Ellis, Young, Quayle, & de Pauw, 1997).

In the third form of disrupted consciousness, the integration of internal and external sensory information is compromised, leading to hallucinations that are often seen in schizophrenia, as well as severe forms of depression and bipolar disorder. Hallucinations are thought to result from an increase in burst-like processing in the thalamus, which inhibits the relay of external sensory information to the rest of the cortex (Behrendt, 2006). As a result, conscious percepts are based primarily on cortical activity not being driven by the external world. Again, given the architecture of the circuitry involved, it is possible to speculate that disruptions in core affect may be in part responsible for this schism between what is going on outside in the external world and what neural assemblies are being formed inside the person's head. Hallucinations can be seen as an extreme form of naïve realism, where the contribution of internal information drastically outweighs the contribution of external sensory information in forming a conscious percept.

CORE AFFECT AS A DIMENSION OF PSYCHOLOGICAL MEANING

Because core affect modulates sensory processing, any psychological process that draws on sensory information will have an affective quality to it. As a result, core affect influences forms of cognitive activity that are traditionally considered distinct from emotion. Perhaps the most discussed example of affect's role in cognition comes from the literature on decision making (e.g., Bechara, 2004; Janis & Mann, 1977; Kahneman & Tversky, 1979), but there is also evidence for affect's contribution to normal consciousness, language and memory. As we discuss here, core affect makes external information from the world personally relevant to people, providing them with a first-person experience of the world, a fluency with language so that they can describe those experiences, and enhances how those experiences are encoded for future use.

Core affect is a precondition for first-person experiences of the world

Perception without an affective component lacks the first-person, subjective quality that is the hallmark of conscious awareness of external sensory information. Blindsight patients offer a particularly clear illustration of perception without affect. Blindsight is a condition caused by lesions in primary visual cortex (V1), leading patients to report complete lack of vision even when they are able to detect the movement, orientation, and colour of objects at above chance levels (Weiskrantz, 1986, 1987). People with blindsight have objective awareness of the world in the absence of subjective awareness. Even with massively impoverished vision, they can detect and act upon visual features of objects at better than chance levels, but they have no conscious experience of those objects. In signal-detection terms, their sensitivity to visual information is above chance, but they have a conservative threshold for reporting the presence of an object (i.e., their response bias is to report no visual awareness for the object; Weiskrantz, 2001). For example, blindsight patients often report that they "know" an object is present, but that they definitely cannot "see" it (Weiskrantz, 1991).

We propose that core affect, through direct and indirect projections to striate cortex, provides individuals with the subjective sense of certainty comes with consciously seeing an object. "Seeing" an object can be equated with perception that has an "about me" quality to it, meaning that the perception is personally relevant in some basic way (probably achieved via the binding of somatovisceral information with sensory information from the external world that occurs in the evaluation circuit involving the OFC and amygdala). In the absence of core affective modulation, a person will remain uncertain of whether or not they consciously experience an object. In fact, Humphrey (2006) calls blindsight "affectless vision" (p. 67). For blindsight patients, who seem to have perception without an affective dimension,[3] seeing is similar to a third-person experience of an object: the person knows that the object is there (as if they were told by someone else), but they do not experience themselves as having seen it.

---

[3] We are not claiming that sensory input is inaccessible to core affective circuitry in blindsight patients. Sensory information could still cause changes in core affective experience, helping blindsight patients to make affect-based discriminations in their environment such as categorising facial configurations depicting fear—as observed by de Gelder and colleagues (de Gelder, Morris, & Dolan, 2005). Our discussion focuses on the output from core affective circuitry to sensory cortex.

Humphrey and colleagues (Ackroyd, Humphrey, & Warrington, 1974) have reported on a patient with an unusual form of blindsight, HD, whose experience speaks to the importance of affect in conscious awareness. Functionally blind from the age of 3, HD had cataracts removed from her eyes at the age of 27, with the presumption that this operation would restore her sight. Indeed, HD had some functional increase in her vision after the operation—she could successfully navigate her world by avoiding obstacles (e.g., curbs on the street), and could point towards and even grasp objects without prompting or instruction. She did not, however, report any conscious visual awareness of these objects. It seems that her vision lacked the affective quality and subjectivity of normal conscious vision. Presumably, the connectivity between core affective circuitry and visual cortex had no opportunity to develop normally in the absence of experience. Eventually, HD returned to wearing dark glasses, since perception without affective quality was more disturbing than no vision at all. Although this is just a single case study, it makes a compelling case for the idea that core affect is a necessary precondition for normal conscious experience.

The importance of core affect in language

Core affect is not only necessary for first-person conscious experience, but it is an integral component of normal linguistic functioning as well. All words have an affective dimension of meaning. Valence (positive/negative), for example, appeared as the most stable factor in Osgood's semantic differential studies of words (Osgood, Suci, & Tannenbaum, 1957). When people rated words (particularly nouns; e.g., "tornados", "mother", "sponges", etc.) on bipolar, adjective-based Likert scales (e.g., hard–soft; slow–fast; ugly–beautiful; etc.), and these ratings were subjected to factor analysis, a valence dimension accounted for nearly 45% of the variance observed in the ratings, even across cultures (smaller "potency" and "activity" factors are also commonly found; Osgood, 1962; Osgood et al., 1957). Osgood interpreted these findings to suggest that each word and the object that the word represents has a pleasant or unpleasant connotation that is not part of the descriptive, technical definition of word. Although some philosophers have taken these findings to mean that valence represents a social, moral, or desirability-based form of evaluation (e.g., Charland, 2005; Solomon & Stone, 2002), Osgood's research suggests that people cannot use words to communicate with others without also (perhaps inadvertently) communicating affective meaning. Furthermore, there is some evidence that the relationships observed between psychological phenomena, such as personality and emotion, might be driven by connotative (as opposed to descriptive) properties (Fossum & Barrett, 2000).

Just as it is not possible to use words without communicating affective connotation, it is also not possible to understand language based on denotation alone. The affective dimension in language makes communication personal and easy to accomplish, and is an important contributor to language fluency (Altarriba & Mathis, 1997). For people who speak two languages, words with strong affective connotation presented in their first language are more likely to capture attention than words presented in their second language. In an emotional Stroop task, an interference effect (i.e., a temporal delay in speaking the colour of the printed word) indicates that attention is captured by the affective meaning of a word. In bilingual individuals, interference effects are only observed when words are presented in their native language; affectively evocative words presented in the second language are processed like neutral words (Altarriba & Mathis, 1997; Rosselli et al., 2002), where diminished interference effects are typically observed (Pratto & John, 1991; Wentura, Rothermund, & Bak, 2000).

There is also evidence that words presented in a fluent language produce greater affective responses than words spoken in a second language. Reprimands (e.g., "Shame on you") spoken in a native language, for example, elicit greater electrodermal responses than reprimands spoken in a second language (Harris, Ayçiçegi, & Gleason, 2003). Since first languages contain an affective dimension that is missing in second languages, bilingual individuals often resort to their native language when communicating their core affective states. For example, bilingual individuals feel more comfortable discussing embarrassing topics in their native language (Bond & Lai, 1986), and prefer to use their native language to swear (particularly when they want swear words to have affective weight; Dewaele, 2004). One important component of language fluency, then, is the ability to derive affective meaning from words, and to use language to communicate that meaning.

Affective meaning is a crucial dimension even in non-linguistic forms of communication. Nonhuman animals, for example, utilise a host of vocalisations to either directly or indirectly change the affect in the perceiving animal (Owren & Rendall, 1997, 2001). The basic acoustical properties of animal calls, including abrupt onsets, upward frequency sweeps, high or noisy frequency sounds, or sounds rapid amplitude fluctuations (called "squeaks", "shrieks", and "screams") directly act on the nervous system of the perceiving animal to change its core affective state (Owren & Rendall, 1997). The acoustical properties that reflect the identity of the caller (reflected in "sonants" and "gruffs") can indirectly influence the core affective state of the perceiving animal as the result of its prior experience with the caller (Owren & Rendall, 1997). Similar types of non-linguistic affectively mediated communication are also found in humans. For example, humans can use laughter to induce positive core affective states in others (Bachorowski & Owren, 2001; Owren & Bachorowski, 2003; Smoski & Bachorowski, 2003).

Affect memory: Encoding and retrieval of experience for future use

Core affect is not only a key feature of consciousness, and necessary for communication, but it also helps determine which experiences with the world are encoded in the brain for later use. Core affect acts as a filter, giving preference to sensory information that affects the somatovisceral state of the organism, thereby helping to select which sensory information is processed more fully and therefore encoded in memory. This information is then available and used for the interpretation of incoming sensory information in the future, in what Edelman calls "the remembered present" (Edelman, 1989). In a sense, conscious experience is bootstrapped by memory (Edelman, 1989) that is directed and infused by affective content. The amygdala appears to be particularly important in this bootstrapping process. Neuroimaging studies have shown a strong correlation between amygdala activity when an object is first seen and successful recognition of the object at a later time (Cahill et al., 1996; Canli, Zhao, Brewer, Gabrieli, & Cahill, 2000; Hamman, 2001; Kensinger, Garoff-Eaton, & Schacter, 2006; Phelps, 2004). Not only does core affect enhances awareness of objects (see The amygdala directly modulates sensory processing), but it also appears to increase the quantity and vividness of memories as well (see Kensinger & Schacter, in press, for a discussion).

Core affect may not only help to determine the content of memories, but it may play a role in the confidence people place in those memories. Events that are associated with large changes in core affect are often remembered vividly, with great contextual detail, and confidence (Kensinger & Schacter, in press; Phelps, 2006). People's memories of Challenger or Columbia space-shuttle explosions (Bohannon, 1988; Kensinger et al., 2006; Neisser & Harsch, 1992; Talarico & Rubin, 2003) or the September 11th attacks (Budson et al., 2004; Paradis, Solomon, Florer, & Thompson, 2004; Pezdek, 2003; Smith, Bibi, & Sheard, 2003) are more vivid and detailed. Controlled laboratory studies confirm that affect increases the confidence and vividness of memories. In tasks where participants were asked whether they "know" that an item is familiar (subjective report of memory with low confidence), or specifically "remember" the item (subjective report of memory with high confidence), participants reported greater confidence in remembering evocative words and images (i.e., more "remember" responses) than less evocative stimuli (Dewhurst & Parry, 2000; Kensinger & Corkin, 2003; Ochsner, 2000; Sharot & Phelps, 2004).

While it is clear that affect influences what people remember and their confidence in those memories, the evidence remains mixed as to whether affect influences the accuracy of memories. Neuroimaging studies show that activity in the amygdala is associated with improved recognition of images, whereas field and behavioural studies find that people are no more accurate in remembering affect-laden autobiographical events (Neisser & Harsch, 1992; Talarico & Rubin, 2003) or images (Ochsner, 2000; Sharot & Phelps, 2004) than less evocative material. In some cases, focusing on one's own affective state during a task can even lead to source memory errors (Johnson, Nolde, & De Leonardis, 1996). Although resolving this debate is outside of the scope of this paper, Kensinger & Schacter (in press) have recently proposed that affect increases the accuracy of memory not by changing the quantity of items or aspects remembered correctly, but by influencing the quality of what is remembered (more important or central details are remembered with more detail, sometimes at the expense of non-central details). Regardless of the outcome, it is clear that affect increases the confidence and vividness of memory. Accordingly, one thing that might distinguish implicit from explicit memories is their affective component. When core affective circuitry enhances sensory processing, events are conscious and are remembered vividly and with confidence.

CONCLUSION

Although feelings seem different than thoughts, we resurrect Neisser's (1967) definition of cognition to argue that affect is a form of cognition. The circuitry that instantiates a core affective state is widely distributed throughout the brain, and includes so-called "cognitive" areas. This circuitry projects to and modulates sensory processing. Via this modulation, affect is an intrinsic part of sensory experience, not a separate cognitive function that is later performed on sensations. As a result, affect is an intrinsic property in all psychological phenomena that result from so-called "cognitive" processes (such as consciousness, language, and memory). Affect and cognition, then, are not ontologically separate, but they are, perhaps, phenomenologically distinct. This is distinction in experience, however, rather than a distinction that exists in the structure of the brain or the psychological processes that produce that experience.

In psychology, we often take distinctiveness in experience as evidence for distinctiveness in process. In appraisal theories of emotion, for example, theorists use specific contents of what is experienced as evidence for distinct cognitive processes that produce the content (e.g., the fact that people experience their goals as blocked when experiencing anger is taken as evidence for the existence of an internal cognitive mechanism for deciding whether or not their goals are blocked). Similarly, appraisal theorists assume that in the apperception of an object, affective processing is separate from sensory processing. Arnold, for example, stated that, "to know or perceive something and to estimate its effect on us are two distinct processes, and appraisal necessarily presupposes perception" (Arnold, 1960, p. 176). Others have followed this trend, but in our view, following Dewey (1894), it may be problematic to regard the perception of an object and the affective meaning of an object as ontologically separate phenomena. Affective experiences are not sequenced, discriminable conscious events distinct from experiences that seem devoid of affect (i.e., perceptual or intellectual experiences). Any thought or action can be said to be more or less affectively infused, so that there is no ontological distinction between, say, affective and non-affective behaviours, or between "hot" and "cold" cognitions. This line of reasoning is very consistent with recent embodiment views of cognition, which argue that affective states are incorporated into the conceptual knowledge that we use to categorise objects and events in the world (Barsalou, 1999, 2002, Barsalou, Niedenthal, Barbey, & Ruppert, 2003a). How you see an object and how you feel about an object may be the same concrete experience, but their distinction is introduced in reflection upon this experience (Dewey, 1895). A phenomenological distinction might exist between thinking and feeling, but they are actually two sides of the same coin.

To understand the distinction between affect and cognition, then, is to understand the nature, causes and functions of this phenomenological distinction. We suggest that core affect can be a central or a background feature (figure or ground) of consciousness, depending on where and how attention is applied. When core affect is in the background, it functions as background feelings (Lane & Garfield, 2005) or background emotions (Damasio, 1999) that colour conscious experience in a less direct fashion, but presumably have the potential to influence behaviour implicitly (Berridge & Winkielman, 2003; Winkielman, Berridge, & Wilbarger, 2005). Backgrounded core affect is experienced as a property of the external world, rather than as the person's reaction to it. We experience some people as nice and others as mean, some foods as delicious but others as unappetising, some pictures as aesthetically pleasing and others as unpleasant or disturbing. It may be under these circumstances that core affect directly translates into a behavioural response. When core affect is backgrounded, as in the Winkielman et al. (2005) study, the contribution of core affect to sensation and cognition goes unnoticed, Thirsty participants in their study valued a fruit-flavoured beverage more (i.e., drank more, were willing to pay more) when they had been exposed to subliminal presentations of smiling compared to frowning faces, even though there was no change in self-reported affective experience. Unconscious affect, in contrast, is not experienced at all.

When brought into the foreground of consciousness, core affect will be experienced directly as pleasant or unpleasant content with some degree of arousal (e.g., "drinking juice makes me feel good), and can serve as information for making explicit judgements and decisions (Clore & Schnall, 2005; Schwarz & Clore, 1983). In addition, core affective feelings will perhaps be attributed to some situational cause, thereby forming the basis of an emotion experience (cf. Barrett, 2006; Russell, 2003; but see Frijda, 2005; Lambie & Marcel, 2002, who characterise backgrounded affect as emotion experience).

When affect is backgrounded and seen as property of the world, it has its effects on cognition in stealth. We experience a world of facts rather than feelings, and affect gives us a sense of confidence in those facts. As we have discussed throughout this paper, the validity of experience (both in conscious awareness and in memory) is rooted in core affect. Core affect provides the necessary components that gives force to beliefs and gives people a sense that what they know is correct or right. It seems plausible, then, that core affect would contribute to confidence in people's beliefs about political topics (e.g., global warming, abortion), world view (belief in a just world) or even form the core of religious faith (a strong affective response is how you believe in something that you cannot see). Given that core affect helps to determine the contents of conscious experience, it is no surprise that the most affectively loaded topics are the ones that produce the most steadfast opinions, even in the face of contrary evidence.

The fact that thoughts and feelings are experienced as different is important, and needs to be explained, but is not, in and of itself, evidence that they are fundamentally different kinds of phenomena. Why the phenomenological boundary between affect and cognition exists remains an important, but perhaps overlooked, question in psychological science. Understanding the conditions under which people foreground or background core affect, and knowing why doing one or the other is functional, will provide us with the best answer to the question of how cognition and affect are different.

REFERENCES

Abercrombie, H. C., Schaefer, S. M., Larson, C. L., Oakes, T. R., Lindgren, K. A., Holden, J. E., et al. (1998). Metabolic rate in the right amygdala predicts negative affect in depressed patients. *Neuroreport, 9*, 3301–3307.

Ackroyd, C., Humphrey, N., & Warrington, E. K. (1974). Lasting effects of early blindness: A case study. *Quarterly Journal Experimental Psychology, 26*, 114–124.

Altarriba, J., & Mathis, K. (1997). Conceptual and lexical development in second language acquisition. *Journal of Memory and Language, 36*, 550–568.

Amaral, D. G., Behniea, H., & Kelly, J. L. (2003). Topographical organization of projections from the amygdala to the visual cortex in the Macaque monkey. *Neuroscience, 118,* 1099–1120.

Amaral, D. G., & Price, J. L. (1984). Amygdalo-cortical projections in the monkey (*Macaca fascicularis*). *Journal of Comparative Neurology, 230,* 465–496.

Anderson, A. K., Chistoff, K., Panitz, D., De Rosa, E., & Gabrieli, J. D. (2003). Neural correlates of the automatic processing of threat facial signals. *Journal of Neuroscience, 23,* 5627–5633.

Aristotle (1991). *The art of rhetoric* (Transl. H. C. Lawson-Tancred). London: Penguin.

Arnold, M. B. (1960). *Emotion and personality.* New York: Columbia University Press.

Azmitia, E. C., & Gannon, P. J. (1986). The primate serotonergic system: A review of human and animal studies and a report on *Macaca fascicularis. Advances in Neurology, 43,* 407–468.

Bachorowski, J. A., & Owren, M. J. (2001). Not all laughs are alike: Voiced but not unvoiced laughter elicits positive affect in listeners. *Psychological Science, 12,* 252–257.

Bar, M., Tootell, R. B., Schacter, D. L., Greve, D. N., Fischl, B., Mendola, J. D., et al. (2001). Cortical mechanisms specific to explicit visual object recognition. *Neuron, 29,* 529–535.

Barbas, H., Saha, S., Rempel-Clower, N., & Ghashghaei, T. (2003). Serial pathways from primate prefrontal cortex to autonomic areas may influence emotional expression. *BMC Neuroscience, 4,* 25–37.

Barnard, P. J., Duke, D. J., Byrne, R. W., & Davidson, I. (2007). Differentiation in cognitive and emotional meanings: An evolutionary analysis. *Cognition and Emotion, 21,* 1155–1184.

Barrett, L. F. (2006). Solving the emotion paradox: Categorization and the experience of emotion. *Personality and Social Psychology Review, 10,* 20–46.

Barrett, L. F., Mesquita, B., Ochsner, K. N., & Gross, J. J. (2007). The experience of emotion. *Annual Review of Psychology, 58,* 373–403.

Barrett, L. F., Ochsner, K., & Gross, J. (2006). The automaticity of emotion. In J. Bargh (Ed.), *Social psychology and the unconsciousness: The automaticity of higher mental processes* (pp. 173–218). New York: Psychology Press.

Barsalou, L. W. (1999). Perceptual symbol systems. *Behavioral and Brain Sciences, 22,* 577–660.

Barsalou, L. W. (2002). Being there conceptually: Simulating categories in preparation for situated action. In N. L. Stein, P. J. Bauer, & M. Rabinowitz (Eds.), *Representation, memory, and development: Essays in honor of Jean Mandler* (pp. 1–15). Mahwah, NJ: Lawrence Erlbaum Associates, Inc.

Barsalou, L. W. (in press). Embodied cognition. *Annual Review of Psychology.*

Barsalou, L. W., Niedenthal, P. M., Barbey, A. K., & Ruppert, J. A. (2003a). Social embodiment. In B. H. Ross (Ed.), *The psychology of learning and motivation* (Vol. 43 pp. 43–92). San Diego, CA: Academic Press.

Barsalou, L. W., Simmons, W. K., Barbey, A. K., & Wilson, C. D. (2003b). Grounding conceptual knowledge in modality-specific systems. *Trends in Cognitive Sciences, 7,* 84–91.

Bauman, M. D., & Amaral, D. G. (2005). The distribution of serotonergic fibers in the macaque monkey amygdala: An immunohistochemical study using antisera to 5-hydroxytryptamine. *Neuroscience, 13,* 193–203.

Bechara, A. (2004). The role of emotion in decision making: Evidence from neurological patients with orbitofrontal damage. *Brain and Cognition, 55,* 30–40.

Behrendt, R. P. (2006). Vocalization in verbal hallucinations: Case report and theoretical model. *Psychopathology, 39,* 38–44.

Berridge, K. C., & Winkielman, P. (2003). What is an unconscious emotion? (the case for unconscious "liking"). *Cognition and Emotion, 17*(2), 181–211.

Bohannon, J. N. (1988). Flashbulb memories for the space shuttle disaster: A tale of two theories. *Cognition, 29*(2), 179–196.

Bond, M. H., & Lai, T. (1986). Embarrassment and code-switching into a second language. *Journal of Social Psychology, 126*(2), 179–186.

Breiter, H. C., Etcoff, N. L., Whalen, P. J., Kennedy, W. A., Rauch, S. L., Buckner, R. L., et al. (1996). Response and habituation of the human amygdala during visual processing of facial expression. *Neuron, 17*, 875–887.

Bridges, K. M. B. (1932). Emotional development in early infancy. *Child Development, 3*, 324–334.

Brown, R. M., Crane, A. M., & Goldman, P. S. (1979). Regional distribution of monoamines in the cerebral cortex and subcortical structures of the rhesus monkey concentrations and in vivo synthesis rates. *Brain Research, 168*, 133–150.

Budson, A. E., Simons, J. S., Sullivan, A. L., Beier, J. S., Solomon, P. R., Scinto, L. F., et al. (2004). Memory and emotions for the September 11, 2001, terrorist attacks in patients with Alzheimer's disease, patients with mild cognitive impairment, and healthy older adults. *Neuropsychology, 18*, 315–327.

Cabanac, M. (2002). What is emotion? *Behavioural Processes, 60*, 69–83.

Cahill, L., Haier, R., Fallon, J., Alkire, M., Tang, C., Keator, D., et al. (1996). Amygdala activity at encoding correlated with long-term, free recall of emotional information. *Proceedings of the National Academy of Sciences, 93*, 8016–8021.

Canli, T., Zhao, Z., Brewer, J., Gabrieli, J. D. E., & Cahill, L. (2000). Event-related activation in the human amygdala associates with later memory for individual emotional response. *Journal of Neuroscience, 20*, RC99.

Cardinal, R. N., Parkinson, J. A., Hall, J., & Everitt, B. J. (2002). Emotion and motivation: The role of the amygdala, ventral striatum, and prefrontal cortex. *Neuroscience and Behavior Reviews, 26*, 321–352.

Carmichael, S. T., & Price, J. L. (1996). Connectional networks within the orbital and medial prefrontal cortex of macaque monkeys. *Journal of Comparative Neurology, 371*, 179–207.

Charland, L. C. (2005). Emotion experience and the indeterminacy of valence. In L. F. Barrett, P. M. Niedenthal, & P. Winkielman (Eds.), *Emotion and consciousness* (pp. 231–254). New York: Guilford Press.

Clore, G. L., & Schnall, S. (2005). *The influence of affect on attitude.* Hillsdale, NJ: Lawrence Erlbaum Associates, Inc.

Craig, A. D. (2002). Opinion: How do you feel? Interoception: The sense of the physiological condition of the body. *Nature Reviews Neuroscience, 3*, 655–666.

Damasio, A. (1999). *The feeling of what happens: Body and emotion in the making of consciousness.* New York: Harcourt.

Davidson, R. J., Irwin, W., Anderle, M. J., & Kalin, N. H. (2003). The neural substrates of affective processing in depressed patients treated with venlafaxine. *American Journal of Psychiatry, 160*, 64–75.

Davis, M., & Whalen, P. J. (2001). The amygdala: Vigilance and emotion. *Molecular Psychiatry, 6*, 13–34.

de Gelder, B., Morris, J. S., & Dolan, R. J. (2005). Unconscious fear influences emotional awareness of faces and voices. *Proceedings of the National Academy of Sciences, 102*, 18682–18687.

Dewaele, J. (2004). The emotional force of swearwords and taboo words in the speech of multilinguals. *Journal of Multilingual and Multicultural Development, 25*, 204–222.

Dewey, J. (1894). The ego as cause. *Philosophical Review, 3*, 337–341.

Dewey, J. (1895). The theory of emotion. (2) The significance of emotions. *Psychological Review, 2*, 13–32.

Dewhurst, S. A., & Parry, L. A. (2000). Emotionality, distinctiveness and recollective experience. *European Journal of Cognitive Psychology, 12*, 541–551.

Dolan, R. J., & Morris, J. S. (2000). The functional anatomy of innate and acquired fear: Perspectives from neuroimaging. In R. D. Lane & L. Nadel (Eds.), *Cognitive neuroscience of emotion* (pp. 225–241). New York: Oxford University Press.

Drevets, W. C., Videen, T. O., MacLeod, A. K., Haller, J. W., & Raichle, M. E. (1992). PET images of blood flow changes during anxiety. *Science, 256*, 1696.

Duncan, S., & Barrett, L. F. (2006). *The relationship between personality and visual awareness of valenced stimuli.* Unpublished raw data, Boston College, Boston, MA, USA.

Edelman, G. M. (1987). *Neural Darwinism: The theory of neuronal group selection.* New York: Basic Books.

Edelman, G. M. (1989). *The remembered present: A biological theory of consciousness.* New York: Basic Books.

Edelman, G. M. (2004). *Wider than the sky: The phenomenal gift of consciousness.* London: Yale University Press.

Edelman, G. M., & Tononi, G. (2000). *A universe of consciousness: How matter becomes imagination.* New York: Basic Books.

Elliott, R., Friston, K. J., & Dolan, R. (2000). Dissociable neural responses in human reward systems. *Journal of Neuroscience, 20*, 6159–6165.

Elliott, R., Rees, G., & Dolan, R. J. (1999). Ventromedial prefrontal cortex mediates guessing. *Neuropsychologia, 37*, 403–411.

Ellis, H. D., & Young, A. W. (1990). Accounting for delusional misidentifications. *British Journal of Psychiatry, 157*, 239–248.

Ellis, H. D., Young, A. W., Quayle, A. H., & de Pauw, K. W. (1997). Reduced autonomic responses to faces in Capgras delusion. *Proceedings of the Royal Society of London: Biological Sciences, 264*, 1085–1092.

Emde, R. N., Gaensbauer, T. J., & Harmon, R. J. (1976). Emotional expression in infancy: A biobehavioral study. *Psychological Issues* (Monograph 37). New York: International Universities Press.

Fellows, L. K., & Farah, M. J. (2003). Ventromedial frontal cortex mediates affective shifting in humans: Evidence from a reversal learning paradigm. *Brain, 126*, 1830–1837.

Fossum, T., & Barrett, L. F. (2000). Evaluation and description in the personality–emotion relationship. *Personality and Social Psychology Bulletin, 26*, 669–678.

Freese, J. L., & Amaral, D. G. (2005). The organization of projections from the amygdala to visual cortical areas TE and V1 in the macaque monkey. *Journal of Comparative Neurology, 486*, 295–317.

Freese, J. L., & Amaral, D. G. (2006). Synaptic organization of projections from the amygdala to visual cortical areas TE and V1 in the macaque monkey. *Journal of Comparative Neurology, 496*, 655–667.

Frijda, N. H. (2005). Emotion experience. *Cognition and Emotion, 19*, 473–497.

Ghashghaei, H. T., & Barbas, H. (2002). Pathways for emotion: Interactions of prefrontal and anterior temporal pathways in the amygdala of the rhesus monkey. *Neuroscience, 115*, 1261–1279.

Goel, V., & Dolan, R. J. (2003). Explaining modulation of reasoning by belief. *Cognition, 87*, 11–22.

Hamman, S. (2001). Nosing in on the emotional brain. *Nature Neuroscience, 6*, 106–108.

Harris, C. L., Ayçiçegi, A., & Gleason, J. B. (2003). Taboo words and reprimands elicit greater autonomic reactivity in a first language than in a second language. *Applied Psycholinguistics, 24*, 561–579.

Hirstein, W., & Ramachandran, V. S. (1997). Capgras syndrome: A novel probe for understanding the neural representation of identity and familiarity of persons. *Proceedings of the Royal Society of London: Biological Sciences, 264*, 437–444.

Holland, P. C., & Gallagher, M. (1999). Amygdala cirtuitry in attentional processes. *Trends in Cognitive Sciences, 3*, 67–73.

Holt, D. J., Kunkel, L., Weiss, A. P., Goff, D. C., Wright, C. I., Shin, L. M., et al. (2006a). Increased medial temporal lobe activation during the passive viewing of emotional and neutral facial expressions in schizophrenia. *Schizophrenia Research, 82*, 153–162.

Holt, D. J., Titone, D., Long, L. S., Goff, D. C., Cather, C., Rauch, S. L., et al. (2006b). The misattribution of salience in delusional patients with schizophrenia. *Schizophrenia Research, 83*, 247–256.

Humphrey, N. (2006). *Seeing red: A study in consciousness.* Cambridge, MA: Harvard University Press.

Hurliman, E., Nagode, J., & Pardo, J. (2005). Double dissociation of exteroceptive and interoceptive feedback systems in the orbital and ventromedial prefrontal cortex of humans. *Journal of Neuroscience, 25*, 4641–4648.

James, W. (1950). The methods and snares of psychology. In *The principles of psychology* (Vol. 1, pp. 183–198). New York: Dover. (Original work published 1890).

Janis, I., & Mann, L. (1977). *Decision making: A psychological analysis of conflict, choice and commitment.* New York: Free Press.

Johnson, M. K., Nolde, S. F., & De Leonardis, D. M. (1996). Emotion focus and source monitoring. *Journal of Memory and Language, 35*, 135–156.

Kahneman, D., & Tversky, A. (1979). Prospect theory: An analysis of decision under risk. *Econometrica, 47*, 263–291.

Kensinger, E. A., & Corkin, S. (2003). Memory enhancement for emotional words: Are emotional words more vividly remembered than neutral words? *Memory & Cognition, 31*, 1169–1180.

Kensinger, E. A., Garoff-Eaton, R. J., & Schacter, D. L. (2006). Memory for specific visual details can be enhanced by negative arousing content. *Journal of Memory and Language, 54*, 99–112.

Kensinger, E. A., & Schacter, D. L. (in press). Memory and emotion. In M. Lewis, J. M. Haviland-Jones, & L. F. Barrett (Eds.), *The handbook of emotion* (3rd ed). New York: Guilford Press.

Kim, H., Somerville, L. H., Johnstone, T., Alexander, A. L., & Whalen, P. J. (2003). Inverse amygdala and medial prefrontal cortex responses to surprised faces. *Neuroreport, 14*, 2317–2322.

Koski, L., & Paus, T. (2000). Functional connectivity of the anterior cingulate cortex within the human frontal lobe: A brain-mapping meta-analysis. *Experimental Brain Research, 133*, 55–65.

Kring, A. M., & Germans, M. K. (2004). Subjective experience of emotion in schizophrenia. In J. H. Jenkins & R. J. Barrett (Eds.), *The edge of experience: Schizophrenia, culture, and subjectivity* (pp. 329–348). New York: Cambridge University Press.

Kring, A. M., & Werner, K. H. (2004). Emotion regulation in psychopathology. In P. Philippot & R. S. Feldman (Eds.), *The regulation of emotion* (pp. 359–385). New York: Lawrence Erlbaum Associates, Inc.

Kringelbach, M. L. (2005). Linking reward to hedonic experience. *Nature Reviews Neuroscience, 6*, 691–702.

Kringelbach, M. L., & Rolls, E. T. (2004). The functional neuroanatomy of the human orbitofrontal cortex: Evidence from neuroimaging and neuropsychology. *Progress in Neurobiology, 72*, 341–372.

Lambie, J. A., & Marcel, A. J. (2002). Consciousness and the varieties of emotion experience: A theoretical framework. *Psychological Review, 109*, 219–259.

Lane, R. D., Chua, P. M., & Dolan, R. J. (1999). Common effects of emotional valence, arousal and attention on neural activation during visual processing of pictures. *Neuropsychologia*, *37*, 989–997.

Lane, R. D., & Garfield, D. A. S. (2005). Becoming aware of feelings: Integration of cognitive-developmental, neuroscientific, and psychoanalytic perspectives. *Neuro-psychoanalysis*, *7*, 5–30.

Lang, P. J., Bradley, M. M., Fitzsimmons, J. R., Cuthbert, B. N., Scott, J. D., Moulder, B., et al. (1998). Emotional arousal and activation of the visual cortex: An fMRI analysis. *Psychophysiology*, *35*, 199–210.

LeDoux, J. (1996). Emotional networks and motor control: A fearful view. *Progress in Brain Research*, *107*, 437–446.

Lucas, R. E., & Baird, B. M. (2004). Extraversion and emotional reactivity. *Journal of Personality and Social Psychology*, *86*, 473–485.

MacLean, P. D. (1949). Psychosomatic disease and the visceral brain: Recent developments bearing on the Papez theory of emotion. *Psychosomatic Medicine*, *11*, 338–353.

McDonald, A. J. (1998). Cortical pathways to the mammalian amygdala. *Progress in Neurobiology*, *55*, 257–332.

Mesquita, B. (2003). Emotions as dynamic cultural phenomena. In R. Davidson & K. Scherer (Eds.), *Handbook of the affective sciences* (pp. 871–890). New York: Oxford University Press.

Mesulam, M. (2000). Behavioral neuroanatomy: Large-scale networks, association cortex, frontal syndromes, the limbic system, and hemispheric specializations. In M. Mesulam (Ed.), *Principles of behavioral and cognitive neurology* (2nd ed., pp. 1–120). New York: Oxford University Press.

Milad, M. R., Quinn, B. T., Pitman, R. K., Orr, S. P., Fischl, B., & Rauch, S. L. (2005). Thickness of ventromedial prefrontal cortex in humans is correlated with extinction memory. *Proceedings of the National Academy of Sciences*, *102*, 10706–10711.

Moll, J., de Oliviera-Souza, R., Eslinger, P. J., Bramati, I. E., Mourão-Miranda, J., Andreiuolo, P. A., et al. (2002). The neural correlates of moral sensitivity: A functional magnetic resonance imaging investigation of basic and moral emotions. *Journal of Neuroscience*, *22*, 2730–2736.

Morris, J. S., Friston, K. J., Buchel, C., Frith, C. D., Young, A. W., Calder, A. J., et al. (1998). A neuromodulatory role for the human amygdala in processing emotional facial expressions. *Brain*, *121*, 47–57.

Nauta, W. (1971). The problem of the frontal lobe: A reinterpretation. *Journal of Psychiatric Research*, *8*, 167–187.

Neisser, U. (1967). *Cognitive psychology*. New York: Appleton-Century-Crofts.

Neisser, U., & Harsch, N. (1992). Phantom flashbulbs: False recollections of hearing the news about challenger. In E. Winograd & U. Neisser (Eds.), *Affect and accuracy in recall: Studies of "flashbulb" memories* (pp. 9–31). New York: Cambridge University Press.

Ochsner, K. N. (2000). Are affective events richly recollected or simply familiar? The experience and process of recognizing feelings past. *Journal of Experimental Psychology*, *129*, 242–261.

Ochsner, K. N., & Gross, J. J. (2005). The cognitive control of emotion. *Trends in Cognitive Sciences*, *9*, 242–249.

Ongur, D., Ferry, A. T., & Price, J. L. (2003). Architectonic subdivision of the human orbital and medial prefrontal cortex. *Journal of Comparative Neurology*, *460*, 425–449.

Ongur, D., & Price, J. L. (2000). The organization of networks within the orbital and medial prefrontal cortex of rats, monkeys and humans. *Cerebral Cortex*, *10*, 206–219.

Osgood, C. E. (1962). Studies of the generality of affective meaning systems. *American Psychologist*, *17*, 10–28.

Osgood, C. E., Suci, G. J., & Tannenbaum, P. H. (1957). *The measurement of meaning*. Chicago: University of Illinois Press.

Owren, M. J., & Bachorowski, J. A. (2003). Reconsidering the evolution of nonlinguistic communication: The case of laughter. *Journal of Nonverbal Behavior, 27,* 183–200.

Owren, M. J., & Rendall, D. (1997). An affect-conditioning model of nonhuman primate vocal signaling. In D. H. Owings, M. D. Beecher, & N. S. Thompson (Eds.), *Perspectives in ethology* (Vol. 12, pp. 299–346). New York: Plenum Press.

Owren, M. J., & Rendall, D. (2001). Sound on the rebound: Bringing form and function back to the forefront in understanding nonhuman primate vocal signaling. *Evolutionary Anthropology, 10,* 58–71.

Papez, J. W. (1937). A proposed mechanism of emotion. *Journal of Neuropsychiatry and Clinical Neurosciences, 7,* 103–112.

Paradis, C. M., Solomon, L. Z., Florer, F., & Thompson, T. (2004). Flashbulb memories of personal events of 9/11 and the day after for a sample of New York City residents. *Psychological Reports, 95,* 304–310.

Parvizi, J., & Damasio, A. R. (2001). Consciousness and the brainstem. *Cognition, 79,* 135–160.

Pessoa, L., Japee, S., Sturman, D., & Ungerleider, L. G. (2006). Target visibility and visual awareness modulates amygdala responses to fearful faces. *Cerebral Cortex, 16,* 366–375.

Pessoa, L., McKenna, M., Gutierrez, E., & Ungerleider, L. G. (2002). Neural processing of emotional faces requires attention. *Proceedings of the National Academy of Sciences, 99,* 11458–11463.

Pessoa, L., & Ungerleider, L. G. (2004). Neuroimaging studies of attention and the processing of emotion-laden stimuli. *Progress in Brain Research, 144,* 171–182.

Pezdek, K. (2003). Event memory and autobiographical memory for the events of September 11, 2001. *Applied Cognitive Psychology, 17*(9), 1033–1045.

Phelps, E. A. (2004). Human emotion and memory: Interactions of the amygdala and hippocampal complex. *Current Opinion in Neurobiology, 14,* 198–202.

Phelps, E. A. (2006). Emotion and cognition: Insights from studies of the human amygdala. *Annual Review of Psychology, 57,* 27–53.

Phelps, E. A., Delgado, M. R., Nearing, K. I., & LeDoux, J. E. (2004). Extinction learning in humans: Role of the amygdala and vmPFC. *Neuron, 43,* 897–905.

Pinkham, A. E., Penn, D. L., Perkins, D. O., & Lieberman, J. (2003). Implications for the neural basis of social cognition for the study of schizophrenia. *American Journal of Psychiatry, 160,* 815–824.

Plato (1992). *Republic* (Transl. G. Grube & C. Reeve). Indianapolis, IN: Hackett Publishing.

Pratto, F., & John, O. P. (1991). Automatic vigilance: The attention-grabbing power of negative social information. *Journal of Personality and Social Psychology, 61,* 380–391.

Quirk, G. J., Russo, G. K., Barron, J. L., & Lebron, K. (2000). The role of ventromedial prefrontal cortex in the recovery of extinguished fear. *Journal of Neuroscience, 20,* 6225–6231.

Rainnie, D. G. (2003). Inhibitory and excitatory circuitries in amygdala nuclei: A synopsis of session II. *Annals of the New York Academy of Sciences, 985,* 59–66.

Rolls, E. T. (1999). *The brain and emotion.* Oxford: Oxford University Press.

Rolls, E. T. (2000). Précis of "The Brain and Emotion". *Behavioral and Brain Sciences, 23,* 177–191.

Rosselli, M., Ardila, A., Santisi, M., Arecco, M., Salvatierra, J., Conde, A., et al. (2002). Stroop effect in Spanish–English bilinguals. *Journal of the International Neuropsychological Society, 8,* 819–827.

Russell, J. A. (1983). Pancultural aspects of the human conceptual organisation of emotions. *Journal of Personality and Social Psychology, 45,* 1281–1288.

Russell, J. A. (2003). Core affect and the psychological construction of emotion. *Psychological Review, 110,* 145–172.

Russell, J. A., & Barrett, L. F. (1999). Core affect, prototypical emotional episodes, and other things called emotion: Dissecting the elephant. *Journal of Personality & Social Psychology*, *76*, 805–819.

Sadikot, A. F., & Parent, A. (1990). The monoaminergic innervation of the amygdala in the squirrel monkey: An immunohistochemical study. *Neuroscience*, *36*, 431–447.

Scherer, K. (1997). Profiles of emotion-antecedent appraisal: Testing theoretical predictions across cultures. *Cognition and Emotion*, *11*, 113–150.

Schneirla, T. (1959). An evolutionary and developmental theory of biphasic processes underlying approach and withdrawal. In M Jones (Ed.), *Nebraska symposium on motivation* (7, pp. 27–58). Lincoln: University of Nebraska Press.

Schnider, A., Treyer, V., & Buck, A. (2000). Selection of currently relevant memories by the human posterior medial orbitofrontal cortex. *Journal of Neuroscience*, *20*, 5880–5884.

Schnyer, D. M., Nicholls, L., & Verfaellie, M. (2005). The role of VMPC in metamemorial judgments of content retrievability. *Journal of Cognitive Neuroscience*, *17*, 832–846.

Schwarz, N., & Clore, G. L. (1983). Mood, misattribution, and judgments of well-being: Informative and directive functions of affective states. *Journal of Personality and Social Psychology*, *45*, 513–523.

Searle, J. (1992). *The rediscovery of the mind*. Cambridge, MA: MIT Press.

Searle, J. (2004). *Mind: A brief introduction*. New York: Cambridge University Press.

Shamay-Tsoory, S. G., Tomer, R., Berger, B. D., Goldsher, D., & Aharon-Peretz, J. (2005). Impaired "affective theory of mind" is associated with right ventromedial prefrontal damage. *Cognitive and Behavioral Neurology*, *18*, 55–67.

Sharot, T., & Phelps, E. A. (2004). How arousal modulates memory: Disentangling the effects of attention and retention. *Cognitive, Affective & Behavioral Neuroscience*, *4*(3), 294–306.

Sheline, Y. I., Barch, D. M., Donnelly, J. M., Ollinger, J. M., Snyder, A. Z., & Mintun, M. A. (2001). Increased amygdala response to masked emotional faces in depressed subject resolves with antidepressant treatment: An fMRI study. *Biological Psychiatry*, *50*, 651–658.

Siegle, G. J., Steinhauer, S. R., Thase, M. E., Stenger, V. A., & Carter, C. S. (2002). Can't shake that feeling: Event-related fMRI assessment of sustained amygdala activity in response to emotional information in depressed individuals. *Biological Psychiatry*, *51*, 693–707.

Smith, M. C., Bibi, U., & Sheard, D. E. (2003). Evidence for the differential impact of time and emotion on personal and event memories for September 11, 2001. *Applied Cognitive Psychology*, *17*, 1047–1055.

Smoski, M. J., & Bachorowski, J. A. (2003). Antiphonal laughter between friends and strangers. *Cognition and Emotion*, *17*, 327–340.

Solomon, R., & Stone, L. (2002). On "positive" and "negative" emotions. *Journal for the Theory of Social Behaviour*, *32*, 417–435.

Spelke, E. S. (2000). Core knowledge. *American Psychologist*, *55*, 233–1243.

Spitz, R. A. (1965). *The first year of life*. New York: International Universities Press.

Sroufe, L. A. (1979). Socioemotional development. In J. D. Osofsky (Ed.), *Handbook of infant development* (pp. 462–516). New York: Wiley.

Stefanacci, L., & Amaral, D. G. (2002). Some observations on cortical inputs to the macaque monkey amygdala: An anterograde tracing study. *The Journal of Comparative Neurology*, *451*, 301–323.

Stolarova, M., Keil, A., & Moratti, S. (2006). Modulation of the C1 visual event-related component by conditioned stimuli: Evidence for sensory plasticity in early affective perception. *Cerebral Cortex*, *16*, 876–887.

Storbeck, J., & Clore, G. L. (2007). On the interdependence of cognition and emotion. *Cognition and Emotion*, *21*, 1213–1238.

Talarico, J. M., & Rubin, D. C. (2003). Confidence, not consistency, characterizes flashbulb memories. *Psychological Science*, *14*, 455–461.

Taylor, S. F., Liberzon, I., & Koeppe, R. A. (2000). The effect of graded aversive stimuli on limbic and visual activation. *Neuropsychologia, 38*, 1415–1425.

Thompson-Schill, S. L. (2003). Neuroimaging studies of semantic memory: Inferring "how" from "where". *Neuropsychologia, 41*, 280–292.

Titchener, E. B. (1909). *Lectures on the experimental psychology of the thought-processes.* New York: Macmillan.

Tong, F., Nakayama, K., Vaughan, J. T., & Kanwisher, N. (1998). Binocular rivalry and visual awareness in human extrastriate cortex. *Neuron, 21*, 753–759.

Tononi, G., & Edelman, G. M. (2000). Schizophrenia and the mechanisms of conscious integration. *Brain Research Reviews, 31*, 391–400.

Vuilleumier, P., Armony, J. L., Driver, J., & Dolan, R. J. (2001). Effects of attention and emotion on face processing in the human brain: An event-related fMRI study. *Neuron, 30*, 829–841.

Vuilleumier, P., Richardson, M. P., Armony, J. L., Driver, J., & Dolan, R. J. (2004). *Nature Neuroscience, 7*, 1271–1278.

Weiskrantz, L. (1986). *Blindsight. A case study and implications.* Oxford, UK: Oxford University Press.

Weiskrantz, L. (1987). Residual vision in a scotoma: A follow-up study of "form" discrimination. *Brain, 110*, 77–92.

Weiskrantz, L. (1991). Disconnected awareness for detecting, processing, and remembering in neurological patients. *The Hughlings Jackson Lecture. Journal of the Royal Society of Medicine, 84*, 466–470.

Weiskrantz, L. (2001). Commentary responses and conscious awareness in humans: The implications for awareness in non-human animals. *Animal Welfare, 10*, 41–46.

Wentura, D., Rothermund, K., & Bak, P. (2000). Automatic vigilance: The attention-grabbing power of approach- and avoidance-related social information. *Journal of Personality and Social Psychology, 78*, 1024–1037.

Whalen, P. J. (1998). Fear, vigilance, and ambiguity: Initial neuroimaging studies of the human amygdala. *Current Directions in Psychological Science, 7*, 177–188.

Wierzbicka, A. (1992). *Semantics, culture, and cognition: Universal human concepts in culture-specific configurations.* Oxford, UK: Oxford University Press.

Williams, M., Morris, A., McGlone, F., Abbott, D., & Mattingley, J. (2004). Amygdala responses to fearful and happy facial expressions under conditions of binocular suppression. *The Journal of Neuroscience, 24*, 2898–2904.

Winkielman, P., Berridge, K. C., & Wilbarger, J. L. (2005). Unconscious affective reactions to masked happy versus angry faces influence consumption behavior and judgments of value. *Personality and Social Psychology Bulletin, 31*, 121–135.

Wright, I., Rabe-Hesketh, S., Woodruff, P., David, A., Murray, R., & Bullmore, E. (2000). Meta-analysis of regional brain volumes in schizophrenia. *American Journal of Psychiatry, 157*, 16–25.

Wundt, W. M. (1897). *Outlines of psychology* (Transl. C. H. Judd). (Available at: http://www.yorku.ca/dept/psych/classics/index.htm)

COGNITION AND EMOTION
2007, 21 (6), 1212–1237

On the interdependence of cognition and emotion

Justin Storbeck and Gerald L. Clore

University of Virginia, Charlottesville, VA, USA

Affect and cognition have long been treated as independent entities, but in the current review we suggest that affect and cognition are in fact highly interdependent. We open the article by discussing three classic views for the independence of affect. These are (i) the *affective independence hypothesis*, that emotion is processed independently from cognition, (ii) the *affective primacy hypothesis*, that evaluative processing precedes semantic processing, and (iii) the *affective automaticity hypothesis*, that affectively potent stimuli commandeer attention and evaluation is automatic. We argue that affect is not independent from cognition, that affect is not primary to cognition, nor is affect automatically elicited. The second half of the paper discusses several instances of how affect influences cognition. We review experiments showing affective involvement in perception, semantic activation, and attitude activation. We conclude that one function of affect is to regulate cognitive processing.

Different views of the relationship between cognition and emotion can be seen in the comments of two prominent psychologists upon receipt of distinguished scientist awards.

Robert Zajonc (1980, p. 151) in a paper titled "Preferences Need No Inferences", proclaimed: "Affect and cognition ... constitute independent sources of effects in information processing". A year later, upon receipt of the same award, Gordon Bower (1981, p. 147), in a paper on "Mood and Memory", stated, "I am a cognitive psychologist, and ... the emotional effects we have found so far seem understandable to me in terms of ideas that are standard fare in cognitive psychology". These two pivotal papers both argued for the importance of studying emotion, but they proposed different meta-theories. Zajonc argued that affect and cognition are processed independently and that affect has temporal priority over even basic cognitive

---

Correspondence should be addressed to: Justin Storbeck, 102 Gilmer Hall, PO Box 400400, Charlottesville, VA 22904–4400, USA. E-mail: storbeck@virginia.edu

Support for this research is acknowledged from National Institute of Mental Health Grant MH 50074 to GLC.

© 2007 Psychology Press, an imprint of the Taylor & Francis Group, an Informa business
www.psypress.com/cogemotion   DOI: 10.1080/02699930701438020

processes. In contrast, Bower argued that cognitive processing could be used to understand emotional phenomena. We agree with Bower's conception, and we extend it to suggest that cognitive processes are necessary for the processing, elicitation, and experience of emotions.

The concepts of "cognition" and "emotion" are, after all, simply abstractions for two aspects of one brain in the service of action. Zajonc believed that emotion is independent from cognition. Our own view is that the study of emotion and cognition should be integrated, because the phenomena themselves are integrated (Dewey, 1894; Parrott & Sabini, 1989). We argue against the notion that discrete emotions have separate and distinct areas in the brain (Duncan & Barrett, 2007 this issue). Rather, emotions emerge from a combination of affective and cognitive processes (see Moors, this issue).[1] Moreover, in agreement with Bower (1981), we suggest that emotion can be studied using cognitive paradigms. Both laboratory findings and everyday observation suggest a unity and inter-relatedness of cognitive and affective processes, and that trying to dissect them into separate faculties would neglect the richness of mental life (Roediger, Gallo, & Geraci, 2002, p. 319). We suggest, like others, that the interconnections found within the brain provide no obvious basis for divorcing emotion from cognition (Erickson & Schulkin, 2003; Halgren, 1992; Lane & Nadel, 2000; Phelps, 2004).

This article has two parts. The first part is a critical review of what recent neuroscience and social psychological research tells us about three popular ideas about cognition and emotion.[2] These include the *affective independence hypothesis*, that emotion is processed independently of cognition via a subcortical "low route", the *affective primacy hypothesis*, that affective and evaluative processing takes precedence over semantic processing, as evident in the mere exposure effect and affective priming, and the *affective automaticity hypothesis*, that affectively potent stimuli commandeer attention and that affective processes are especially likely to be automatic. In the second part, we suggest that rather than being processed independently, affect modifies and regulates cognitive processing, as illustrated in a review of some recent research from our own lab.

---

[1] That is, we, along with others (e.g., Barrett, 2006), suggest that there is not a brain centre dedicated to specific emotions such as fear, happiness, etc. But, there are specific areas critically involved in emotion processing. For instance, the amygdala is critically involved in the emotion of fear, but is not specifically dedicated to fear.

[2] The conception of emotion we raise, affective independence and affective primacy, comes mainly from Zajonc (1980, 2000). The affective automaticity derives from arguments made by Bargh and colleagues (Bargh, 1997; Ferguson & Bargh, 2003).

I. ASSESSING THREE HYPOTHESES ABOUT AFFECT AND COGNITION

A. The affective independence hypothesis: The low route

Zajonc (2000) lists ten ways in which affect and cognition differ and suggests that they arise from separate systems. Papers in this tradition sometimes cite LeDoux's (1996) proposal that the amygdala can elicit emotion before information reaches the cortex. In this section, we suggest (a) that the low route does not play a role in processing the complex stimuli typically used in social and emotional research (e.g., faces, ideographs, objects), and (b) that the amygdala, and emotion in general, does not function independently of perceptual and cognitive processes.

The "low route" (LeDoux, 1996; LeDoux, Romanski, & Xagoraris, 1989) is a pathway that allows stimulus processing without cortical influence as studied in rats. When light hits the retina, the signal is relayed to the amygdala through the thalamus without going first to the visual cortex. The pathway is adequate to support fear conditioning between illumination changes and fear-invoking events (e.g., shock). Based on studies with the auditory cortex, which have similar relay pathways as the visual cortex, information can reach the amygdala within 20 ms (Quirk, Armony, & LeDoux, 1997; Quirk, Repa, & LeDoux, 1995).

LeDoux and colleagues used rat models to examine the low route to emotion, and the question remains whether a similar pathway exists in humans. First, comparative anatomical studies (Linke, De Lima, Schwegler, & Pape, 1999) and behavioural studies (Shi & Davis, 2001) using rat-based models suggest that this pathway may be functionally relevant only when cortical areas have been lesioned or damaged. In humans, converging evidence suggests that the low route may not be functionally important for emotion processing (Halgren, 1992; Kudo, Glendenning, Frost, & Masterson, 1986; Rolls, 1999; Shi & Davis, 2001; Storbeck, Robinson, & McCourt, 2006). However, the existence of the low route in humans is still debated (see LeDoux, 2001).[3]

---

[3] In particular, the strongest evidence for such a route comes from affective blindsight individuals. Individuals have damage to area V1 of the visual cortex and as a result have no conscious perception of the world. However, these individuals still demonstrate affective reactions to fear-inducing visual stimuli. In the literature though, this is still a debated issue. First, the pathways involved are unclear. That is, although information may not be visually conscious to blindsight individuals, areas of the visual cortex still receive visual information (area V4 and extrastriate) from subcortical structures such as the pulvinar and superior colliculus. Therefore, although the area V1 is damaged, areas of the visual cortex still receive the same visual information. Storbeck, Robinson, and McCourt (2006) examine this issue more extensively.

Can the low route discriminate emotional vs. non-emotional stimuli without cortical involvement? That is, can the low route sufficiently discriminate a snake from a bunny without cortical involvement? We say No. The low route has limited capacity for stimulus discrimination. Fear conditioning studies that find support for the low route typically require only detection of the presence or absence of a stimulus (Duvel, Smith, Talk, & Gabriel, 2001; LeDoux et al., 1989; Shi & Davis, 2001). When the task requires discriminating one stimulus from another (e.g., CS+ = high freq. tone, CS − = low freq. tone), then cortical analysis appears to be necessary (Butler, Diamond, & Neff, 1957; Duvel et al., 2001; Komura et al., 2001; McCabe, McEchron, Green, & Schneiderman, 1993; Nicholson & Freeman, 2000; Thompson, 1962).

One way to test the affective independence hypothesis is to temporarily inactivate the visual cortex to determine whether it is necessary for the amygdala to determine affective significance of stimuli. Fukuda, Ono, and Nakamura (1987) did just that in awake, behaving monkeys. They observed that when the visual cortex (representing early cognitive processing) was temporarily inactivated, monkeys failed to learn and failed to demonstrate appropriate affective associations to visual cues of edible vs. inedible objects. But, the amygdala was still intact, because the monkeys could determine the affective significance of the same stimuli based on taste. This study suggests that in order to determine whether a peanut or a baseball is edible based on visual properties and prior experience, the visual cortex is necessary.

Another way to determine whether the amygdala is independent of initial cognitive processing is to record single-cell activity within the visual cortex and the amygdala. Again, if the amygdala can process visual stimuli independent of cortical input, then amygdala neurons should still remain active to visually presented objects that have affective significance when the visual cortex is temporarily inactivated. Nishijo, Ono, Tamura, and Nakamura (1993) recorded such vision-relevant neurons in the amygdala of monkeys. They discovered that these neurons failed to respond to affectively significant visual stimuli when the visual cortex was temporarily inactivated. They suggested that amygdala activity is not related directly to sensory inputs, but rather it relies on view-invariant representations of objects from the visual cortex. That is, the goal of the visual cortex is to create unique neural signatures for unique objects regardless of its orientation, background lighting, etc. Therefore, the same affective significance can be retrieved regardless of the visual state the object is in. Halgren offers similar conclusions as Nishijo et al. by suggesting that when "the amygdala performs emotional evaluation, it does so within the cognitive system. This could explain why it has been so difficult to dissociate emotional from cognitive processing in humans" (Halgren, 1992, p. 212).

Faces have always received special attention in the study of emotion due to their possible evolutionary connection to survival (Davey, 1995; Öhman, 1997). Adolphs (2002) suggested that processing and recognising a fear face requires a network of various structures and that the low route alone is incapable of such processing. He proposed that the visual cortex first grossly identifies the face, and in particular determines whether the face contains an expression or not. Support for this model comes from the fact that there are two areas in the monkey visual cortex dedicated to face processing, areas STS and IT. Area STS (superior temporal sulcus) is involved in encoding facial expressions, while the IT (inferotemporal cortex) is involved in encoding facial identity (see Allison, Puce, & McCarthy, 2000; Kanwisher, McDermott, & Chun, 1997; Narumoto, Okada, Sadato, Fukui, & Yonekura, 2001; Rotshtein, Malach, Hadar, Graif, & Hendler, 2001, for related literature on humans). Both areas, STS and IT, have strong reciprocal connections to the amygdala, suggesting the amygdala receives highly processed facial information pertaining to both facial identity and facial expression (Baylis, Rolls, & Leonard, 1987; Fukuda et al., 1987; Nishijo, Ono, & Nishino, 1988b; Rolls, 1992). For example, Rotshtein et al. (2001) found that lateral occipital cortex in humans, which processes facial expressions, is concerned with the configuration for each expression, rather than with its affective value. That is, the visual cortex does not code for affective significance (Rolls, 1999; Rotshtein et al., 2001), but rather codes for facial configurations and these configurations are sent to the amygdala for affective processing. Thus, the visual cortex is needed for the amygdala to correctly identify and respond to emotional stimuli.

For emotional stimuli used by psychologists (e.g., snakes; emotional faces) the processing capacities of the low route would appear to be inadequate (see Rolls, 1999; Smith, Cacioppo, Larsen, & Chartrand, 2003, for similar concerns). But, the low route is still cited to help explain particular affective phenomena (e.g., Bargh, 1997; Berkowitz & Harmon-Jones, 2004; Zajonc, 2000). However, we suggest that the fact that the amygdala relies on cortical input to make an evaluation requires reconsideration of whether emotion at initial levels of processing can be dissociated from cognitive processing. We should also note that the same processes occur regardless of whether stimuli are presented subliminally or supraliminally (Rolls & Tovee, 1994; Rolls, Tovee, Purcell, Stewart, & Azzopardi, 2004; Storbeck et al., 2006).

Conclusions. Davidson (2003) claimed that one of seven deadly sins of cognitive neuroscience is to assume that affect is independent from cognition. We and several others agree that emotion should not be divorced from cognition (Adolphs & Damasio, 2001; Barnard, Duke, Byrne, &

Davidson, 2007 this issue; Davidson, 2003; Duncan & Barrett, 2007 this issue; Eder & Klauer, this issue; Erickson & Schulkin, 2003; Lane & Nadel, 2000; Lavender & Hommel, this issue; Lazarus, 1995; Parrott & Sabini, 1989; Phelps, 2004; Storbeck et al., 2006). For instance, based on anatomical connections alone (Ghashghaei & Barbas, 2002) areas necessary for cognition and emotion are highly interconnected, and these connections are bidirectional, suggesting integrated processing of emotion and cognition. Halgren (1992) suggests that emotion and cognition are so interconnected that it is not practical to try to disentangle the temporal and casual relations of emotion and cognition.

B. The affective primacy hypothesis

In addition to the idea that affect and cognition are independent sources of influence, is the allied idea of affective primacy (Zajonc, 1980, 2000). The mere exposure phenomenon (Zajonc, 1968) was an important source of evidence for the hypothesis, because mere exposure involves an affective reaction that is not dependent on conscious categorisation or identification of the liked stimulus.

One problem with accepting the grand conclusions, that affective processing occurs without cognitive processing, drawn from mere exposure research is that they rest on an equation of consciousness with cognition (Lazarus, 1995). However, single-cell recording shows that the visual cortex can readily identify stimuli presented below subjective thresholds. Therefore, lack of conscious awareness has no bearing on whether the visual cortex categorises and identifies a stimulus. In fact, studies have demonstrated that the only difference between a stimulus presented for 30 ms as opposed to 1000 ms is the strength at which a neural population fires (Rolls, 1999; Rolls & Tovee, 1994; Rolls et al., 1994). But the response pattern output remains the same, which is thought to reflect a unique neural signature for a given stimulus type. That is, the neural population identifies X whether presented for 30 ms or 1000 ms, but the firing is stronger so that the system is more confident for 1000 ms presentations than for 30 ms presentations.

Another problem is that the mere exposure effect gets weaker the longer stimuli are presented, as respondents have time to process the identity of the stimulus and to realise that they have seen it before. The mere exposure effect is, therefore, a mistake based on a misattribution of fluency as liking instead of as familiarity (Winkielman, Schwarz, Fazendeiro, & Reber, 2003). Of course, most real-world emotional reactions are not errors of this kind, so that its appeal as a model of how affect is related to cognition is limited.

More importantly, Zajonc (2000) assumed that the mere exposure effect does not rely on cognitive or cortical involvement, suggesting the effect may rely on the low route to emotion. The low route to emotion would allow for affective processing without cortical or cognitive input. However, available evidence suggests that the effect does not rely on processing by the amygdala. For example, Greve and Bauer (1990) report the case of a patient, GY, who had an accident that severed the connection between the visual cortex and the amygdala. They found that GY showed the mere exposure effect even though visual information was not getting to the amygdala. Elliott and Dolan (1998) also report that the mere exposure effect relies more on frontal cortical networks. They failed to observe any relevant amygdala activation. These data suggest that the mere exposure effect is not a phenomenon that requires the amygdala, let alone one that could be based in the low route to the amygdala.

Affective priming as evidence for affective primacy. Another phenomenon that has been interpreted as demonstrating a special status for affect is affective priming. Research suggests that people routinely evaluate objects in their environment (Murphy & Zajonc, 1993; Niedenthal, 1990). For example, in sequential priming studies, briefly presented prime words are followed by target words that participants categorise (e.g., as positive or negative) as quickly as possible (Bargh, Chaiken, Govender, & Pratto, 1992; Bargh, Chaiken, Raymond, & Hymes, 1996; Fazio, Sanbonmatsu, Powell, & Kardes, 1986). Priming is then seen when, for example, positive primes facilitate responses to positive targets and interfere with responses to negative targets. Such affective priming suggests that people may automatically evaluate stimuli without an intention to do so.

In an effort to rule out the possibility that the response facilitation is really due to some semantic dimension, investigators typically choose primes and targets that have no association other than being similar or dissimilar in evaluative meaning. However, Storbeck and Robinson (2004) point out that this practice of limiting the relationship between primes and targets to evaluation may force respondents into evaluative priming. If so, it would lose its value as evidence that affect is independent of cognition or has primacy over semantic meaning.

To test this hypothesis, Storbeck and Robinson (2004) used "a comparative priming method" in which words were selected to vary not only evaluatively but also categorically. For example, primes or targets might be positively or negative valenced animals (e.g., puppies, snakes) or positive or negatively valenced texture words (smooth, rough). Thus, prime-target pairs were related evaluatively (good vs. bad), but also descriptively (animals vs. textures).

Two tasks were used, an evaluation task and a lexical decision task, and both revealed semantic but not affective priming. In addition, the same result was found when they used pictures instead of words. To verify that the practice of artificially limiting the relationship between primes and targets to evaluation had promoted affective priming in prior studies, Storbeck and Robinson (2004) then repeated their experiment but removed any systematic descriptive relationship between primes and targets, such that all words were now animal exemplars. As expected, the usual affective priming results reappear when participants are given only evaluation as a possible basis for relating primes and targets.

Another comparative priming study was performed by Klauer and Musch (2002). They used primes and targets that could be categorised based on affect or another non-affective dimension, and manipulated only the task demand (i.e., to evaluate or categorise). They concluded that affective priming is not based on a special evaluation system. Rather, affective priming relies on the same mechanisms responsible for semantic priming.

These experiments suggest that affective priming is not obligatory. The evaluative meaning on which affective priming is based is represented within a larger semantic network in which it is not the dominant mode of semantic categorisation. Evaluation is doubtlessly a very basic level of analysis, but evaluative meaning is not processed apart from other dimensions of semantic meaning, nor does it invoke a special automatic evaluator.

The Storbeck and Robinson experiments used supraliminal exposures of primes, but Erdley and D'Agostino (1988) used subliminal exposures. In a very different paradigm, they too found that when both affective and descriptive features were present, priming occurred along semantic rather than evaluative lines, suggesting that categorisation may often have priority over evaluation.

One might hypothesize that affect is elicited automatically at the onset of a stimulus and degrades from that point. If so, the use of a relatively long Stimulus Onset Asynchrony (SOA) (300 ms) by Storbeck and Robinson (2004) might conceivably have prevented detection of affective priming. To assess this possibility, studies might again use the comparative-priming approach and shorten either stimulus durations or response times, either of which might allow early components of the priming process to be visible. A study by Klinger, Burton, and Pitts (2000) satisfied these two requirements, and concluded that when primes are presented subliminally and response-window procedures are used, finding semantic or affective priming depends mainly on task requirements and response competition.

The Klinger et al. study is unique in the use of the response-window procedure. Since spreading activation builds up over hundreds of milliseconds (Perea & Rosa, 2002), such procedures tend to reduce any effects due to spreading activation within the semantic network, making it likely that any priming effects obtained are due to response compatibility, rather than spreading activation. It is interesting to note, though, that both semantic and affective priming were sensitive to similar task constraints, suggesting that both result from similar mechanisms. Other studies using similar comparative methods and response-window procedures also found both affective and categorical priming (Klauer & Musch, 2002; Klinger et al., 2000). However, crucially, these studies failed to equate semantic and affective features, and in each, affect was the most salient feature. Together these studies suggest that with response-window procedures, regardless of prime duration, priming is driven by response compatibility.

Since the use of a response window shortens the time available for effects due to spreading activation, what happens when spreading activation is allowed to build up over time, by presenting primes subliminally without a response window. Kemp-Wheeler and Hill (1992) performed such a study with a lexical decision task, and found both affective and semantic priming. But they also found that affective priming occurred mostly when people could detect the prime. Such detection did not facilitate semantic priming. They argued that affective priming is a subform of semantic priming and occurs when more time is given to revealing the affective significance of primes and targets.

Moving away from the priming procedure, Storbeck, Robinson, Ram, Meier, and Clore (2004) examined evaluations and categorisations of single target words using a response-window procedure. The window of response varied from 100 ms to 2000 ms and the dependent measure was accuracy. The experiment included nine participants over five days with over 500 trials per day. This allowed us to produce predictive models for the rise of semantic and affective accuracy. The results revealed that in shorter response windows, participants were more accurate in detecting semantic information than affective information. Other studies have found that semantic distinctions can occur as early as 80 ms, while evaluative distinctions start around 100 ms (Van Rullen & Thorpe, 2001).

EEG measures can also be used to discriminate semantic and affective aspects of processing without involving motor output processes. Cacioppo, Crites, and Gardner (1996) and Ito and Cacioppo (2001) found that ERP potentials always tracked semantic relations, even when semantic analysis was not the focus of the task. ERPs also tracked affective features, but only when the task had an explicitly evaluative focus, unless the evaluative components were quite potent. More critically, evidence suggests that the same discriminative processing based on semantic features performed by the visual cortex occurs whether stimuli are presented subliminally or supraliminally, regardless of conscious experience (Dehaene et al., 2001; Rolls & Tovee, 1994; Rolls et al., 1994; Stenberg, Lindgren, & Johansson, 2000). ERP and single-cell recordings both demonstrate that semantic information appears to be represented regardless of the task at hand and whether or not there is conscious perception of the stimuli. That is, semantic information always gets activated, regardless of the explicit task, whereas affective information is processed mainly when evaluation is an explicit part of the task or a highly salient aspect of the stimulus.

To be clear, in this view, the system needs an identification stage before an evaluation stage, and identification occurs in later stages of processing in the visual cortex. Even in classical conditioning, some kind of identification is required by the cortex (e.g., visual cortex) to discriminate a conditioned stimulus from all other stimuli. By "identification stage" we mean simply that a view invariant, neural signature of an object is activated in the visual cortex. Only then can the object activate affective and other associations.

Conclusions. These studies suggest that both semantic[4] and affective features are represented in a single semantic network, and that semantic information (which is not to say lexical information, see footnote 3) has a necessary priority. That is, we feel that affective priming is a special case of semantic priming and can be obtained when affect is part of the task demand, the salient feature of the stimuli, or the focus of attention (Storbeck & Robinson, 2004). Under the right set of circumstances, affective relations can be made more accessible than semantic relations (e.g., Bargh et al., 1992, 1996; Klinger et al., 2000; Storbeck & Robinson, 2004). For example, Storbeck and Robinson (2004) found that when they crossed descriptive and evaluative features of stimuli in an evaluative priming task, semantic but not affective priming was observed. But when the relations between primes and targets stimuli were limited to their evaluative features, then affective priming was observed. Thus, under the right set of conditions, affective priming can readily be observed, but such evaluative priming is in no way obligatory. Thus, the fact that evaluative priming can be found when evaluative meaning is made salient, provides little support for ideas about affective primacy or about the separate nature of affective and cognitive processing.

C. The affective automaticity hypothesis

Although the automatic–controlled distinction arose in cognitive psychology (Shiffrin & Schneider, 1977), a special association is often assumed between affect and automaticity. Perhaps the idea was that thoughts can be more easily controlled than feelings has made affect seem to have a life of its

---

[4] We will use the term "semantic" to describe the meaning analysis that we propose precedes affective analysis. What we have in mind specifically are at least three achievements: (1) the integration of multiple features of the object into a single "object" code; (2) the identification of this object; and (3) the categorisation of the object (e.g., as animate or not). The term semantic, then, refers somewhat more directly to the achievements of area IT (especially invariance, identification, and categorisation) that seem to occur in order for a person to retrieve affective associations.

own. One can decide to think about one particular topic rather than another, but one cannot decide to feel one way or another, except by guiding thoughts. Is automaticity a key distinction that makes affect and emotion separate from cognition?

Cognitive psychologists have recently become critical of the term "automaticity". Recent reviews have concluded that the initial demonstrations of what was purported to be automaticity may actually have required attention after all (see, Lavie & De Fockert, 2003; Logan, 2002; Pashler, Johnston, & Ruthruff, 2001; Stolz & Besner, 1999). For example, Pashler et al. (2001, p. 648) stated that, "A variety of proposals for 'wired-in' attention capture by particular stimulus attributes have been effectively challenged; attention, it turns out, is subject to a far greater degree of top-down control than was suspected 10 years ago". Generally, the relevant data have come from studies of cognition rather than affect. In this section, we suggest that the same conclusion applies in the case of affective stimuli.

Harris, Pashler, and Coburn (2004) examined whether affective words could be processed automatically. Their data indicated that affective words can slow responses down on a primary task, suggesting that affect may capture attention. However, when the primary task was made difficult, thus reducing attentional resources, affective words failed to slow responses, suggesting that affect did not capture attention. These results suggest that under high-load conditions, when attention is occupied, affective words should not be expected to "grab" attention in a bottom-up manner. Instead, affect appears to be processed by top-down networks. Similar results have been found when emotional faces were used in a modified Posner cueing paradigm (Fox, Russo, Bowles, & Dutton, 2001) and when threat-related words and faces were used in a variation of the Stroop task (White, 1996). Moreover, examining the affective pronunciation priming task, De Houwer and Randell (2002) observed affective priming only when attention was focused on the primes. When attention was not focused on the primes, affective priming was not observed in the pronunciation paradigm.

These studies all presented evidence to suggest that affective stimuli require attention and that they do not grab attention in a bottom-up manner. However, Lundqvist and Öhman (2005) have argued that evolutionarily relevant threat stimuli (e.g., snakes, spiders, faces) should be especially likely to be processed pre-attentively (see Davey, 1995, for a relevant criticism to evolutionary preparedness account).

Relevant data are limited, but, the data available would suggest that even faces require attention in order to be processed. As discussed above, Fox et al. (2001) found that angry, happy, and neutral faces failed to capture attention when the effects of attention capture versus disengagement were disentangled. Narumoto et al. (2001) found that when faces were presented, area STS, which processes facial expressions, was significantly activated only when the task required facial expression discrimination, but not when identity or gender discriminations were required for the emotional faces (see also Critchley et al., 2000). Pessoa, Kastner, and Ungerleider (2002) performed a study similar to the Harris et al. study, but they used pictures with facial expressions and collected neuroimaging data. They observed that under low-load conditions, amygdala activation was observed to task-irrelevant fear faces. But, under high-load conditions, when processing resources were limited, the amygdala failed to show significant activation to task-irrelevant fear faces, suggesting that attention was driven by top-down influences. These findings suggest that even the amygdala needs attentional resources in order to process fear faces and that fear faces can fail to capture attention.

Amygdala evaluation requires attention. It has been suggested that emotional stimuli are processed automatically, namely, without attention (LeDoux, 1996; Öhman, Esteves, & Soares, 1995; Vuilleumier, Armony, Driver, & Dolan, 2003), and that the amygdala plays a key role in automatic stimulus evaluation (Morris, Öhman, Dolan, 1998; Whalen et al., 1998). This process is often cited as the basis of affective primacy (e.g., Bargh & Chartrand, 1999; Zajonc, 2000). However, cortical input appears to be more important in amygdala processing than has sometimes been emphasised (as discussed earlier), and the data reviewed below suggest that the amygdala requires attention to process threatening and novel stimuli.

Several studies have tested the hypothesis that exposure to affective words should elicit amygdala activation, reflecting the automatic evaluation process (Beauregard et al., 1997; Canli, Desmond, Zhao, Glover, & Gabrieli, 1998). No evidence was found of the hypothesised amygdala activation unless attention was explicitly drawn to the affective content of words by asking participants to evaluate them. Such results suggest that the amygdala does not continuously evaluate all incoming stimuli.

These studies involved lexical stimuli, but the same turns out to be true for the evaluation of pictures.[5] When presented with affective pictures,

---

[5] A host of fMRI studies have demonstrated the activation of the amygdala to masked fear faces and other emotional stimuli. Such studies are interesting because individuals do not have a conscious perception of the image. However, the amygdala only shows enhanced activation to arousing images (e.g., fear faces), but not to non-arousing faces (e.g., houses). Although such evidence suggests that amygdala activation can occur without perceptual awareness, we still suggest that the visual system still codes that image and sends its input forward to the amygdala in the same manner as if the stimulus was presented supraliminally. Moreover, imaging studies have a weakness of comparative activity. Therefore, it is difficult to gage how much processing is done between masked and non-masked fear faces. In addition, there is plenty of evidence to suggest that the visual cortex processes masked and non-masked images in a similar manner.

(continued overleaf)

Keightley et al. (2003) found no amygdala activation. When participants were explicitly asked to evaluate affective stimuli, amygdala activation was found only for negative information (Keightley et al., 2003; Lane, Chua, & Dolan, 1999). For fearful faces, however, even passive viewing showed amygdala activation (Critchley et al., 2000; Morris et al., 1998; Vuilleumier et al., 2003; Whalen et al., 1998). However, with other face stimuli there was no amygdala activation even when participants explicitly evaluated them (Critchley et al., 2000; Keightley et al., 2003). Happy and angry faces also showed no amygdala activation for either passive viewing or active evaluation (Blair, Morris, Frith, Perrett, & Dolan, 1999; Morris et al., 1998; Surguladze et al., 2003).

(Continued)
Moreover, evidence from single-cell recording suggests that the visual system can still determine whether a face or a house was presented regardless of whether each image was presented with a mask and subliminally. Therefore, studies demonstrating that the amygdala activates for a subliminal, but not a supraliminal picture does not mean that the visual cortex did not send the same information. There is no reason to believe that the categorisation processes performed by area IT are conscious. Indeed, on the basis of ERP data, we might conclude that unconscious categorisation routinely precedes conscious categorisation. Furthermore, unconscious categorisation by the visual system may occur extremely quickly after stimulus exposure, in as little as 48 ms for "global templates" (Sugase, Yamane, Ueno, & Kawano, 1999) and 70–80 ms for classes of stimuli (Van Rullen & Thorpe, 2001). Interestingly, Van Rullen and Thorpe (2001) also found that the initial (70–80) categorisation-related ERP component was not highly correlated with a participant's response to the task at hand, whereas an ERP component that occurred at 190 ms post-stimulus onset was. Thus, categorisation appears to occur quite rapidly and seems to occur independently of later, possibly more conscious, categorisation processes. Relatedly, people can classify objects on the basis of category membership even with no awareness of the distinct categories guiding their response (e.g., Reed, Squire, Patalano, Smith, & Jonides, 1999). In summary, we conclude that categorisation occurs within later stages of the visual cortex, specifically area IT. Moreover, other data suggest that these same visual areas are not sensitive to the affective significance of objects (Iwai et al., 1990; Nishijo, Ono, & Nishino, 1988a; Rolls, 1999; Rolls, Judge, & Sanghera, 1977). Thus, within area IT and other later stages of the visual cortex we appear to have considerable evidence for categorisation prior to affect retrieval. Recall that studies have found distinct category-related ERPs within 70–80 ms post-stimulus onset (e.g., Van Rullen & Thorpe, 2001). Object identification also appears to occur rapidly, perhaps within 100 ms of stimulus onset (Lehky, 2000; Rolls & Tovee, 1994). These findings suggest that categorisation tends to occur prior to identification. Nevertheless, studies that present masked stimuli have demonstrated that even stimuli presented as briefly as 20–60 ms with pre- and postmasks are still sufficiently processed by area IT to support object identification (Dehaene et al., 2001; Rolls, 1999; Vogels & Orban, 1996). In the latter connection, Rolls, Tovee, Purcell, Stewart, and Azzopardi (1994) argued that such subliminal presentations reduce the amplitude of neural responses to stimuli, but do not change fundamental neural identification processes (see also Kovacs, Vogels, & Orban, 1995, for similar results). Thus, the primary difference between subliminal and optimal viewing conditions pertains to the amplitude of the neuronal responses within area IT, but sufficient processing still occurs to produce an invariant neural code (i.e., identification). From this perspective, demonstrations of "unconscious" cognition or affect are not particularly special from a neurological point of view.

Conclusions. These results suggest that valence is not automatically processed by the amygdala, but the amygdala may be sensitive to arousing stimuli such as fearful faces. Other research groups have also suggested that the amygdala is important for encoding arousal, but not the valence, dimension of stimuli (Adolphs & Damasio, 2001; Adolphs, Russell, & Tranel, 1999; Cahill et al., 1996; Lane et al., 1999; McGaugh, 2004; Morris et al., 1998; Surguladze et al., 2003). Moreover, the evidence suggests that when affect is salient and processing demands are relatively low, emotional information may engage attention. But when processing demands are high and affective stimuli are not of attention, affect will not "capture" attention. Such findings limit the conditions for automaticity, and, as cognitive psychology has already discovered, processing relies on attention, even for affective stimuli.

II. THE AFFECT–COGNITION CONNECTION

Throughout history, people's optimism or pessimism about the human condition has often turned on their beliefs about the possibility of rational thought unsullied by emotion. Gradually, however, cognition and emotion are coming to be viewed as complementary rather than antagonistic processes. Our current research is informed by an affect-as-information approach (Schwarz & Clore, 1983; Clore & Storbeck, in press), which assumes that affective reactions provide useful feedback both explicitly and implicitly from emotional appraisal processes. Evidence in support of such a view comes from observations that the inability to use affective feedback as a result of brain damage has profoundly negative consequences for judgement and decision making (Damasio, 1994). Conversely, expertise at using affective information seems to be associated with effective personal and social functioning (Mayer, Salovey, & Caruso, 2004).

A. Emotion modulates cognition[6]

In Part I, we argued against the idea that cognition and emotion involved distinct brain areas or that they operate independently. The strongest claim for independence relied on the "low route" to emotion (LeDoux, 1996), a direct pathway from the sensory thalamus to the amygdala. However, by all available evidence, the low route does not appear to be a candidate for explaining any instance of human emotion. If it operates at all in humans, it appears incapable of even basic affective discriminations without cognitive

---

[6] The section title implies that cognition does not modulate emotion. We would suggest, like others have, that in fact cognition does modulate emotion (e.g., Ochsner & Gross, 2005), but such a discussion is beyond the scope of this article.

input. Rather, the evidence from neuroscience suggests that evaluations of the amygdala are dependent upon input from the visual cortex. We suggested that affect probably does not proceed independently of cognition, nor precede cognition in time.

How, then, do we see the relationship between emotion and cognition? At the most general level, emotion modulates and mediates basic cognitive processes. The brain, of course, accomplishes numerous tasks all at once, including automatic processes (Barnard et al., 2007 this issue; Robinson, 1998). As the sensory cortex identifies stimuli in the environment, the visual cortex processes it in a view-invariant manner, allowing it to determine attributes of the object, including its affective significance, regardless of the position the object happens to be in. Once the visual cortex creates a view-invariant code for the object, it projects that information to other areas in the brain.

One of the primary pathways of the visual cortex is to the amygdala, and the role of the amygdala is in part to determine the urgency of the stimulus, which eventuates in the marking of apparently important experiences hormonally and in terms of experienced arousal. The amygdala retrieves the affective value of the stimulus or determines that it is novel and guides subsequent cognitive processing. The amygdala has extensive back projections to all areas of the visual cortex, which we believe modulate visual perception, attention, and memory for affectively significant stimuli. Note that the amygdala is probably not the only area involved in emotional processing that can modulate cognition. The visual cortex also has extensive projections to areas such as the orbitofrontal cortex, prefrontal cortex, and cingulate cortex, all of which can guide cognitive processing based on affective value.

In this section, we illustrate how we believe affect regulates cognition by briefly reviewing several recent studies from our lab. The studies discussed focus on two problems—the role of affect in perception and the affective regulation of styles of information processing. We note that in performance situations, emotional cues regulate cognitive processing, serving to adjust the mix of cognition and perception. Of special interest are several recent experiments that ask about affective consequences for implicit processes of learning, memory, priming, and attitude.

B. The affective regulation of perception

The "New Look" in perception, a movement in the 1950s (Bruner, 1957), maintained that rather than being a passive registration of reality, perception reflected internal expectations and motivations as part of an adaptive process. That movement quickly ran its course without having much impact, but, today, research again suggests that perception of the physical world is influenced by emotion and other internal factors. For example, Proffitt and colleagues (e.g., Bhalla & Proffitt, 1999; Proffitt, Stefanucci, Banton & Epstein, 2003; Witt, Proffitt, & Epstein, 2004) have found that hills appear steeper and distances farther to people with reduced physical resources, either from wearing a heavy backpack, being physically tired, or being elderly. Recent research shows that emotion can have similar effects. In one study (Riener, Stefanucci, Proffitt, & Clore, 2003) participants listened to happy or sad music as they stood at the bottom of a hill. The results showed that sadness can make mountains out of molehills. Sad mood led to overestimation of the incline on verbal and visual measures, but not on a haptic measure. That is, the sad individuals were more likely to say that the hill was steeper compared to happy individuals, but both groups provided similar haptic responses.

Affective feelings thus appear to inform explicit, but not implicit measures of perception. That is, when asked to estimate the incline verbally in degrees (i.e., verbal measure) and when indicating the incline analogically with a sort of protractor (i.e., visual measure), individuals feeling sad estimated the hill to be significantly steeper than individuals who were feeling happy or who had not heard any music. Such perceptual measures are thought to reflect conscious visual perception that relies on processing in the ventral visual stream, or "what" system, concerned with visual identification (Milner & Goodale, 1995). A reasonable argument can be made for why this system might be sensitive to resources for coping with inclines and distances (Proffitt, 2006). The third, haptic measure involved tilting a palm board (without looking at it) to match the incline of the hill. This haptic measure of incline is generally found to be quite accurate and to be immune from the influence of resource depletion such as physical exhaustion. It was also unaffected by sad mood. The measure is thought to reflect unconscious visual perception and relies on processing in the dorsal visual stream, or "how" system, engaged in the visual control of motor behaviour. Whereas it might be adaptive for one's perception of a hill to reflect one's resources, as decisions on whether to take action or not might hinge on such information, but for regulation of one's actual foot placement, such overestimations might be disastrous.

In extensions of this work, Stefanucci, Proffitt, and Clore (2005) also examined the effect of fear on hill estimates. They had individuals on top of the hill and to manipulate fear, some individuals stood on a skateboard, whereas others stood on a stable platform. They found that individuals on the skateboard provided steeper verbal hill estimates again on both the verbal and visual measures when compared to individuals standing on the stable platform. As expected, the haptic measure was again unaffected by the manipulation of emotion.

C. Affective regulation of processing

At the beginning of the cognitive revolution, Jerome Bruner (1957) famously concluded that people are active processors who typically "go beyond the information given". A number of experiments have been conducted in our lab over the past five years in which emotions and moods were added to classic experiments in cognitive psychology. One way to summarise our results is to say that happy affect appears to promote this "going beyond" through its influence on "relational processing". In contrast, negative affect leads to more item-specific processing. Such results lead us to conclude that Bruner's dictum, and all that it implies, may not be applicable when emotional cues of sadness are present. The experiments from our lab suggest (perhaps ironically) that the cognitive revolution had a hidden emotional trigger.

Many of the classic phenomena on which cognitive psychology was founded turn out to depend on affect. For instance, we observed that individuals in happy moods, but not those in sad moods, demonstrate schema effects on constructive memory of the kind introduced by Bartlett in 1932 (Gasper & Clore, 2002). Other classic phenomena also turn out to be more pronounced in happy moods than in sad moods. These include semantic priming (Storbeck & Clore, 2006), script processing (Bless et al., 1996), schema-guided memory (Gasper & Clore, 2002), stereotype use (Isbell, 2004), heuristic reasoning (Gasper, 2000), the global superiority effect (Gasper & Clore, 2002), and false memory generation (Storbeck & Clore, 2005). These results do not arise from general performance deficits caused by sad mood. On the contrary, general reaction times, overall memory accuracy, and basic performance levels often show no mood-based differences. Moreover, since the classic paradigms often rely on particular errors to show the mediating role of knowledge structures, individuals in sad moods may perform better in certain ways than those in happy moods.

These observations are compatible with findings demonstrating that positive moods are associated with processing that is generative (e.g., Erez & Isen, 2002), constructive (e.g., Fiedler, 2001), and broad (e.g., Fredrickson & Branigan, 2005). Our own account of these effects emphasises the informational properties of affect. For example, during task performance, positive affect may be experienced as efficacy and negative affect as difficulty. Feeling that one is effective confers value on one's own generative thoughts and goals resulting in the reliance on them to process incoming information (relational processing). On the other hand, experiences of difficulty and lack of efficacy reduce the apparent value of one's own cognitions and goals, leading to a focus on more-specific, literal aspects of stimuli.

D. Affective regulation of implicit processes

Priming. In other research, Storbeck and Clore (2006) tested whether this relational processing of associations can carry over to semantic knowledge. They observed that happy individuals were more likely to relate primes and targets together, demonstrating both category and evaluative priming, depending on the nature of the task. However, sad individuals failed to demonstrate priming on the same tasks, suggesting they were impaired in relating the descriptive meaning from primes to targets. Again, the results suggest that negative affective cues act as though they undermine confidence in using accessible cognitions. In the implicit learning situation, it prevented expression of what had been learned, and in the priming situation, it allowed sad participants to respond to target stimuli independently from the descriptive meaning of the primes.

False memory effects. To investigate further the hypothesis that negative affect impairs the formation and use of implicit associations, Storbeck and Clore (2005) induced positive and negative moods before a false-memory task. The task produces false memories by presenting word lists in which the lists are composed of words that are highly associated to a non-presented word, referred to as the critical lure. False memories are engendered because as individuals are relating the words from the list together, the critical lures should come to mind and are then likely to be falsely recalled. We observed that, in fact, negative moods led to a decrease in activation and subsequent recall of critical lures compared to the positive mood group and the control group. In addition, no differences were observed for the recall of presented items between the three groups. Ironically, the observed effect demonstrated that negative affect can improve memory performance by inhibiting the use of lexical associations during learning. Such findings suggest that affect from mood can influence the expression of implicit associations (Storbeck & Clore, 2005, 2006).

Affective involvement in implicit attitudes. The previous experiments show that affective states modulate the use of implicit associations in cognitive performance situations. Extensive prior research has already shown that affective states can influence evaluative judgements or attitudes expressed in self-report measures. But the intense interest in implicit attitude measurement raises the question of whether or not affect influences attitudes when assessed on implicit measures such as the Implicit Association Test or IAT (Greenwald, McGhee, & Schwartz, 1998).

Several experiments (Huntsinger, Sinclair, Dunn, & Clore, 2006) tested the hypothesis that positive affect would serve as a "go" sign and negative affect as a "stop" sign for acting on goals that were either chronically or temporarily activated. The goal in one experiment concerned taking an egalitarian stance regarding sexist attitudes, and in the other experiment the goal was either to adopt or not to adopt the racial attitudes held by an experimenter. Implicit measures of attitude were employed (a lexical decision task and an IAT). An elaborate set of effects neatly confirmed the predictions, showing that in each case, happy moods prompted participants to act on their chronic or temporarily activated goals, whereas sad moods interfered with goal expression. Importantly, the goals had been activated implicitly as a subtle part of the social situation, and the attitudes were measured implicitly using two different measures—see also DeSteno, Dasgupta, Bartlett, and Cajdric (2004) for a demonstration of the effects of anger on implicitly measured prejudice toward an outgroup. Thus, affective states appear to regulate not only the expression of implicit learning and implicit lexical associations, but also the expression of implicitly measured attitudes.

In summary, our main goal of this section was to demonstrate that affect and cognition should be thought of as fundamentally interactive. In this view, affect is potential moderator of all kinds of cognitive operations from perception and attention to implicit learning and implicit associations (see also, Duncan & Barrett, this issue). We have argued against conceptualising emotion as a separate force in opposition to cognition in favour of viewing cognition and emotion as inherently integrated. We included examples of recent research in our own lab showing affective moderation of basic cognitive processes.

REFERENCES

Adolphs, R. (2002). Recognizing emotion from facial expressions: Psychological and neurological mechanisms. *Behavioral and Cognitive Neuroscience Reviews, 1*, 21–62.

Adolphs, R., & Damasio, A. (2001). The interaction of affect and cognition: A neurobiological perspective. In J. P. Forgas (Ed.), *Handbook of affect and social cognition* (pp. 27–49). Mahwah, NJ: Lawrence Erlbaum Associates, Inc.

Adolphs, R., Russell, J., & Tranel, D. (1999). A role for the human amygdala in recognizing emotional arousal from unpleasant stimuli. *Psychological Science, 10*, 167–171.

Allison, T., Puce, A., & McCarthy, G. (2000). Social perception from visual cues: Role of the STS region. *Trends in Cognitive Sciences, 4*, 267–278.

Bargh, J. (1997). The automaticity of everyday life. In R. S. Wyer Jr. (Ed.), *The automaticity of everyday life: Advances in social cognition* (Vol. 10, pp. 1–61). Mahwah, NJ: Lawrence Erlbaum Associates, Inc.

Bargh, J., Chaiken, S., Govender, R., & Pratto, F. (1992). The generality of the automatic attitude activation effect. *Journal of Personality and Social Psychology, 62*, 893–912.

Bargh, J., Chaiken, S., Raymond, P., & Hymes, C. (1996). The automatic evaluation effect: Unconditional automatic attitude activation with a pronunciation task. *Journal of Experimental Social Psychology, 32*, 104–128.

Bargh, J., & Chartrand, T. (1999). The unbearable automaticity of being. *American Psychologist, 54*, 462–479.

Barnard, P. J., Duke, D. J., Byrne, R. W., & Davidson, I. (2007). Differentiation in cognitive and emotional meanings: An evolutionary analysis. *Cognition and Emotion, 21,* 1155–1183.

Barrett, L. F. (2006). Emotions as natural kinds? *Perspectives on Psychological Science, 1,* 28–58.

Bartlett, F. C. (1932). *Remembering: A study in experimental and social psychology.* Cambridge: Cambridge University Press.

Baylis, G., Rolls, E. T., & Leonard, C. (1987). Functional subdivisions of the temporal lobe neocortex. *Journal of Neuroscience, 7,* 330–342.

Beauregard, M., Chertkow, H., Bub, D., Murtha, S., Dixon, R., & Evans, A. (1997). The neural substrate for concrete, abstract, and emotional word lexica: A positron emission tomography study. *Journal of Cognitive Neuroscience, 9,* 441–461.

Berkowitz, L., & Harmon-Jones, E. (2004). More thoughts about anger determinants. *Emotion, 4,* 107–130.

Bhalla, M., & Proffitt, D. (1999). Visual-motor recalibration in geographical slant perception. *Journal of Experimental Psychology: Human Perception and Performance, 25,* 1076–1096.

Blair, R., Morris, J., Frith, C., Perrett, D., & Dolan, R. (1999). Dissociable neural responses to facial expressions of sadness and anger. *Brain, 122,* 883–893.

Bless, H., Clore, G. L., Schwarz, N., Golisano, V., Rabe, C., & Wolk, M. (1996). Mood and the use of scripts: Does a happy mood really lead to mindlessness? *Journal of Personality & Social Psychology, 71,* 665–679.

Bower, G. H. (1981). Mood and memory. *American Psychologist, 36,* 129–148.

Bruner, J. S. (1957). Going beyond the information given. In J. S. Bruner et al. (Eds.), *Contemporary approaches to cognition* (pp. 41–69). Cambridge, MA: Harvard University Press.

Butler, R., Diamond, I., & Neff, W. (1957). Role of auditory cortex in discrimination of changes in frequency. *Journal of Neurophysiology, 20,* 108–120.

Cacioppo, J., Crites, S., & Gardner, W. (1996). Attitudes to the right: Evaluative processing is associated with lateralized late positive event-related brain potentials. *Personality & Social Psychology Bulletin, 22,* 1205–1219.

Cahill, L., Haier, R., Fallon, J., Alkire, M., Tang, C., Keator, D., et al. (1996). Amygdala activity at encoding correlated with long-term, free recall of emotional information. *Proceedings of the National Academy of Sciences, 93,* 8016–8021.

Canli, T., Desmond, J., Zhao, Z., Glover, G., & Gabrieli, J. (1998). Hemispheric asymmetry for emotional stimuli detected with fMRI. *Neuroreport, 9,* 3233–3239.

Chaiken, S., & Trope, Y. (1999). *Dual-process theories in social psychology.* New York: Guilford Press.

Clore, G. L., & Storbeck, J. (in press). Affect as information about liking, efficacy, and importance. In J. P. Forgas (Ed.), *Hearts and minds: Affective influences on social cognition and behaviour.* New York: Psychology Press.

Critchley, H., Daly, E., Phillips, M., Brammer, M., Bullmore, E., Williams, S., et al. (2000). Explicit and implicit neural mechanisms for processing of social information from facial expressions: A functional magnetic resonance imaging study. *Human Brain Mapping, 9,* 93–105.

Damasio, A. (1994). *Descartes' error: Emotions, reason, and the human brain.* New York: Avon Books.

Davey, G. C. L. (1995). Preparedness and phobias: Specific evolved associations or a generalized expectancy bias? *Behavioral and Brain Sciences, 18,* 289–325.

Davidson, R. J. (2003). Seven sins in the study of emotion: Correctives from affective neuroscience. *Brain and Cognition, 52,* 129–132.

De Houwer, J., & Randell, T. (2002). Attention to primes modulates affective priming of pronunciation responses. *Experimental Psychology, 49,* 163–170.

Dehaene, S., Naccache, L., Cohen, L., Bihan, D., Mangin, J., Poline, J., et al. (2001). Cerebral mechanisms of word masking and unconscious repetition priming. *Nature Neuroscience, 4,* 752–758.

DeSteno, D., Dasgupta, N., Bartlett, M. Y., & Cajdric, A. (2004). Prejudice from thin air: The effect of emotion on automatic intergroup attitudes. *Psychological Science, 15,* 319–324.

Dewey, J. (1894). The ego as cause. *Philosophical Review, 3,* 337–341.

Duncan, S., & Barrett, L. F. (2007). Affect is a form of cognition: A neurobiological analysis. *Cognition and Emotion, 21,* 1184–1211.

Duvel, A., Smith, D., Talk, A., & Gabriel, M. (2001). Medial geniculate, amygdalar and cingulate cortical training-induced neuronal activity during discriminative avoidance learning in rabbits with auditory cortical lesions. *Journal of Neuroscience, 21,* 3271–3281.

Elliott, R., & Dolan, R. J. (1998). Neural response during preference and memory judgments for subliminally presented stimuli: A functional imaging study. *Journal of Neuroscience, 18,* 4697–4704.

Erdley, C., & D'Agostino, P. (1988). Cognitive and affective components of automatic priming effects. *Journal of Personality & Social Psychology, 54,* 741–747.

Erez, A., & Isen, A. (2002). The influence of positive affect on the components of expectancy motivation. *Journal of Applied Psychology, 87,* 1055–1067.

Erickson, K., & Schulkin, J. (2003). Facial expressions of emotion: A cognitive neuroscience perspective. *Brain and Cognition, 52,* 52–60.

Fazio, R., Sanbonmatsu, D., Powell, M., & Kardes, F. (1986). On the automatic activation of attitudes. *Journal of Personality and Social Psychology, 50,* 229–238.

Ferguson, M., & Bargh, J. (2003). The constructive nature of automatic evaluation. In J. Musch & K. Klauer (Eds.), *The psychology of evaluation: Affective processes in cognition and emotion* (pp. 169–188). Mahwah, NJ: Lawrence Erlbaum Associates, Inc.

Fiedler, K. (2001). Affective states trigger processes of assimilation and accommodation. In L. Martin & G. Clore (Eds.), *Theories of mood and cognition: A user's guidebook* (pp. 86–98). Mahwah, NJ: Lawrence Erlbaum Associates, Inc.

Fox, E., Russo, R., Bowles, R., & Dutton, K. (2001). Do threatening stimuli draw or hold visual attention in subclinical anxiety? *Journal of Experimental Psychology: General, 130,* 681–700.

Fredrickson, B., & Branigan, C. (2005). Positive emotions broaden the scope of attention and thought-action repertoires. *Cognition and Emotion, 19,* 313–332.

Fukuda, M., Ono, T., & Nakamura, K. (1987). Functional relations among inferior temporal cortex, amygdala, and lateral hypothalamus in monkey operant feeding behavior. *Journal of Neurophysiology, 57,* 1060–1077.

Gasper, K. (2000). How thought and differences in emotional attention influence the role of affect in processing and judgment: When attempts to be reasonable fail. *Dissertation Abstracts International: Section B: the Sciences & Engineering, 60,* 5834.

Gasper, K., & Clore, G. L. (2002). Attending to the big picture: Mood and global versus local processing of visual information. *Psychological Science, 13,* 34–40.

Ghashghaei, H. T., & Barbas, H. (2002). Pathways for emotion: Interactions of prefrontal and anterior temporal pathways in the amygdala of the rhesus monkey. *Neuroscience, 115,* 1261–1279.

Greenwald, A. G., McGhee, D. E., & Schwartz, J. L. K. (1998). Measuring individual differences in implicit cognition: The implicit association task. *Journal of Personality and Social Psychology, 74,* 1464–1480.

Greve, K., & Bauer, R. (1990). Implicit learning of new faces in prosopagnosia: An application of the mere-exposure paradigm. *Neuropsychologia, 28,* 1035–1041.

Halgren, E. (1992). Emotional neurophysiology of the amygdala within the context of human cognition. In J. Aggleton (Ed.), *The amygdala: Neurobiological aspects of emotion, memory, and mental dysfunction* (pp. 191–228). New York: Wiley-Liss.

Harris, C., Pashler, H., & Coburn, N. (2004). Moray revisited: High-priority affective stimuli and visual search. *The Quarterly Journal of Experimental Psychology, 57A*, 1–31.

Huntsinger, J. R., Sinclair, S., Dunn, E., & Clore, G. L. (2006). *If it feels good, just do it: Mood shapes conscious and unconscious goal pursuit.* Unpublished Manuscript, University of Virginia, USA.

Isbell, L. (2004). Not all happy people are lazy or stupid: Evidence of systematic processing in happy moods. *Journal of Experimental Social Psychology, 40*, 341–349.

Ito, T., & Cacioppo, J. (2001). Electrophysiological evidence of implicit and explicit categorization processes. *Journal of Experimental Social Psychology, 36*, 660–676.

Iwai, E., Yukie, M., Watanabe, J., Hikosaka, K., Suyama, H., & Ishikawa, S. (1990). A role of amygdala in visual perception and cognition in Macaque monkeys (macaca fuscata and macaca mulatta). *Tohoku Journal of Experimental Medicine, 161*, 95–120.

Kanwisher, N., McDermott, J., & Chun, M. (1997). The fusiform face area: A module in human extrastriate cortex specialized for face perception. *Journal of Neuroscience, 17*, 4302–4311.

Keightley, M., Winocur, G., Graham, S., Mayberg, H., Hevenor, S., & Grady, C. (2003). An fMRI study investigating cognitive modulation of brain regions associated with emotional processing of visual stimuli. *Neuropsychologia, 41*, 585–596.

Kemp-Wheeler, S., & Hill, A. (1992). Semantic and emotional priming below objective detection threshold. *Cognition and Emotion, 6*, 113–128.

Klauer, K., & Musch, J. (2002). Goal-dependent and goal-independent effects of irrelevant evaluations. *Personality and Social Psychology Bulletin, 28*, 802–814.

Klinger, M., Burton, P., & Pitts, S. (2000). Mechanisms of unconscious priming: I. Response competition, not spreading activation. *Journal of Experimental Psychology: Learning, Memory, and Cognition, 26*, 441–455.

Komura, Y., Tamura, R., Uwano, T., Nishijo, H., Kaga, K., & Ono, T. (2001). Retrospective and prospective coding for predicted reward in the sensory thalamus. *Nature, 412*, 546–549.

Kovacs, G., Vogels, R., & Orban, G. (1995). Cortical correlate of pattern backward masking. *Proceedings of the National Academy of Sciences of the USA, 92*, 5587–5591.

Kudo, M., Glendenning, K., Frost, S., & Masterson, R. (1986). Origin of mammalian thalamocortical projections. I. Telencephalic projection of the medial geniculate body in the opossum (*Didelphis virginiana*). *Journal of Comparative Neurology, 245*, 176–197.

Lane, R. D., & Nadel, L. (Eds.). (2000). *Cognitive neuroscience of emotion: Series in affective science.* New York: Oxford University Press.

Lane, R., Chua, P., & Dolan, R. (1999). Common effects of emotional valence, arousal and attention on neural activation during visual processing of pictures. *Neuropsychologia, 37*, 989–997.

Lavie, N., & De Fockert, J. (2003). Contrasting effects of sensory limits and capacity limits in visual selective attention. *Perception & Psychophysics, 65*, 202–212.

Lazarus, R. (1995). Vexing research problems inherent in cognitive-mediational theories of emotion and some solutions. *Psychological Inquiry, 6*, 183–196.

LeDoux, J. (1996). *The emotional brain: The mysterious underpinnings of emotional life.* New York: Simon & Schuster.

LeDoux, J. (2001). *Synaptic self: How our brain becomes who we are.* New York: Viking Publishing.

LeDoux, J., Romanski, L., & Xagoraris, A. (1989). Indelibility of subcortical emotional memories. *Journal of Cognitive Neuroscience, 1*, 238–243.

Lehky, S. (2000). Fine discrimination of faces can be performed rapidly. *Journal of Cognitive Neuroscience, 12*, 848–855.

Linke, R., De Lima, A., Schwegler, H., & Pape, H. (1999). Direct synaptic connections of axons from superior colliculus with identified thalamo-amygdaloid projection neurons in the rat: Possible substrates of a subcortical visual pathway to the amygdala. *Journal of Comparative Neurology, 403*, 158–170.

Logan, G. (2002). An instance theory of attention and memory. *Psychological Review, 109*, 376–400.

Lundqvist, D., & Öhman, A. (2005). Caught by the evil eye: Nonconscious information processing, emotion, and attention to facial stimuli. In L. F. Barrett, P. Niedenthal, & P. Winkielman (Eds.), *Emotion and consciousness* (pp. 97–122). New York: Guilford Press.

Mayer, J., Salovey, P., & Caruso, D. (2004). Emotional intelligence: Theory, findings, and implications. *Psychological Inquiry, 15*, 197–215.

McCabe, P., McEchron, M., Green, E., & Schneiderman, N. (1993). Electrolytic and ibotenic acid lesions of the medial subnucleus of the medial geniculate prevent the acquisition of classically conditioned heart rate to a single acoustic stimulus in rabbits. *Brain Research, 619*, 291–298.

McGaugh, J. L. (2004). The amygdala modulates the consolidation of memories of emotionally arousing experiences. *Annual Reviews in Neuroscience, 27*, 1–28.

Milner, A., & Goodale, M. (1995). *The visual brain in action.* Oxford, UK: Oxford University Press.

Morris, J., Öhman, A., & Dolan, R. (1998). Conscious and unconscious emotional learning in the human amygdala. *Nature, 393*, 467–470.

Murphy, S., & Zajonc, R. (1993). Affect, cognition, and awareness: Affective priming with optimal and suboptimal stimulus exposure. *Journal of Personality and Social Psychology, 64*, 723–739.

Narumoto, J., Okada, T., Sadato, N., Fukui, K., & Yonekura, Y. (2001). Attention to emotion modulates fMRI activity in human right superior temporal sulcus. *Cognitive Brain Research, 12*, 225–231.

Nicholson, D., & Freeman, J. (2000). Lesions of the perirhinal cortex impair sensory preconditioning in rats. *Behavioural Brain Research, 112*, 69–75.

Niedenthal, P. (1990). Implicit perception of affective information. *Journal of Experimental Social Psychology, 26*, 505–527.

Nishijo, H., Ono, T., & Nishino, H. (1988a). Single neuron response in amygdala of alert monkey during complex sensory stimulation with affective significance. *Journal of Neuroscience, 8*, 3570–3583.

Nishijo, H., Ono, T., & Nishino, H. (1988b). Topographic distribution of modality-specific amygdalar neurons in alert monkey. *Journal of Neuroscience, 8*, 3556–3569.

Nishijo, H., Ono, T., Tamura, R., & Nakamura, K. (1993). Amygdalar and hippocampal neuron responses related to recognition and memory in monkey. *Progress in Brain Research, 95*, 339–357.

Ochsner, K., & Gross, J. (2005). The cognitive control of emotion. *Trends in Cognitive Sciences, 9*, 242–249.

Öhman, A. (1997). As fast as the blink of an eye: Evolutionary preparedness for preattentive processing of threat. In P. J. Lang, et al. (Eds.), *Attention and orienting: Sensory and motivational processes* (pp. 165–184). Mahwah, NJ: Lawrence Erlbaum Associates, Inc.

Öhman, A., Esteves, F., & Soares, J. (1995). Preparedness and preattentive associative learning: Electrodermal conditioning to masked stimuli. *Journal of Psychophysiology, 9*, 99–108.

Parrott, G., & Sabini, J. (1989). On the "emotional" qualities of certain types of cognition: A reply to arguments for the independence of cognition and affect. *Cognitive Therapy and Research, 13,* 49–65.

Pashler, H., Johnston, J., & Ruthruff, E. (2001). Attention and performance. *Annual Review of Psychology, 52,* 629–651.

Perea, M., & Rosa, E. (2002). Does the proportion of associatively related pairs modulate the associative priming effect at very brief stimulus-onset asynchronies? *Acta Psychologica, 110,* 103–124.

Pessoa, L., Kastner, S., & Ungerleider, L. (2002). Attentional control of the processing of neutral and emotional stimuli. *Cognitive Brain Research, 15,* 31–45.

Phelps, E. (2004). The human amygdala and awareness: Interactions between emotion and cognition. In M. Gazzaniga (Ed.), *The cognitive neurosciences* (3rd ed., pp. 1005–1015). Cambridge, MA: MIT Press.

Proffitt, D. R. (2006). Embodied perception and the economy of action. *Perspectives on Psychological Science, 1,* 110–122.

Proffitt, D., Stefanucci, J., Banton, T., & Epstein, W. (2003). The role of effort in perceiving distance. *Psychological Science, 14,* 106–112.

Quirk, G., Armony, J., & LeDoux, J. E. (1997). Fear conditioning enhances different temporal components of toned-evoked spike trains in auditory cortex and lateral amygdala. *Neuron, 19,* 613–624.

Quirk, G., Repa, J., & LeDoux, J. E. (1995). Fear conditioning enhances short-latency auditory responses of lateral amygdala neurons: Parallel recordings in the freely behaving rat. *Neuron, 15,* 1029–1039.

Reed, J., Squire, L., Patalano, A., Smith, E., & Jonides, J. (1999). Learning about categories that are defined by object-like stimuli despite impaired declarative memory. *Behavioral Neuroscience, 113,* 411–419.

Riener, C., Stefanucci, J. K., Proffitt, D., & Clore, G. L. (2003). *Mood and the perception of spatial layout.* Poster presented at the 44th Annual Meeting of the Psychonomic Society, Vancouver, BC, Canada.

Robinson, M. D. (1998). Running from William James' bear: A review of preattentive mechanisms and their contributions to emotional experience. *Cognition and Emotion, 12,* 667–696.

Roediger, H. L., Gallo, D., & Geraci, L. (2002). Processing approaches to cognition: The impetus from the levels-of-processing framework. *Memory, 10,* 319–332.

Rolls, E. T. (1992). Neurophysiological mechanisms underlying face processing within and beyond the temporal cortical visual areas. *Philosophical Transactions of the Royal Society of London, Series B: Biological Sciences, 335,* 11–21.

Rolls, E. T. (1999). *The brain and emotion.* Oxford, UK: Oxford University Press.

Rolls, E. T., Judge, S., & Sanghera, M. (1977). Activity of neurons in the inferotemporal cortex of the alert monkey. *Brain Research, 130,* 229–238.

Rolls, E. T., & Tovee, M. (1994). Processing speed in the cerebral cortex and the neurophysiology of visual masking. *Proceedings of the Royal Society of London, Series B: Biological Sciences, 257,* 9–15.

Rolls, E. T., Tovee, M., Purcell, D., Stewart, A., & Azzopardi, P. (1994). The responses of neurons in the temporal cortex of primates, and face identification and detection. *Experimental Brain Research, 101,* 473–484.

Rotshtein, P., Malach, R., Hadar, U., Graif, M., & Hendler, T. (2001). Feeling or features: Different sensitivity to emotion in high-order visual cortex and amygdala. *Neuron, 32,* 747–757.

Schwarz, N., & Clore, G. L. (1983). Mood, misattribution, and judgments of well-being: Informative and directive functions of affective states. *Journal of Personality and Social Psychology, 45*, 513–523.

Shi, C., & Davis, M. (2001). Visual pathways involved in fear conditioning measured with fear-potentiated startle: Behavioral and anatomic studies. *Journal of Neuroscience, 21*, 9844–9855.

Shiffrin, R., & Schneider, W. (1977). Controlled and automatic human information processing: II. Perceptual learning, automatic attending and a general theory. *Psychological Review, 84*, 127–190.

Smith, N., Cacioppo, J., Larsen, J., & Chartrand, T. (2003). May I have your attention, please: Electrocortical responses to positive and negative stimuli. *Neuropsychologia, 41*, 171–183.

Stefanucci, J. K., Proffitt, D. R., & Clore, G. (2005, May). *Skating down a steeper slope: The effect of fear on geographical slant perception.* Poster presented at the 5th Annual Meeting of the Society for Vision Sciences, Sarasota, FL, USA.

Stenberg, G., Lindgren, M., & Johansson, M. (2000). Semantic processing without conscious identification: Evidence from event-related potentials. *Journal of Experimental Psychology: Learning, Memory, and Cognition, 26*, 973–1004.

Stolz, J., & Besner, D. (1999). On the myth of automatic semantic activation in reading. *Current Directions in Psychological Science, 8*, 61–65.

Storbeck, J., & Clore, G. L. (2005). With sadness come accuracy, with happiness, false memory: Mood and the false memory effect. *Psychological Science, 16*, 785–791.

Storbeck, J., & Clore, G. L. (2006). *Turning on and off affective and categorical priming with mood.* Manuscript submitted for publication.

Storbeck, J., & Robinson, M. D. (2004). Preferences and inferences in encoding visual objects: A systematic comparison of semantic and affective priming. *Personality and Social Psychology Bulletin, 30*, 81–93.

Storbeck, J., Robinson, M. D., & McCourt, M. E. (2006). Semantic processing precedes affect retrieval: The neurological case for cognitive primacy in visual processing. *Review of General Psychology, 10*, 41–55.

Storbeck, J., Robinson, M. D., Ram, N., Meier, B., & Clore, G. L. (2004). [Unpublished raw data]. University of Virginia.

Sugase, Y., Yamane, S., Ueno, S., & Kawano, K. (1999). Global and fine information coded by single neurons in the temporal visual cortex. *Nature, 400*, 869–873.

Surguladze, S., Brammer, M., Young, A., Andrew, C., Travis, M., Williams, S., et al. (2003). A preferential increase in the extrastriate response to signals of danger. *NeuroImage, 19*, 1317–1328.

Thompson, R. (1962). The role of the cerebral cortex in stimulus generalization. *Journal of Comparative and Physiology Psychology, 55*, 279–287.

Van Rullen, R., & Thorpe, S. (2001). The time course of visual processing: From early perception to decision-making. *Journal of Cognitive Neuroscience, 13*, 454–461.

Vogels, R., & Orban, G. (1996). Coding of stimulus invariance temporal neurons. *Progress in Brain Research, 112*, 195–211.

Vuilleumier, P., Armony, J., Driver, J., & Dolan, R. J. (2003). Distinct spatial frequency sensitivities for processing faces and emotional expressions. *Nature Neuroscience, 6*, 624–631.

Whalen, P., Rauch, S., Etcoff, N., McInerney, S., Lee, M., & Jenike, M. (1998). Masked presentations of emotional facial expressions modulate amygdala activity without explicit knowledge. *Journal of Neuroscience, 18*, 411–418.

White, M. (1996). Automatic affective appraisal of words. *Cognition and Emotion, 10*, 199–211.

Winkielman, P., Schwarz, N., Fazendeiro, T., & Reber, R. (2003). The hedonic marking of processing fluency: Implications for evaluative judgment. In J. Musch & K. Klauer (Eds.),

The psychology of evaluation: Affective processes in cognition and emotion (pp. 189–217). Mahwah, NJ: Lawrence Erlbaum Associates, Inc.

Witt, J. K., Proffitt, D. R., & Epstein, W. (2004). Perceiving distance: A role of effort and intent. *Perception, 33*, 577–590.

Zajonc, R. (1968). Attitudinal effects of mere exposure. *Journal of Personality and Social Psychology, 9*, 1–27.

Zajonc, R. (1980). Feeling and thinking: Preferences need no inferences. *American Psychologist, 35*, 151–175.

Zajonc, R. (2000). Feeling and thinking: Closing the debate over the independence of affect. In J. P. Forgas (Ed.), *Feeling and thinking: The role of affect in social cognition. Studies in emotion and social interaction* (Vol. 2., pp. 31–58). New York: Cambridge University Press.

COGNITION AND EMOTION
2007, 21 (6), 1238–1269

Can cognitive methods be used to study the unique aspect of emotion: An appraisal theorist's answer

Agnes Moors

Ghent University, Ghent, Belgium

I address the questions of whether cognitive methods are suited to the study of emotion, and whether they are suited to the study of the unique aspect of emotion. Based on a definition of cognitive processes as those that mediate between variable input–output relations by means of representations, and the observation that the relation between stimuli and emotions is often variable, I argue that cognition is often involved in emotion and that cognitive methods are suited to study them. I further propose that the unique feature of emotion has to do with the content of the representations involved in the transition from stimulus input to emotion. Emotions are elicited when stimuli contain information about the satisfaction status of goals (i.e., when they are goal relevant). Given that cognitive methods are fit to study any representation-mediated process regardless of their content, they can a fortiori be used to study a process that operates on representations with goal-relevant content. I compare this process to processes that have no or a different relation to goals, including the process that deals with purely valenced information.

Are cognitive methods suited to the study of emotion? And, if so, do they capture the unique aspect of emotion? I address these two questions in the first and second parts of the paper. If a cognitive method is understood as one that is suited or at least designed to investigate cognitive processes, the answer to the first question, whether cognitive methods can be used to investigate emotion, depends on whether cognitive processes are involved in emotion. Therefore, in the first part of the paper, I examine various views about the role of cognition in emotion. Special attention will be given to an analysis of the definitions of cognition employed in these views. The answer to the second question, whether cognitive methods can be used to study the

Correspondence should be addressed to: Agnes Moors, Department of Psychology, Ghent University, Henri Dunantlaan 2, B-9000 Ghent, Belgium. E-mail: agnes.moors@Ugent.ac.be

Agnes Moors is a postdoctoral researcher at the Fund for Scientific Research (Flanders, Belgium).

The author is grateful to Jan De Houwer and Adriaan Spruyt for valuable discussions and comments on an earlier draft of the paper.

© 2007 Psychology Press, an imprint of the Taylor & Francis Group, an Informa business
www.psypress.com/cogemotion   DOI: 10.1080/02699930701438061

unique aspect of emotion, depends on what the unique aspect is. In the second part of the paper, therefore, I examine various proposals about the unique aspect of emotion and I defend a proposal based on appraisal theory. According to this proposal, the unique aspect of emotion is that it is caused by a process that monitors the satisfaction status of goals. In a third part of the paper I delineate this process from processes that have a different or no relation to goals including the process that is concerned with pure valence. In the final part of the paper, I examine whether there are ways to examine the motivational hypothesis empirically.

CAN COGNITIVE METHODS BE USED TO STUDY EMOTION?

Theorists who do not assign a (major) role to cognitive processes in emotion should not expect much use from cognitive methods (e.g., Izard, 1994; Tomkins, 1984). Among those that do assign a role to cognitive processes in emotion, some equate emotion with cognition (e.g., Nussbaum, 1990; Solomon, 1984), whereas others hold that cognition is part of emotion but does not overlap entirely with it. Most contemporary emotion theories are componential in that they view emotion as a compound of action tendency, bodily responses, and emotional experience. Cognition is often held to be part of the experience component (Scherer, 1993). Several brands of componential theory also assume that cognitive processes are involved in the causation of emotion. Network theorists (e.g., Lang, 1985; Leventhal, 1984; Teasdale, 1999) propose that emotions are caused by a process that activates the memory representations of prior emotions. Appraisal theorists (e.g., Frijda, 1986; Lazarus, 1991; Scherer, 1994) propose that emotions are caused by a process that deals with the implications of an event for the person's well-being. The debate about the role of cognition in emotion has often centred on the question of whether cognition is a cause of emotion. In the following sections, I discuss a few arguments against and in favour of cognitive causation of emotion. These arguments cannot be properly understood or compared without understanding the definition of cognition employed (cf. Leventhal & Scherer, 1987; Scherer, 1993). I therefore dedicate some space to exploring various usages of the term cognition.

What is cognition?

Consultation of the literature teaches us that cognition is a contrastive notion: It derives its meaning from the category with which it is contrasted. Various traditions have envisaged different types of non-cognition. I discuss two broad accounts of cognition and three narrow ones (see Table 1 for a schematic overview). After that, I zoom in on the term "cognitive method".

TABLE 1
Taxonomy of definitions for cognitive processes. For each definition, it is indicated what the criterion for inclusion is, and it is specified which processes belong to the category of cognitive processes and which belong to the category of non-cognitive processes

Accounts	Criterion for inclusion in terms of	Cognitive process	Non-cognitive process
Broad accounts			
(1) Topological account	- anatomical location	internal (=inside the brain)	external (=outside the brain)
(2) Mentalist account	- presence of representations	internal (=mental)	external (=physical/ behavioural)
Narrow accounts			
(1) Family of accounts		part of the brain/the mental	part of the brain/the mental (=subcognition)
1st Functional account	- functions (i.e., what the process does, the relation between input and output)	e.g., processes that transform the input	processes that preserve the input
Condition account	- conditions	e.g., nonautomatic in sense of conscious or controlled	automatic in sense of unconscious or uncontrolled
Mechanism account	- mechanisms	e.g., rule based	associative
Code account	- representational format/code	e.g., conceptual	nonconceptual
Neuroanatomical account	- neuroanatomical structures	e.g., cortical	subcortical
(2) 2nd Functional account	- functions	processes producing cognitive output = information unrelated to emotion (e.g., colour, location, gender, size, letter case, grammatical category, semantic category)	processes producing emotional output = (a) emotions (e.g., anger, fear, sadness, joy) (b) information related to emotion (e.g., valence)
(3) Intentional account	- presence of Intentionality	Intentional part of the mental	phenomenal part of the mental

Broad accounts

Proponents of broad accounts have equated cognition with internal processes contrasting them with external ones such as those going on in the body. According to a first broad account, the category of internal processes is equated with everything that goes on in the brain, including the physical aspects. The contrasting category in this case is peripheral (but not central) physical processes and overt behaviour. I dub this account the topological account: cognition is a matter of location; it is what is inside the brain.

According to a second broad account, internal processes are equated with mental processes and delineated from all physical ones (including central physical ones) and overt behaviour (cf. Green, 1996). This "mentalist" view was endorsed by the originators of cognitive psychology (Miller, 1962; Neisser, 1967). They reacted against the then-dominant S–R view of psychological explanation by inserting intermediate variables between stimulus and response (S–O–R). Positive formulations of this view present cognitive processes as ones that are mediated by representations (e.g., Miller, Galanter, & Pribram, 1960).

Representation is a functional notion. It is something we need in order to explain certain types of input–output relations. Representations are required in cases in which the relation between input and output is not fixed (Bermudéz, 1995; Fodor, 1986). In cases in which the same stimulus always leads to the same response, there is no need for mediating representations. An input–output relation can be variable in different ways. First, repeated encounters with the same stimulus can lead to a change in response—e.g., faster; more positive (cf. mere exposure); less intense (cf. habituation); more intense (cf. sensitisation). Second, the same stimulus can lead to a change in response due to (repeated) co-occurrence with other stimuli (cf. classical and evaluative conditioning). Third, the same stimulus can lead to different responses depending on varying internal states such as motivation (e.g., food is approached when a person is hungry, but avoided when he/she is satiated). In the first two cases, a representation of the stimulus must be something that can be used on more than one occasion; it must be stored in long-term memory. In the first case, the stimulus representation must also be able to alter its quantitative parameters (e.g., activation strength, distinctiveness, and stability in time; Cleeremans & Jiménez, 2002) resulting in increased or diminished accessibility. Increased accessibility may explain faster and even more positive responses (Mandler, Nakamura, & Shebo-Van Zandt, 1987). In the second case, the stimulus representation must also be able to be associated with other representations. In the third case, stimulus representations must be able to be integrated with other representations (e.g., goal representations) to produce new representations or new behavioural output. In the third case, pre-existing long-term memory representations are not a must. A representation may be newly built, but it must be something that can be held in short-term memory long enough to become integrated with other pre-existing representations (e.g., of goals) or other newly built ones.

Narrow accounts

Proponents of more narrow accounts of cognition reserve the term for a restricted part of the brain or a restricted part of the mental. In a first family of narrow accounts, cognitive processes are delineated from what one might call subcognitive processes. Researchers have proposed various criteria to mark the distinction between cognitive and subcognitive. The criteria used are best understood when they are placed within a levels-of-analysis framework (e.g., Marr, 1982). This framework rests on the idea that one process can be described at three levels of analysis. The first level is the functional level. At this level, a process is described as a relation between the contents of its input and output; it tells what the process does. For example, the process of evaluation links a stimulus (i.e., the input) to a positive or negative valence (i.e., the output). At this level can also be situated the conditions under which the process operates (in addition to the stimulus input). Examples of conditions are that the stimulus input is conscious, that the person has the intention to evaluate the stimulus, that the person's attention is focused on the stimulus input, and that there is ample time. The second level is the formal level. At this level, a process is described in terms of the mechanisms that translate input into output (i.e., what is in the black box). Examples of mechanisms are associative processes and rule-based ones (Sloman, 1996). This level also articulates the representational format (i.e., codes) of inputs and outputs. Examples of codes are conceptual (verbal-like) and non-conceptual (image-like) codes. The third level is the implementational level. This level is concerned with the physical realisation of a process in the brain. On this level may be specified neuroanatomic details of the process, such as the brain structures or circuits involved.

Criteria to separate cognitive from subcognitive processes have been formulated in functional terms (e.g., cognitive processes transform rather than preserve input, Duncan & Barrett, 2007 this issue; Scherer, 1993[1]), in terms of the conditions under which they operate (e.g., cognitive processes are conscious, Baars, 1986; cognitive processes are under organismic control, Prinz, 2004; cognitive processes are goal dependent, Lavender & Hommel, 2007 this issue), in terms of mechanisms (e.g., cognitive processes are rule-based rather than associative), in terms of representational format (e.g., cognitive processes operate on conceptual rather than non-conceptual

---

[1] This functional account and the broad representation-mediated account discussed above are both concerned with change and variation. Whereas the former considers change within a single encounter with the stimulus (the output is different from the input), the latter considers change over the course of several actual or possible encounters with the stimulus (the input–output relation at time t_1 is different from that at time t_2, or it is different from one context to another).

codes, Armon-Jones, 1989), and in neuroscientific terms (e.g., cognitive processes are cortical rather than subcortical, e.g., Murphy & Zajonc, 1993).

According to a second narrow account, cognitive processes are ones that produce a cognitive output. Used as a predicate to output, the term cognitive is contrasted with the term emotional. Cognitive output is information that is not related to emotion, so-called "cold" information. Classic examples are colour, location, semantic category membership (e.g., profession, animal, tool), and identity. Emotional output includes emotions (e.g., anger) as well as information related to emotions (e.g., valence). This account is similar to the functional variant of the first narrow account in that cognitive processes are delineated from non-cognitive ones on functional grounds (the distinction is a matter of the content of inputs and/or outputs). It differs from it, however, in that the contrasting class here does not consist of subcognitive processes but of processes with an emotional output. This second functional account of cognition is very popular among experimental researchers concerned with the role of cognition in emotion (e.g., Bargh, 1997; Klauer & Musch, 2002; Murphy & Zajonc, 1993; see below).

A third narrow account of cognition can be found in philosophy of mind. There, the term has been coined to refer to the Intentional[2] part of the mental and has been contrasted with the phenomenal part (Green, 1996). I call this the Intentional account. An Intentional state is one that is about or directed toward something. It is a state that has an object. Examples are thinking, believing, and desiring. A being can be directed toward something by forming a representation of it. Cognitive processes have therefore been equated—here also—with representation-mediated processes. Phenomenal states or qualia belong to the part of the mental that cannot be captured in representations (but see Crane, 1998, and Tye, 2003, for a representationalist view of qualia) and therefore cannot be objectified. They refer to states or qualities that are entirely subjective such as what it is like to experience red colour or pain.

Cognitive method

A cognitive *method* is one that is suited or at least designed to measure cognitive processes. The meaning of the term cognitive method is thus parasitic on the meaning of the term cognitive process. For example, on the topological account of cognition, cognitive methods are those suited to investigate internal processes, not peripheral physical ones. On the

---

[2] I capitalise *Intentional* in philosophical use, but not *intentional* in ordinary use, following Searle (1983).

mentalist account, cognitive methods are those suited to study representation-mediated processes. Some of these methods focus on the *content* of the representations (i.e., the functional level of process description), whereas others focus on the *mechanisms* or on the *format of the representations* (i.e., formal level of process description). For example, most research conducted by appraisal theorists examines what kind of information must be minimally or typically processed before specific emotions such as anger and fear can be produced. This research focuses on the *content* of the representations that form the inputs and outputs of emotion-eliciting processes (e.g., Scherer, 1997). A handful of appraisal theorists have begun to investigate the *mechanisms* and the *format of the representations* involved in emotion elicitation using experimental techniques (e.g., Moors, De Houwer, & Eelen, 2004; Smith & Kirby, 2001). According to more narrow accounts of cognition, cognitive methods are those suited to investigate conscious or controlled processes, rule-based ones, neocortical ones, or processes with a cold output. On the Intentional account of cognition, cognitive methods are those fit to study the objectifiable part of the mental (Green, 1996).

Conclusion

Several of the accounts discussed converge on the idea that cognitive processes are ones that are mediated by representations, whether this feature serves to shield them from non-mental (i.e., physical and behavioural, cf. mentalist view) processes or, more narrowly, from the phenomenal part of the mental (cf. Intentional view). Other narrow views are more restrictive in that they take cognitive processes to be those that are mediated by representations with a specific format (e.g., conceptual), those with specific functional (e.g., producing cold output) or formal (e.g., rule-based) properties, and those that occur under specific conditions (e.g., under organismic control). I side with the broad representation-mediated view because I find the distinction between processes generating fixed vs. variable input–output relations useful. As explained above, the notion of representation is key to understanding this distinction (Bermudéz, 1995). Moreover, I do not want to restrict the definition further because I think there is nothing in the functional notion of representation that compels us to say that representations must be conceptual or propositional. Different types of input–output variability require representations with different functional properties: some must be capable of quantitative change, others of becoming associated with other representations, and still others of becoming integrated with other representations (cf. above). In principle, none of these properties demand representations of a specific format or with a specific content and none of them require specific operating conditions.[3]

I now turn to a discussion of some experimental arguments adduced against and in favour of the idea that cognitive processes are involved in emotion, and more in particular, in the causation of emotion. The aim is not to give an exhaustive literature review but to show that the issue has not been settled in favour of either view yet. Another aim is to examine the definitions of cognition used in this kind of research and to situate them within the taxonomy of definitions presented above.

Arguments against cognitive causation of emotion

In this section I discuss four types of arguments against cognitive causation of emotion as well as some counterarguments. A first type of observations seeks support for the claim that in some cases the processing of valence precedes that of cognitive features. Given that valence processing is often considered a first step in the development of an emotion, the claim is that in some cases the start of the emotion process is not caused by cognition. A second type of observation purports to show that emotions can be caused directly by physical stimulation. A third argument is neuroanatomical evidence for the direct causation of emotion by simple stimuli. A fourth type of argument is dissociation data obtained with experimental and neuroanatomical techniques. These are aimed at showing that different mechanisms are responsible for the processing of cognitive vs. emotional information, and hence that cognition is not likely to cause emotions.

Valence comes first

Murphy and Zajonc (1993) reported that the influence of the valence of primes on preferences for neutral targets came about at shorter exposure times than did the influence of cognitive features of the primes such as symmetry, size, and gender. They concluded that valence is processed prior to cognitive features. However, there is evidence that the order in which different aspects of the stimulus material come to *influence* other processes does not necessarily reflect the order in which they were *processed* (Marcel,

---

[3] Note that this idea challenges the widespread view that integration of representations demands representations of a propositional format (e.g., Bermúdez, 1995) and cannot take place under conditions of automaticity. It may be so that different types of input–output variability (functional process level) demand different mechanisms (formal process level): some must only be capable of handling a single input and suffice with a simple associative process, whereas others must be capable of integrating a double (or multiple) input and require a complex associative process or a rule-based one (Moors, 2006). In any case, all three types of formal processes (simple associative, complex associative, and rule based) are representation mediated and count as cognitive on my use of the term.

1983). It is thus possible that cognitive features were processed simultaneously or even before valence but that their influence on the target responses was slower. Of importance, the account of cognition employed here corresponds to the second functional account discussed above. Cognitive processes are defined as those producing a cognitive output and contrasted to those producing an emotional output. It should be mentioned that Murphy and Zajonc (1993, p. 738) considered valence to be an emotional output in the sense that it is related to emotion, but they did not consider it to be a full-blown emotion.

Emotions caused directly by physical stimuli

Another type of experimental study was taken to demonstrate a direct effect (unmediated by cognitive processing) of physical stimuli on emotions and preferences. For example, Strack, Martin, and Stepper (1988) showed that participants evaluated cartoons more positively when they took on a smiling face (due to the instruction to hold a pen between their teeth) than when they took on a serious face (due to the instruction to hold a pen between their lips). Critics, however, demonstrated that facial expressions do not cause but rather intensify relevant emotions (Clore, Storbeck, Robinson, & Centerbar, 2005; Tamir, Robinson, Clore, Martin, & Whitaker, 2004). Another example is data suggesting that drugs can directly cause emotions. Here also, it is difficult to establish that drugs cause rather than intensify emotions or that when they actually do cause emotions, they do so directly, bypassing cognition. Drugs may enhance the perceptual salience of certain stimuli so that they are more easily interpreted as threatening or satisfying.

Neuroanatomical data for the direct causation of emotion

Many researchers have taken LeDoux's (1989) subcortical route to the amygdala (which is said to be the locus of stimulus evaluation) as evidence that evaluation can occur without cognitive mediation. Because of the direct connections between the amygdala and motor centres, the subcortical route even leads to emotional responses (particularly fear responses) without cognitive mediation. Critics do not exactly deny the existence of the subcortical route to stimulus evaluation and emotional responses, but they contend that it is rarely used (Storbeck, Robinson, & McCourt, 2006). The use of the subcortical route to fear responses seems to be limited to simple stimuli (light) that were previously associated with negative stimuli (shocks) in a non-differential conditioning procedure (LeDoux, Romanski, & Xagoraris, 1989). In the experimental studies that are typically adduced as supporting the evaluation-without-cognition hypothesis (cf. the studies of Murphy & Zajonc, 1993), the stimuli presented are more complex (words, pictures of faces or objects). These stimuli require identification via cortical structures (e.g., area IT) before they can be evaluated (Storbeck et al., 2006).

The debate in this neuroanatomical research is characterised by the use of three accounts of cognition. First, there is the second functional account, according to which cognitive processes are those with a cognitive output (such as semantic categories and identity) that are contrasted to those with an emotional output (such as valence and fear responses; e.g., Storbeck et al., 2006). Second, there is the neuroanatomical account, which equates cognitive with cortical and subcognitive with subcortical. It should be noted that authors often assume strong overlap between the second functional account and the neuroanatomical account: Cognitive functions such as categorisation and identification are often thought to take place in cortical brain areas (but see Crosson, 1992, for the role of subcortical areas in cognitive functions). Finally, there is the first functional account, which defines cognition as computation or transformation (i.e., the first functional account, cf. Table 1). Scherer (1993, p. 12) opted for this possibility and LeDoux (1989, p. 271) imagined it when he wrote that "the processes involved in stimulus evaluation could, if one chose, be called cognitive processes. The meaning of the stimulus is not given in physical character-istics but instead is determined by computations performed by the brain. As computation is the benchmark of the cognitive, the computation of affective significance could be considered a cognitive process". Separating between these different definitions of cognition is useful because asking whether cognitive functions such as categorisation and identification take place prior to evaluation (cf. the second functional account) is not the same thing as asking whether evaluation is itself cognition (cf. the first functional account).

Dissociation data

Experimental dissociation studies are set up to show that processes producing valenced versus cognitive (or non-valenced) output obey to different rules and hence that they are of a different nature (Bargh, 1997; Klauer & Musch, 2002; Zajonc, 1980). It is reasoned that if processes with valenced output obey different rules than processes with cognitive output, the former must be non-cognitive. Bargh (1997) reported a failure to find priming effects for potency and activity,[4] contrasting this with the fact that priming effects for valence are robust. Klauer and Musch (2002), however, pointed out that the strength of this argument depends in part on null-findings and on the comparability of the stimuli used as valenced and non-valenced material.

---

[4] Potency and activity are non-valenced features but they are not unrelated to emotion.

Further, several investigators reported that, contrary to semantic priming effects, affective priming effects became more likely or stronger when conscious or strategic aspects were eliminated from the task (Bargh, 1997; Murphy & Zajonc, 1993). However, Clore et al. (2005) argued that conscious input generally leads to stronger emotions than unconscious input. The observation that priming effects are sometimes weaker with conscious input can be explained by the fact that conscious input makes the purpose of the experiment more transparent. As a result, participants may no longer experience their feelings as reactions to the targets and deny them.

Finally, Klauer and Musch (2002) reported a series of studies (Experiments 4 to 8) showing priming effects for valence when the task consisted in matching primes and targets with regard to a cognitive feature such as location, colour, letter case, and grammatical category. They failed to observe priming effects for any of these other features when the task consisted of matching prime and target with regard to valence. They concluded that valence is the only feature that is processed independent of the goal to do so (see also Eder, Hommel, & De Houwer, 2007 this issue). Even in the Klauer and Musch experiments, however, there may have been characteristics of the procedure that favour the occurrence of a priming effect for valence over the occurrence of a priming effect for the non-valenced features. For instance, it could be argued that the "yes" and "no" responses that participants give on the basis of the match between primes and targets have an intrinsic positive and negative valence. This element may have enhanced the salience of valence relative to the other, non-valenced features. An imbalance in salience of one feature relative to others may induce in participants the goal to process this feature and this goal may be necessary to engage in the processing of this feature (see also Lavender & Hommel, 2007 this issue). A handful of observations are in line with this argument. Duscherer, Holender, and Molenaar (in press) reported that the affective Simon effect disappeared when trials with valenced stimuli were embedded in a large set of trials with neutral stimuli. These results suggest that in a standard affective Simon task (and perhaps also affective priming task) the salience of stimulus valence encourages participants to intentionally evaluate the stimuli. Storbeck and Robinson (2004; see also Storbeck & Clore, 2007 this issue) obtained semantic but not affective priming effects (even in the evaluation task) when the stimulus material varied systematically with regard to valence as well as with regard to a non-valenced feature (semantic category: religion vs. texture). They only obtained an affective priming effect when words were chosen from one semantic category (e.g., religion) and when an evaluation task was administered. The authors argued that valence is just part of the semantic meaning of a stimulus and that it only serves as the basis for categorisation when no other, more salient, feature is available.

Taken together, the dissociation data described above present a mixed picture. Some researchers believe that the dissociations they obtained reflect systematic differences between processes with valenced and those with cognitive output. Others have argued that the dissociations that are sometimes observed are due to confounding factors that have nothing to do with valence per se, such as characteristics of the procedure (instructions, stimulus set) that enhance the salience of valence relative to that of other features. Even if one maintains that the data do reflect systematic differences between processes with valenced and those with cognitive output, these differences only concern the conditions (e.g., conscious stimulus input, the goal to engage in the process) under which these processes can take place. They do not show differences in the mechanisms involved. I argued elsewhere (Moors & De Houwer, 2006b) that conditions and mechanisms must be kept separate and that conditions do not reliably inform us about mechanisms.

Dissociations between processes with emotion-related output and those with cognitive output are also suggested by data coming from neuroanatomical studies. Damage to certain neural structures causes impairment in processes with emotional output, but leaves processes with cognitive output intact. For example, LaBar, LeDoux, Spencer, and Phelps (1995) showed that subjects with lesions to the medial temporal lobe (including the amygdala) showed impaired fear conditioning as measured by skin conductance responses (emotional output), but no impairment of awareness of the CS–US relation (cognitive output). Neuroanatomical dissociations of this kind more convincingly argue that processes with emotional versus cognitive output have different underlying mechanisms. However, several authors have argued on logical grounds that neuroanatomical dissociation data, even double dissociations, are not proof of different underlying mechanisms or modular architecture (Dunn & Kirsner, 2003). Moreover, recent neuroanatomic studies seem to increasingly challenge the idea of specialised brain structures for cognition versus emotion (e.g., Duncan & Barrett, 2007 this issue; Storbeck & Clore, 2007 this issue).

In summary, behavioural dissociation studies at best reveal differences or similarities regarding the conditions under which processes with valenced versus cognitive output occur. Conditions, however, do not inform us about the mechanisms involved. Neuroanatomical dissociation studies seem more persuasive in demonstrating that different mechanisms underlie processes with cognitive versus emotional output, but they have recently been under fire.

As with the previous arguments against the cognitive causation of emotion hypothesis, the guiding account of cognition seems to be the second functional one. Cognitive processes are defined as those that have a cognitive output and contrasted with those that have an emotional output.

There is little overlap between this functional account of cognition and the broad representation-mediated account of cognition that I adopt in the present paper. There is no reason to suspect that processes with a cognitive output are representation-mediated and those with an emotional output are not. Even if future research shows that different mechanisms are responsible for delivering cognitive versus emotional output, both mechanisms can still be representation-mediated and hence cognitive within my use of the term.

Arguments in favour of cognitive causation of emotion

In the previous sections, I listed a number of arguments against cognitive causation of emotion. These arguments were followed by counterarguments that questioned the validity of them. Some but not all of these counterarguments can themselves be considered arguments in favour of cognitive causation of emotion, at least according to the functional definition of cognition often employed in that type of research. On the broad definition of cognition that I proposed, however, to answer the question whether cognitive processes are involved in emotion elicitation, one should consult research concerning the degree of flexibility in emotion elicitation. Saying that cognition is a cause of emotion amounts to saying that emotions are not invariably produced by a fixed set of stimuli and that representations must intervene. Empirical research does show that emotional responses are flexible. Habituation and sensitisation effects illustrate that emotional responses to stimuli can diminish or increase as a result of repeated exposure to these stimuli (Rose & Rankin, 2001). Fear-conditioning research shows that fear to initially neutral stimuli comes and goes as a consequence of prior presentation with other fear-eliciting stimuli or safety signals (Hamm & Vaitl, 1996). Appraisal research tells us that emotions vary as a function of the relevance of the stimulus for goals or concerns (Scherer, 1997).

To answer the question whether cognition is a *necessary* cause of emotion, one should look for cases in which an emotion is not caused by cognition. This comes down to finding stimuli that invariably lead to the same emotional response. The observation that rats' fearful responses to a cat's odour do not habituate or cannot be modified in another way (Zangrossi & File, 1994) would count as an example of emotion without cognition on the broad representation-mediated definition of cognition employed here (McNaughton, 1997). It remains to be seen whether such stimuli also exist for humans. I argued that to judge the usefulness of cognitive methods for the study of emotion, one must ascertain that cognition is involved in emotion or its causation. It may not be necessary, however, to ascertain that cognition is always involved in emotion or its causation. If not all emotions are caused by cognition, cognitive methods can still be used to study those emotions that are.

Until now I have discussed the problem that most research dedicated to the cognitive causation of emotion contrasts processes with cognitive output to those with emotional output and that this research does not inform us about whether processes with an emotional output are representation-mediated and hence cognitive within my use of the term. Another problem has to do with the fact that processes with emotional output are often restricted to those with valenced output. Earlier, I distinguished between two types of output that can be labelled emotional: genuine emotions (e.g., anger) and information related to emotions (e.g., valence). I believe that it is the first type of emotional output, the genuine emotions, that matter to emotion research. Many investigators consider the assessment of valence to be the first and most important step in the development of genuine emotions. They therefore consider research concerning processes with valenced output to be relevant for emotion research. In the next section, I defend the position that the assessment of valence independent of the person's goals may have no actual emotion-eliciting power (Lazarus, 1991). In other words, valence can be totally disconnected from emotions. Thus, I propose shifting the focus of processes with valenced output to ones with emotions as output (see below).

To sum up, research dedicated to the cognitive causation of emotion is characterised by several elements: First, most research is guided by the narrow functional definition of cognitive processes as those with cognitive output (e.g., colour, size, location, non-valenced semantic meaning) and these are contrasted to processes with emotional output (e.g., emotions, valence). Second, much research contrasts processes with cognitive output to those with *valenced* output instead of those with *emotions* as output. Third, much research centres on the question whether or not there exist cases in which emotions are not caused by cognition. To decide whether cognitive methods can be used to study emotion or its causation, one should focus instead on whether there exist instances of emotions that involve cognition or that are caused by cognitive processes. On the basis of the account of cognition adopted in the present paper, emotions are caused by cognitive processes when they are mediated by representations. A useful guide to assessing whether a process is representation-mediated is to see whether the relation between input and output is flexible. The available evidence (coming from habituation studies, classical conditioning research, and appraisal research) suggests that there is a fair amount of flexibility in the causation of emotion. I therefore believe that cognitive methods can be used to study it. The next section deals with the second question, which is to know whether cognitive methods can also be used to study the *unique* aspect of emotion.

CAN COGNITIVE METHODS BE USED TO STUDY THE UNIQUE ASPECT OF EMOTION?

For theorists who assume partial overlap among cognition and emotion, cognitive methods can be used to study the overlapping parts. One may object that by studying the cognitive part of emotion, researchers miss out on the non-cognitive part, the part that is unique to emotion. Theorists have identified different constructs as the unique non-cognitive part of emotion. Some authors have chosen action or other bodily responses (e.g., Dolan, 2002), whereas others have stressed the phenomenal (as opposed to Intentional) aspect of emotional experience (e.g., Oatley & Johnson-Laird, 1987). I agree that the aspects of body and phenomenal experience can be considered non-cognitive (at least according to certain definitions of the term cognition) and that they cannot be studied with cognitive methods. Physical processes cannot be studied with methods developed to study mental processes, and phenomenal aspects of experience cannot be studied with methods aimed at studying the Intentional aspect of experience. I disagree, however, that physical and phenomenal aspects are unique to emotions. Emotion is not the only phenomenon that has a physical component. Consider intentional action as another example of such a phenomenon. Phenomenal quality is not exclusive to emotions either. Perceptions (e.g., seeing red or green colours), bodily sensations (e.g., feeling physical pain), and even thoughts (e.g., thinking of the concept circle) are all infused with phenomenal quality.

Several theorists have proposed that the unique aspect of emotion has to do, not with the presence of one or another component of emotion (bodily responses, emotional experience), but rather with the causes of emotion. Among the theorists who agree that both cognitive outputs and emotions are caused by representations, some posit that the format of the representations differs in the two cases. Leventhal (1984) argued that nonconceptual (i.e., image-like), but not conceptual (verbal-like) representations have emotion-eliciting power. This view was shared by Teasdale (1999; see also Barnard, Duke, Byrne, & Davidson, 2007 this issue) who equated nonconceptual representations with memories *of* emotions and conceptual representations with memories *about* emotions. This proposal raises two problems. First, it remains obscure why nonconceptual representations would be more likely to elicit emotions than conceptual ones (Frijda & Zeelenberg, 2001). According to Leventhal (1984) this is because the abstractions of conceptual representations are often based on the most salient features of an emotion episode and tend to leave out familiar cues and context information, which are crucial for the actual elicitation of emotions. Frijda (1988) suggested that it may have to do with the fact that nonconceptual representations have a higher degree of reality or vividness than conceptual ones. The second problem is that nonconceptual representations are not unique to emotions. For instance, perceptual representations of objects are considered nonconceptual but they do not necessarily elicit emotions.

Other theorists have argued that it is not the format, but the content of the representations that marks the difference between processes with cognitive output and those with emotions as output. According to Lang (1985), only representations that contain response information can elicit emotions. Recent research on embodied cognition, however, suggests that representations or schemata containing motor information are not unique to emotions. This research is guided by the thesis that most if not all of our representations contain motor information and that action and perception share the same representations. For example, Spivey, Tyler, Richardson, and Young (2000) showed that activation of the concept skyscraper influenced eye-movements, suggesting that representations of neutral concepts may in fact include motor information.

Another content proposal comes from appraisal theory and other belief–desire theories of emotion. These theories have suggested that any and only information about the satisfaction status of goals or concerns, that is, stimuli appraised as goal relevant, are capable of eliciting emotions (Buck, 1988; Frijda, 1986, 1988, 1994; Lazarus, 1991; Oatley & Johnson-Laird, 1987; Ortony, Clore, & Collins, 1988; Reisenzein, 2006; Roseman, 1984; Scherer, 1994; Smith & Lazarus, 1993). Emotion-related information that is not goal relevant is emotionally inert. Information about components of emotion, such as bodily responses and action tendencies are not capable of eliciting emotions unless they are themselves appraised as relevant for a goal. For example, a stimulus signalling a pending mismatch with one's goal for safety may elicit fear, and the consequent trembling of one's body may itself constitute a mismatch with one's goal of making a good impression and elicit shame. Further, a mismatch with an expected state will not provoke an emotion, unless the expected state is also desired, or unless being able to predict the outcome of events in general is desired. Finally, a stimulus with positive or negative valence (e.g., the word "dumb") will not lead to an emotion unless and until it is appraised as affecting one's goals (e.g., when your boss calls you dumb and your self-esteem is threatened). Lazarus (1991) defended a similar point when he wrote that intrinsic valence, without referring to motives, is incapable of eliciting real emotions. He asserted that the inherent pleasantness or unpleasantness of a stimulus should be considered pure knowledge, which requires additional evaluation in light of goals before resulting in an emotion.

Appraisal theory distinguishes between an appraisal of goal relevance and an appraisal of goal congruence (Lazarus, 1991). Goal relevance refers to whether or not (or the extent to which) a stimulus conveys information about the satisfaction status of goals and determines whether or not an emotion will occur (or the intensity of the emotion that will occur). Goal congruence refers to the kind of information that is conveyed by the stimulus (whether the stimulus matches or mismatches with the goal) and determines the kind of emotion (positive or negative) that will occur. In the present paper, I do not make separate predictions for the appraisals of goal relevance and goal congruence. On the assumption that emotion always has intensity and quality, it may be difficult to separate them.

In summary, the components of bodily responses and phenomenal experience can be considered non-cognitive aspects on some accounts of cognition, but they are not unique to emotion. Uniqueness is also problematic for the nonconceptual format and response-related content of representations that some believe to be crucial for emotion elicitation. Of the candidate constructs discussed, only the goal-relevant content of emotion-antecedent representations seems unique to emotions. This construct faces another problem, however, which it shares with the constructs of non-conceptual format and response-related content of representations. They are all features of representations and therefore do not fall outside the realm of the cognitive. This may pose a problem for emotion theorists who wish to avoid equating emotion with cognition. One solution may be to say that the cause of emotion can be equated with cognition but that emotions themselves may still include non-cognitive components.

I hypothesise along with appraisal theory that the representations mediating the relation between stimuli and emotions contain information that touches on goals or concerns. This information is the unique aspect of emotion. The question whether cognitive methods can be used to study the unique aspect of emotion can now be answered as follows. A process operating on representations is a cognitive process irrespective of the content of these representations. Thus, methods designed to study cognitive processes can also be used to study cognitive processes operating on goal-relevant information. In the next section, I consider the motivational hypothesis in further detail. The aim is to delineate the process that deals with goal-relevant information from processes that have no relation or a different relation with goals, such as processes that deal with stimuli that are valent but not goal relevant. I also formulate additional predictions regarding the conditions under which goal-relevant or goal (in)congruent information versus purely valenced information can be processed. In the final part of the section, I examine whether there are ways to investigate the motivational hypothesis as well as the additional predictions about conditions.

OUTLINE OF THE MOTIVATIONAL HYPOTHESIS

Before refining the hypothesis that goal-relevant information reliably produces emotions, I clarify some theoretical choices and useful distinctions about the representation, activation, and implementation of goals.

The representation, activation, and implementation of goals

I side with Bargh's (1997) assumption that "goals ... do not exist in some mysterious ether but correspond to mental representations in much the same way as do attitudes and perceptual structures" (Bargh, 1997, p. 7). Goal representations, however, are said to have special dynamic qualities that are not shared by other kinds of representations. For instance, the activation of goal representations accumulates over time and persists in the face of obstacles (Bargh & Barndollar, 1996).

With regard to the content of goal representations, three distinctions are useful. A first distinction is between goals and intentions. Intentions are a subclass of goals. The content of a goal can be any state of affairs; the content of an intention must be an action or process (e.g., James, 1890). One can intend to cook an egg, but one cannot intend the egg to be cooked. An intention must also be carried out by the person who has it. One cannot intend someone else to cook the egg. I define an intentional action or process as one that is caused by the goal to engage in it, and an unintentional action or process as one that is not caused by the goal to engage in it (Moors & De Houwer, 2006a).

A second distinction is between central and peripheral goals (e.g., Frijda, 1986). Central goals define satisfaction conditions for basic needs such as safety, food, appreciation, and optimal physical and cognitive functioning. Peripheral goals are derived from central goals. The central goal for physical survival may induce a series of more peripheral goals that directly or indirectly serve the satisfaction of this goal,[5] such as the goals to earn money, to watch traffic lights, and to eat healthily. These goals may, in turn, trigger subgoals. Together, they form a hierarchical network.

A third useful distinction is between proximal goals and remote goals. These are not fixed categories of goals. The terms proximal and remote refer to the distance between a goal and the process (or action) under study. A goal is proximal when it is directly related to the process under study, meaning that the process figures in the content of the goal. Examples are the goal to engage in the process and the goal to stop or avoid the process.

---

[5] For one part, the satisfaction of a central goal is at the service of a central goal or another peripheral goal. For the other part, peripheral goals may lead a life of their own. For example, the goal to own a nice car may stem from the goal to be appreciated by others, but it may also become a purpose in itself (Frijda, 1986).

A remote goal is one that is not related, content-wise, to the process under study. The notions of proximal and remote goal are useful for explaining the difference between the concepts goal (in)dependent and (un)intentional (Moors & De Houwer, 2006a). A process that is caused by a goal is goal dependent. This goal may be either the proximal goal to engage in the process or another, remote goal. A remote goal may cause the process indirectly, via the proximal goal, or directly, circumventing the proximal goal. A process that is caused by the proximal goal to engage in it is intentional. A process that is directly caused by a remote goal is unintentional but goal dependent. Intentional processes are a subclass of goal-dependent processes (because intentions are a subclass of goals). A process that is not caused by a (proximal or remote) goal is goal independent. As an illustration of these notions, consider the process of evaluating primes in a priming task. The process is intentional when it is caused by the proximal goal to evaluate the primes, otherwise it is unintentional. The process is unintentional but goal dependent when it is directly caused by a remote goal, such as the goal to perform well on the task. Another scenario is that the remote goal to perform well on the task triggers the proximal goal to evaluate the primes, and that the latter goal causes the evaluation process. In this case the process is also intentional. The evaluation process is goal independent when there is not a proximal or a remote goal that causes it.

Another distinction has to do with the way in which goals are activated or chosen among a set of alternatives (i.e., the phase of goal setting; Gollwitzer, 1990). Bargh (1990; Bargh & Barndollar, 1996; Bargh & Gollwitzer, 1994) distinguished between chronic goals and temporary goals. Chronic goals are those that are frequently and enduringly activated in the past, whereas temporary goals are recently induced and their activation is typically short lived. In Bargh's (1990) automotive model, a goal that is repeatedly and enduringly chosen in a specific situation forms associations in memory with stimuli in these situations. These stimuli eventually become sufficient to activate the existing goal representation so that conscious choice of the goal can be circumvented and the goal drops out of consciousness. To activate a temporary goal, other conditions are required in addition to the stimulus, such as instructions or other task features. To illustrate the distinction, when the goal to be egalitarian is chronic, it can be activated upon the mere presentation of a picture of a minority group member (cf. Moskowitz, Gollwitzer, Wasel, & Schaal, 1999). When the goal to be egalitarian is not chronic, its temporary activation requires more than the picture alone. It may require the instruction to be egalitarian or more subtle ways of induction, such as a preceding unobtrusive priming phase (e.g., a scrambled sentence test with egalitarian words; Chartrand & Bargh, 1996). In the case of instructions, the temporary goal is thought to be conscious; in the case of more subtle ways of induction, the goal may remain unconscious.

Once a goal is activated or chosen (phase of goal setting) it must still be translated into real action (phase of goal striving; Gollwitzer, 1990; Heckhausen, 1990/1991). The motivation literature has identified two factors that determine whether an intention will be implemented: strength of the intention and feasibility of the action or process. An intention must be strong enough in comparison to other intentions that are vying for implementation. Feasibility encompasses two subfactors: opportunity and skill. For example, to process a word for meaning, there must be a word (i.e., opportunity), and the person must know how to read (i.e., skill).

Processes can have two kinds of relations with goals

The previous paragraph described how goals to engage in actions or processes are translated into real actions and processes and in this way *serve the satisfaction* of these goals. Goals (of any kind) may also induce processes that serve to *monitor the satisfaction status* of these goals. The goal for survival may lead to a process that determines matches or mismatches with it. The core of the motivational hypothesis is that the output of this monitoring process is, structurally speaking, an emotion. One extra condition that is probably needed to speak of a full-blown (i.e., intense) emotion is that the goal at stake should be sufficiently *central*. Centrality is a relative notion. Some goals are more central than others and hence more likely to serve as the basis for emotions. For example, a mismatch with the goal to survive is more likely to elicit an emotion than a mismatch with the goal to perform a dull task.

According to the motivational hypothesis, processes that have emotions as output deal with goal-relevant information, whereas processes that have no emotions do not. I wish to clearly delineate the terms goal relevant, goal dependent, and goal related. Goal-relevant information is information about the satisfaction status of goals. A goal-dependent process is one that is caused by a goal. A process that does not deal with the satisfaction status of goals may still be caused by a goal. Thus, processes concerned with goal-relevant information and processes that are goal dependent are both goal related, but the type of relation differs.

The motivational hypothesis says that emotions are caused by stimuli that are appraised as goal relevant. It is important to note that goal relevance *as appraised* is not the same thing as *objective* goal relevance (Frijda, 1986, p. 330; Frijda & Zeelenberg, 2001). A goal-relevant stimulus does not lead to an emotion unless the person processes this goal relevance.

This raises the question of what kind of mechanism is required to assess goal relevance (and goal congruence). The most common proposal is a mechanism that compares the incoming stimulus with a goal. The output of this comparison is a match or a mismatch. A match leads to a positive and a mismatch to a negative emotion. Positive and negative emotions may consist of different action tendencies depending on whether matches are potential, partial, or complete, and whether mismatches are revocable or irrevocable. A potential or a partial match leads to the tendency to increase contact with the stimulus (i.e., approach); a perfect match leads to the tendency to cease goal striving or the tendency to increase contact with other stimuli (that offer opportunity for the fulfilment of other goals). A revocable mismatch results in a tendency to turn it into a match (e.g., by means of fight or flight); an irrevocable mismatch results in the tendency to cease goal-striving. The actions resulting from the tendency to reduce the discrepancy between stimulus and goal (in case there is a potential or partial match or a revocable mismatch) may cause a change in the stimulus situation. The changed situation is fed back in the monitoring process and the feedback cycle is repeated until the discrepancy is solved (cf. TOTE model of Miller et al., 1960; also see Carver & Scheier, 1990; Case 4 in Figure 1). As suggested by several authors (Bargh, 1990; Moskowitz, 2001), goal representations need not have a conceptual format nor must they be consciously chosen or even consciously accessible to serve as a standard for comparison. A goal representation may be latent until a discrepant or matching stimulus awakens it. Often, a person is unaware of what is important to her/him until a strong emotional reaction tells her/him so (cf. Buck's, 1988, idea that emotion is a readout of motivational potential). As an alternative to a comparison mechanism, information about the satisfaction status of goals may, in principle, also be delivered by a mechanism of direct memory retrieval. It is not unthinkable that certain stimuli are tagged in memory as goal (ir)relevant or goal (in)congruent as a result of prior learning. Presentation of these stimuli may trigger activation of their associated goal-(ir)relevant or goal-(in)congruent meaning.

Until now, I have defended a strong version of the motivational hypothesis. According to this version, goal-relevant information is necessary for emotion elicitation. One could also defend a weak version, arguing that goal-relevant information is not strictly necessary to elicit emotions but, together with a host of background conditions, it is sufficient. The weak version leaves room for emotions that are not easily explained by making appeal to goal relevance, such as those elicited by music and films (but see Frijda, 1989).

The theoretical possibilities discussed can be summarised as follows (see Figure 1). A process can be: (a) unintentional (i.e., not caused by a proximal goal; Case 1); (b) chronically intentional (i.e., caused by a proximal goal that is chronic; Case 2); or (c) temporarily intentional (i.e., caused by a proximal goal that is temporary; Case 3). In all three cases the process may or may not

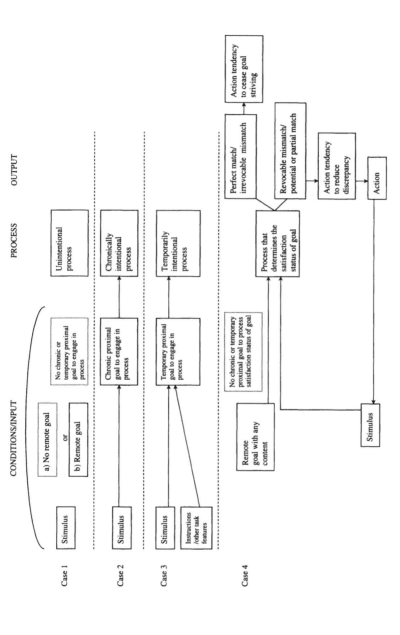

Figure 1. The motivational framework distinguishes between processes that are unrelated to goals (Case 1a); processes that serve the satisfaction of goals (unintentional goal-dependent ones [Case 1b], chronically intentional ones [Case 2], and temporarily intentional ones [Case 3]); and processes that monitor the satisfaction status of goals (Case 4).

(also/still) be caused by a remote goal, but the model is organised around the presence or absence of proximal goals. In addition to processes that directly *serve* the satisfaction of intentions (Cases 2 and 3), there is a process that *monitors* the satisfaction status of intentions and of other goals (Case 4). The core of the (strong version of the) motivational hypothesis is that only the process in Case 4 has emotions as output. An important implication is that valenced stimuli that are not appraised as goal relevant are not capable of eliciting emotions.

The motivational framework sketched above assumes that many processes and actions stem from goals. Most processes and actions do not occur in isolation but are embedded in chains of goals and subgoals. Although the framework does leave room for processes that are not caused by a proximal and/or remote goal, there may be very few cases of entirely goal-independent processes. When researchers argue that their effects are goal independent they often mean that these effects are independent of certain goals, such as the proximal goal to process the feature under study or other, more remote goals that are temporarily induced by features of the experimental procedure.

Conditions under which goal relevance versus valence can be processed

The process that monitors the satisfaction status of goals was presented as goal dependent. The goal to be loved leads to the process to verify whether one is actually loved. In addition, I hypothesise that this process is (or can be) unintentional. From a functionalist perspective, emotions have survival value. They are designed to mobilise the organism in response to the detection of (potential) matches or mismatches with goals. Emotions are most useful for survival when their occurrence is dependent on the least number of processing conditions. I therefore hypothesise that the process that causes emotions can be unintentional. Pursuing the survival argument, I further speculate that processes without survival value are typically intentional; they do not occur unless the person has the intention to engage in them. Several cognitive tasks, such as sorting stimuli in the binary categories of blue versus yellow, upper case versus lower case, and animal versus person, do not usually require priority and I hypothesise that people will not engage in them unless they have an intention to do so. In a similar vein, I hypothesise that valenced stimuli that are not goal relevant will not be sorted in the binary categories of positive versus negative unless people have the intention to do so. In short, I predict a dissociation between processes that have emotions as output and those that have valence as output: the former require no intention to occur, whereas the latter do. In addition, I predict no dissociation between processes that have valence as output and those that have other binary categories as output: both require an intention to occur.

In the next sections, I examine whether there are ways to investigate the core of the motivational hypothesis that emotions are caused by stimuli that provide information about the satisfaction status of goals. I also examine the available empirical support in favour of and against the additional hypotheses that the process that determines the satisfaction status of goals can take place unintentionally, whereas processes that sort stimuli into binary categories (including the binary categories of positive vs. negative) do not.

EMPIRICAL INVESTIGATION OF THE MOTIVATIONAL HYPOTHESIS

Investigating the core assumption

To falsify the strong version of the motivational hypothesis that goal-relevant information is necessary for emotion elicitation entails demonstrating that valenced stimuli that do not provide information about the satisfaction status of goals can also elicit emotions. This enterprise is complicated by two difficulties. First, one has to choose a criterion that indicates the presence or absence of an emotion (dependent variable), and this criterion should be logically independent of the presence or absence of goal relevance (independent variable; Frijda & Zeelenberg, 2001). In other words, in addition to the hypothesised criterion of goal relevance, one has to find a second unique criterion (or set of criteria) to demarcate emotions from phenomena that are not emotions. The literature contains several proposals for criteria. Examples are that emotions: (1) are valenced states (this delineates them from surprise and interest; Ortony & Turner, 1990); (2) are short lived (this delineates them from moods); (3) have arousal (this delineates them from attitudes and preferences); (4) are action tendencies (this delineates them from actions; Frijda, 1986); (5) arise spontaneously (this delineates them from intentions; Frijda, 1986); and (6) have a specific formal object (Hacker, 2004) or core relational theme (Lazarus, 1991) such as danger (for fear), a demeaning offence against me and mine (for anger), and irrevocable loss (for sadness). The latter criterion delineates emotions from bodily sensations (e.g., hunger, pain). Most authors combine several of these criteria to delineate the class of emotions. Unfortunately, there is no consensus among authors. Thus, researchers have to make a choice and state it explicitly.

There is a second difficulty that one encounters when studying the emotion-evoking power of stimuli that have valence but no goal relevance. One has to find a way to operationalise valence in a pure way. This may turn out to be a very tough nut to crack. Indeed, when stimuli are used with a positive or negative valence, one has no guarantee that participants will *not* link these stimuli to their goals, even if goals are not being manipulated. For example, the word "dumb" may have no emotion-evoking power as such, but it may actually make contact with a person's goals via imagination (e.g., she may imagine that someone calls her dumb so that her self-esteem is threatened) and in this way evoke an emotion. Because of this difficulty, direct testing of the strong version of the motivational hypothesis does not seem within immediate reach. It remains possible, however, to seek support for the weaker version of the motivational hypothesis. Despite the difficulty of discarding the goal relevance of a stimulus, it remains possible to manipulate the degree to which the stimulus is relevant for some goal, and assess whether this affects the intensity of the emotional response. Another possibility is to suddenly increase the goal relevance of some stimulus by inducing a new goal or by enhancing the centrality of an existing goal. The emotional consequences of both phases can then be compared.

Investigating the additional assumptions concerning the conditions under which goal relevance versus valence can be processed

In the present section, I further consider the hypotheses that the satisfaction status of goals can be determined unintentionally, whereas processes that sort stimuli into binary categories require an intention. I first compare these new hypotheses with those that have guided previous dissociation research. Authors of previous dissociation studies have addressed the question whether processes with valenced versus cognitive output occur under the same (no-dissociation view) or under different conditions (dissociation view). Advocates of the dissociation view (Bargh, 1997; Zajonc, 1980) assume that processes with valenced output are unintentional and even entirely goal independent (Case 1) and that certain processes with cognitive output are steered by intentions, without specifying whether these intentions are chronic (Case 2) or temporary (Case 3). Advocates of the no-dissociation view (Clore et al., 2005; Storbeck & Robinson, 2004; Storbeck et al., 2006) assume that processes with valenced output are part of semantic encoding, without specifying whether both are unintentional or intentional in some variety of the term.

I propose an alternative account that is still consistent with the no-dissociation view. I first hypothesise that the (semantic) encoding of stimuli is either unintentional (Case 1) or chronically intentional (Case 2). I further propose that the processes underlying priming effects are binary categorisation processes. Priming for valence requires the categorisation of stimuli (both primes and targets) as positive or negative, whereas priming for cognitive features (e.g., animacy, colour) requires categorisation in other binary categories (e.g., living vs. non-living, blue vs. yellow).[6] Target responses are relatively facilitated when prime and target are sorted in the same category, but relatively inhibited when they are sorted in different categories. Categorisation based on valence is just one type of binary categorisation. Crucially, binary categorisation of stimuli entails more than pure encoding; encoding can be a first step. For example, encoding of the word dog can be a first step in categorising it as an animal instead of a person or as a living creature instead of an object. Similarly, encoding of a blue square can be a first step in sorting it in the category of blue instead of yellow or in the category of squares instead of triangles. I hypothesise that binary categorisation of stimuli is temporarily intentional (Case 3). Sorting stimuli in one of two categories on the basis of valence or any other feature requires more than the mere presence of the stimulus; it requires a temporary intention that must be fuelled by an explicit instruction or a more subtle task feature (such as the nature of the target task or the characteristics of the stimulus set).

Empirical support for the idea that valence-based categorisation is (consciously or unconsciously) intentional is mixed. Studies in which task features are removed that might induce the (conscious or unconscious) intention to engage in valence-based categorisation show sometimes that affective priming (and Simon) effects disappear (De Houwer, Hermans, Rothermund, & Wentura, 2002; Duscherer et al., in press; Klauer & Musch, 2001, 2002; Klinger, Burton, & Pitts, 2000; Lavender & Hommel, 2007 this issue; Spruyt, Hermans, De Houwer, & Eelen, 2002; Spruyt, Hermans, Pandelaere, De Houwer, & Eelen, 2004) and sometimes that they remain intact (Bargh, Chaiken, Raymond, & Hymes, 1996; Hermans, De Houwer, & Eelen, 1994, Klauer & Musch, 2002). Although the latter results are inconsistent with the view proposed here, it could be argued that in none of these studies it can be completely ruled out that the nature of the target responses or the polarised valence of the stimuli (primes and/or targets) enhanced the salience of valence compared to that of other dimensions and induced the intention to engage in valence-based categorisation. It must be emphasised, however, that the proposed account is speculative and calls for extensive empirical testing.

Until now, there has been only limited empirical support for the hypothesis that the satisfaction status of goals can be determined unintentionally. Several studies with attentional bias tasks support the idea that goal relevance can be processed unintentionally (Moskowitz, 2002; Rothermund, 2003; Wentura, Rothermund, & Bak, 2000). Support for the idea that

---

[6] Priming experiments may, of course, require participants to sort features into more than two categories.

goal congruence can be processed unintentionally is provided by studies conducted at our lab. Using variants of the sequential affective priming task, Moors, De Houwer, Hermans, and Eelen (2005) showed that primes that constituted a match or a mismatch with temporarily induced goals influenced responses to positive and negative target words. Several features of the procedures used supported the idea that these matches and mismatches were determined without the (conscious) intention to do so.

In summary, I have speculated that binary valence-based categorisation requires a conscious or unconscious temporary intention, whereas assessment of the satisfaction status of goals requires no intention. Empirical support in favour of these speculations is either mixed or limited. I see it as a major challenge for future dissociation studies to continue investigation of these speculations. Where most previous studies have focused on dissociations between processes concerned with valence versus non-valenced features, future studies should focus on dissociations between processes concerned with valence versus the satisfactions status of goals. Studies may focus on differences with respect to conditions and test the speculations presented above, or differences with respect to the types of mechanisms involved. Differences or similarities in conditions do not yield an insight in mechanisms but are valuable in their own right. In this way, the motivational framework provides directions for future research.

CONCLUSION

The present paper set out to answer the questions whether cognitive methods are suited to the study of emotion, and whether they are suited to study the unique aspect of emotion. Based on (a) the definition of a cognitive process as one that mediates between flexible input–output relations by means of representations, and (b) observations indicating a flexible relation between stimuli and emotions, I concluded that cognitive processes are involved in the elicitation of many emotions and hence that cognitive methods can be used to study them. I further proposed that the unique aspect of emotion has to do with the content of the representations involved in the process that elicits the emotion. More particularly, these representations contain information about the satisfaction status of central goals. Cognitive methods are fit to study this process, given that such methods work for any representation-mediated process, regardless of the content of the representations.

The core of the motivational hypothesis is that (only) processes that monitor the satisfaction status of goals can elicit emotions. I sketched a broader motivational framework in which this monitoring process was contrasted with processes that serve the direct satisfaction of goals and intentions. I formulated the additional hypotheses that the satisfaction status of goals can be processed unintentionally, whereas processes that sort stimuli into binary categories (e.g., based on valence, colour, semantic category) cannot. These hypotheses were contrasted to the views guiding previous dissociation research. In most of this previous research, the focus was on dissociations between the processing of valence versus cognitive features. The current motivational hypothesis urges researchers to also study processes concerned with goal relevance or goal congruence. In conclusion, processes involved in the causation of emotion can be studied with cognitive methods and I believe they do have a special status, but researchers may have been looking for them in the wrong place.

REFERENCES

Armon-Jones (1989). *Varieties of affect*. Toronto, Canada: University of Toronto Press.

Baars, B. J. (1986). *The cognitive revolution in psychology*. New York: Guilford Press.

Bargh, J. A. (1990). Auto-motives: Preconscious determinants of social interaction. In E. T. Higgins & R. M. Sorrentino (Eds.), *Handbook of motivation and cognition* (Vol. 2, pp. 93–130). New York: Guilford Press.

Bargh, J. A. (1997). The automaticity of everyday life. In R. S. Wyer (Ed.), *Advances in social cognition* (Vol. 10, pp. 1–49). Mahwah, NJ: Lawrence Erlbaum Associates, Inc.

Bargh, J. A., & Barndollar, K. (1996). Automaticity in action: The unconscious as repository of chronic goals and motives. In P. M. Gollwitzer & J. A. Bargh (Eds.), *The psychology of action: Linking cognition and motivation to behavior* (pp. 457–481). New York: Guilford Press.

Bargh, J. A., Chaiken, S., Raymond, P., & Hymes, C. (1996). The automatic evaluation effect: Unconditional automatic activation with a pronunciation task. *Journal of Experimental Social Psychology, 32*, 104–128.

Bargh, J. A., & Gollwitzer, P. M. (1994). Environmental control of goal-directed action: Automatic and strategic contingencies between situations and behavior. In W. D. Spaulding (Ed.). *Nebraska Symposium on Motivation, 41*, 71–124.

Barnard, P., Duke, D., Byrne, R., & Davidson, I. (2007). Differentiation in cognitive and emotional meanings: An evolutionary analysis. *Cognition and Emotion, 21*, 1155–1183.

Bermudéz, J. L. (1995). Nonconceptual content: From perceptual experience to subpersonal computational states. *Mind and Language, 10*, 333–369.

Buck, R. (1988). *Human motivation and emotion*. New York: Wiley.

Carver, C. S., & Scheier, M. F. (1990). Principles of self-regulation: Action and emotion. In E. T. Higgins & R. M. Sorrentino (Eds.), *Handbook of motivation and cognition: Foundations of social behavior* (Vol. 2, pp. 3–52). New York: Guilford Press.

Chartrand, T. L., & Bargh, J. A. (1996). Automatic activation of social information processing goals: Nonconscious priming reproduces effects of explicit conscious instructions. *Journal of Personality and Social Psychology, 71*, 464–478.

Cleeremans, A., & Jiménez, L. (2002). Implicit learning and consciousness: A graded, dynamic perspective. In R. M. French & A. Cleeremans (Eds.), *Implicit learning and consciousness* (pp. 1–40). Hove, UK: Psychology Press.

Clore, G. L., Storbeck, J., Robinson, M. D., & Centerbar, D. (2005). Seven sins in the study of unconscious affect. In L. F. Barrett, P. Niedenthal, & P. Winkielman (Eds.), *Emotion: Conscious and unconscious* (pp. 384–408). New York: Guilford Press.

Crane, T. (1998). Intentionality as the mark of the mental. In A. O'Hear (Ed.), *Contemporary issues in philosophy of mind* (pp. 229–251). Cambridge, UK: Cambridge University Press.

Crosson, B. A. (1992). *Subcortical functions in language and memory.* New York: Guilford Press.

De Houwer, J., Hermans, D., Rothermund, K., & Wentura, D. (2002). Affective priming of semantic categorization responses. *Cognition and Emotion, 16,* 643–666.

Dolan, R. J. (2002). Emotion, cognition, and behavior. *Science, 298,* 1191–1194.

Duncan, S., & Barrett, L. F. (2007). Affect is a form of cognition: A neurobiological analysis. *Cognition and Emotion, 21,* 1184–1211.

Dunn, J. C., & Kirsner, K. (2003). What can we infer from double dissociations? *Cortex, 39,* 1–7.

Duscherer, K., Holender, D., & Molenaar, E. (in press). Revisiting the affective Simon effect. *Cognition and Emotion.*

Eder, A. B., Hommel, B., & De Houwer, J. (2007). How distinctive is affective porcessing? On the implications of using cognitive paradigms to study affect and emotion. *Cognition and Emotion, 21,* 1137–1154.

Frijda, N. H. (1986). *The emotions.* New York: Cambridge University Press.

Frijda, N. H. (1988). The laws of emotion. *American Psychologist, 43,* 349–358.

Frijda, N. H. (1989). Aesthetic emotions and reality. *American Psychologist, 44,* 1546–1547.

Frijda, N. H. (1994). Emotions require cognitions, even if simple ones. In P. Ekman & R. J. Davidson (Eds.), *The nature of emotion: Fundamental questions* (pp. 197–202). New York: Oxford University Press.

Frijda, N. H., & Zeelenberg, M. (2001). What is the dependent? In K. R. Scherer, A. Schorr, & T. Johnstone (Eds.), *Appraisal processes in emotion* (pp. 141–155). New York: Oxford University Press.

Fodor, J. A. (1986). Why Paramecia don't have mental representations. *Midwest Studies in Philosophy, 10,* 3–23.

Gollwitzer, P. M. (1990). Action phases and mind-sets. In E. T. Higgins & R. M. Sorrentino (Eds.), *Handbook of motivation and cognition: Foundations of social behavior* (Vol. 2, pp. 53–92). New York: Guilford Press.

Green, C. D. (1996). Where did the word "cognitive" come from anyway? *Canadian Psychology, 37,* 31–39.

Hacker, P. M. S. (2004). The conceptual framework for the investigation of emotions. *International Review of Psychiatry, 16,* 199–208.

Hamm, A. O., & Vaitl, D. (1996). Affective learning: Awareness and aversion. *Psychophysiology, 33,* 97–107.

Heckhausen, H. (1991). *Motivation and action* (P. K. Leppman, Trans.). Berlin, Germany: Springer-Verlag. (Original work published 1990)

Hermans, D., De Houwer, J., & Eelen, P. (1994). The affective priming effect: Automatic activation of evaluative information in memory. *Cognition and Emotion, 8,* 515–533.

Izard, C. E. (1994). Cognition is one of four types of emotion-activating systems. In P. Ekman & R. J. Davidson (Eds.), *The nature of emotion: Fundamental questions* (pp. 203–207). New York: Oxford University Press.

James, W. (1890). *The principles of psychology.* New York: Holt, Rinehart, & Winston.

Klauer, K. C., & Musch, J. (2001). Does sunshine prime loyal? Affective priming in the naming task. *Quarterly Journal of Experimental Psychology, 54,* 727–751.

Klauer, K. C., & Musch, J. (2002). Goal-dependent and goal-independent effects of irrelevant evaluations. *Personality and Social Psychology Bulletin, 28,* 802–814.

Klinger, M. R., Burton, P. C., & Pitts, G. S. (2000). Mechanisms of unconscious priming: I. Response competition, not spreading activation. *Journal of Experimental Psychology: Learning, Memory, and Cognition, 26,* 441–455.

LaBar, K. S., LeDoux, J. E., Spencer, D. D., & Phelps, E. A. (1995). Impaired fear conditioning following unilateral temporal lobectomy in humans. *The Journal of Neuroscience, 15*, 6846–6855.

Lang, P. J. (1985). The cognitive psychophysiology of fear and anxiety. In A. H. Tuma & J. D. Maser (Eds.), *Anxiety and the anxiety disorders* (pp. 131–170). Hillsdale, NJ: Lawrence Erlbaum Associates, Inc.

Lavender, T., & Hommel, B. (2007). Affect and action: Towards an event-coding account. *Cognition and Emotion, 21*, 1270–1296.

Lazarus, R. S. (1991). *Emotion and adaptation.* New York: Oxford University Press.

LeDoux, J. E. (1989). Cognitive–emotional interactions in the brain. *Cognition and Emotion, 3*, 267–289.

LeDoux, J., Romanski, L., & Xagoraris, A. (1989). Indelibility of subcortical emotional memories. *Journal of Cognitive Neuroscience, 1*, 238–243.

Leventhal, H. (1984). A perceptual-motor theory of emotion. In L. Berkowitz (Ed.), *Advances in experimental social psychology* (Vol. 17, pp. 117–182). New York: Academic Press.

Leventhal, H., & Scherer, K. (1987). The relationship of emotion to cognition: A functional approach to a semantic controversy. *Cognition and Emotion, 1*, 3–28.

Mandler, G., Nakamura, Y., & Shebo-Van Zandt, B. J. (1987). Non-specific effects of exposure on stimuli that cannot be recognized. *Journal of Experimental Psychology: Learning, Memory and Cognition, 13*, 646–648.

Marcel, A. J. (1983). Conscious and unconscious perception: An approach to the relation between phenomenal experience and perceptual processes. *Cognitive Psychology, 15*, 238–300.

Marr, D. (Ed.). (1982). *Vision: A computational investigation into the human representation and processing of visual information.* New York: Freeman.

McNaughton, N. (1997). Cognitive dysfunction resulting from hippocampal hyperactivity—A possible cause of anxiety disorder. *Pharmacology Biochemistry and Behavior, 65*, 603–611.

Miller, G. A. (1962). *Psychology: The science of mental life.* Harmondsworth, UK: Penguin.

Miller, G. A., Galanter, E., & Pribram, K. (1960). *Plans and the structure of behavior.* New York: Holt.

Moors, A. (2006). Investigating the automaticity of constructive appraisals. *Proceedings of the 18th European Meeting on Cybernetics and Systems Research.* Vienna, Austria: Austrian Society for Cybernetic Studies.

Moors, A., & De Houwer, J. (2006a). Automaticity: A theoretical and conceptual analysis. *Psychological Bulletin, 132*, 297–326.

Moors, A., & De Houwer, J. (2006b). Problems with dividing the realm of cognitive processes. *Psychological Inquiry, 17*, 199–204.

Moors, A., De Houwer, J., & Eelen, P. (2004). Automatic stimulus–goal comparisons: Support from motivational affective priming studies. *Cognition and Emotion, 18*, 29–54.

Moors, A., De Houwer, J., Hermans, D., & Eelen, P. (2005). Unintentional processing of motivational valence. *Quarterly Journal of Experimental Psychology, 58A*, 1043–1063.

Moskowitz, G. B. (2001). Preconscious control and compensatory cognition. In G. B. Moskowitz (Ed.), *Cognitive social psychology: The Princeton symposium on the legacy and future of social cognition* (pp. 333–358). Hillsdale, NJ: Lawrence Erlbaum Associates, Inc.

Moskowitz, G. B. (2002). Preconscious effects of temporary goals on attention. *Journal of Experimental Social Psychology, 38*, 397–404.

Moskowitz, G. B., Gollwitzer, P. M., Wasel, W., & Schaal, B. (1999). Preconscious control of stereotype activation through chronic egalitarian goals. *Journal of Personality and Social Psychology, 77*, 167–184.

Murphy, S. T., & Zajonc, R. B. (1993). Affect, cognition, and awareness: Affective priming with optimal and suboptimal stimulus exposures. *Journal of Personality and Social Psychology, 64*, 723–739.

Neisser, U. (1967). *Cognitive psychology.* Englewood Cliffs, NJ: Prentice Hall.

Nussbaum, M. (1990). *Love's knowledge.* Oxford, UK: Oxford University Press.

Oatley, K., & Johnson-Laird, P. N. (1987). Towards a cognitive theory of emotions. *Cognition and Emotion, 1,* 29–50.

Ortony, A., Clore, G. L., & Collins, A. (1988). *The cognitive structure of emotions.* London: Cambridge University Press.

Ortony, A., & Turner, T. J. (1990). What's basic about basic emotions? *Psychological Review, 97,* 315–331.

Prinz, J. (2004). *Gut reactions: A perceptual theory of emotion.* Oxford, UK: Oxford University Press.

Reisenzein, R. (2006). Emotions as metarepresentational states of mind. In R. Trappl (Ed.), *Proceedings of the 18th European Meeting on Cybernetics and Systems Research.* Vienna, Austria: Austrian Society for Cybernetic Studies.

Rose, J. K., & Rankin, C. H. (2001). Analyses of habituation in Caenorhabditis elegans. *Learning & Memory, 8,* 63–69.

Roseman, I. J. (1984). Cognitive determinants of emotions: A structural theory. In P. Shaver (Ed.), *Review of personality and social psychology* (Vol. 5, pp. 11–36). Beverly Hills, CA: Sage.

Rothermund, K. (2003). Automatic vigilance for task-related information: Perseverance after failure and inhibition after success. *Memory & Cognition, 31,* 343–352.

Scherer, K. R. (1993). Neuroscience projections to current debates in emotion psychology. *Cognition and Emotion, 7,* 1–41.

Scherer, K. R. (1994). An emotion's occurrence depends on the relevance of an event to the organism's goal/need hierarchy. In P. Ekman & R. J. Davidson (Eds.), *The nature of emotion: Fundamental questions* (pp. 227–231). New York: Oxford University Press.

Scherer, K. R. (1997). Profiles of emotion–antecedent appraisals: Testing theoretical predictions across cultures. *Cognition and Emotion, 11,* 113–150.

Searle, J. R. (1983). *Intentionality: An essay in the philosophy of mind.* Cambridge, UK: Cambridge University Press.

Sloman, S. A. (1996). The empirical case for two systems of reasoning. *Psychological Bulletin, 119,* 3–22.

Smith, C. A., & Kirby, L. D. (2001). Toward delivering on the promise of appraisal theory. In K. R. Scherer, A. Schorr, & T. Johnstone, *Appraisal processes in emotion* (pp. 121–138). New York: Oxford University Press.

Smith, C. A., & Lazarus, R. S. (1993). Appraisal components, core relational themes, and the emotions. *Cognition and Emotion, 7,* 233–269.

Solomon, R. (1984). *The passions: The myth and nature of human emotions.* New York: Doubleday.

Spivey, M., Tyler, M., Richardson, D., & Young, E. (2000). Eye movements during comprehension of spoken scene descriptions. *Proceedings of the 22nd Annual Conference of the Cognitive Science Society* (pp. 487–492). Mahwah, NJ: Lawrence Erlbaum Associates, Inc.

Spruyt, A., Hermans, D., De Houwer, J., & Eelen, P. (2002). On the nature of the affective priming effect: Affective priming of naming responses. *Social Cognition, 20,* 227–256.

Spruyt, A., Hermans, D., Pandelaere, M., De Houwer, J., & Eelen, P. (2004). On the replicability of the affective priming effect in the pronunciation task. *Experimental Psychology, 51,* 109–115.

Storbeck, J., & Clore, G. L. (2007). On the interdependence of cognition and emotion. *Cognition and Emotion, 21*, 1212–1237.

Storbeck, J., & Robinson, M. D. (2004). Preferences and inferences in encoding visual objects: A systematic comparison of semantic and affective priming. *Personality and Social Psychology Bulletin, 30*, 81–93.

Storbeck, J., Robinson, M. D., & McCourt, M. E. (2006). Semantic processing precedes affect retrieval: The neurological case for cognitive primacy in visual processing. *Review of General Psychology, 10*, 41–55.

Strack, F., Martin, L. L., & Stepper, S. (1988). Inhibiting and facilitating conditions of the human smile: A nonobtrusive test of the facial feedback hypothesis. *Journal of Personality and Social Psychology, 54*, 768–777.

Tamir, M., Robinson, M. D., Clore, G. L., Martin, L. L., & Whitaker, D. (2004). Are we puppets on a string? The contextual meaning of unconscious expressive cues. *Personality and Social Psychology Bulletin, 30*, 237–249.

Teasdale, J. D. (1999). Multi-level theories of cognition–emotion relations. In T. Dalgleish & M. Power (Eds.), *Handbook of cognition and emotion* (pp. 665–682). Chichester, UK: Wiley.

Tomkins, S. S. (1984). Affect theory. In K. R. Scherer & P. Ekman (Eds.), *Approaches to emotion* (pp. 163–196). Hillsdale, NJ: Lawrence Erlbaum Associates, Inc.

Tye, M. (2003). A theory of phenomenal concepts. In O'Hear A. (Ed.), *Minds and persons* (pp. 91–106). Cambridge, UK: Cambridge University Press.

Wentura, D., Rothermund, K., & Bak, P. (2000). Automatic vigilance: The attention-grabbing power of approach and avoidance-related social information. *Journal of Personality and Social Psychology, 78*, 1024–1037.

Zajonc, R. B. (1980). Feeling and thinking: Preferences need no inferences. *American Psychologist, 3*, 151–175.

Zangrossi, H., & File, S. E. (1994). Habituation and generalization of phobic responses to cat odor. *Brain Research Bulletin, 33*, 189–194.

COGNITION AND EMOTION
2007, 21 (6), 1270–1296

Affect and action: Towards an event-coding account

Tristan Lavender and Bernhard Hommel

Leiden University, Leiden, The Netherlands

Viewing emotion from an evolutionary perspective, researchers have argued that simple responses to affective stimuli can be triggered without mediation of cognitive processes. Indeed, findings suggest that positively and negatively valenced stimuli trigger approach and avoidance movements automatically. However, affective stimulus–response compatibility phenomena share so many central characteristics with nonaffective stimulus–response compatibility phenomena that one may doubt whether the underlying mechanisms differ. We suggest an "affectively enriched" version of the theory of event coding (TEC) that is able to account for both affective and nonaffective compatibility, and that can account for the observation that both types of compatibility seem to be modulated by goals and intentions. Predictions from the model are tested in an experiment where participants carried out approach and avoidance responses to either the valence or the orientation of emotionally charged pictures. Under affective instruction the positive-approach/negative-avoid mapping yielded faster responses than the positive-avoid/negative-approach mapping, but no such effect was observed under spatial instruction. Conversely, spatial compatibility effects were obtained under spatial, but not under affective instruction. We conclude that affective and nonaffective compatibility effects reflect the same mechanism.

INTRODUCTION

In the early 1980s, Robert Zajonc (1980, 1984) launched a devastating attack on the then prevalent view in cognitive psychology that cognitive processes are a necessary precursor to affect. Zajonc drew attention to the effortless and inescapable nature of affective (overt or covert) responses, arguing that evaluations can be elicited automatically, without mediation of cognitive processes or conscious awareness (see Lazarus, 1982, 1984, for a cognitivistic reply). The idea that affective processes can be triggered automatically gains much in plausibility when viewed from an evolutionary perspective (LeDoux, 1996; Öhman, Flykt, & Lundqvist, 2000, Zajonc, 1980). The

Correspondence should be addressed to: Bernhard Hommel, Leiden University, Department of Psychology, Cognitive Psychology Unit, Wassenaarseweg 52, NL-2333 AK Leiden, The Netherlands. E-mail: hommel@fsw.leidenuniv.nl

© 2007 Psychology Press, an imprint of the Taylor & Francis Group, an Informa business
www.psypress.com/cogemotion   DOI: 10.1080/02699930701438152

evolutionary perspective on affect contends that humans are endowed with a primitive set of wired-in basic affective responses. Environmental stimuli that proved to be dangerous or valuable to our ancestors are systematically linked to certain behavioural responses (e.g., fleeing from a predator or approaching food).

Adopting an evolutionary perspective, neuroscientists such as LeDoux (1996) and Damasio (1999) have argued that emotions did not evolve as conscious feelings but, rather, as adaptive bodily responses controlled by the brain. According to LeDoux (1996), "the basic building blocks of emotions are neural systems that mediate behavioral interactions with the environment, particularly behaviors that take care of fundamental problems of survival" (p .125). Building on extensive research on fear conditioning, LeDoux (1996) proposed two separate neural pathways mediating between sensory stimuli and affective responses. First, there is a subcortical pathway that transmits emotional stimuli directly to the amygdala, a brain structure that regulates behavioural, autonomic and endocrine responses by way of connections to the brain stem. This "low road" bypasses higher cortical areas believed to be involved in cognition and consciousness. It is this processing route that allows us to withdraw our hand from fire and to shrink back from a snake long before we have realised that we are in danger. Operating in parallel with the subcortical pathway, there is a second pathway to the amygdala that passes through the higher cortical areas. Although (or because) this "high road" allows for much more fine-grained processing of stimuli than the subcortical pathway, it has one major drawback: it is much slower. The existence of a subcortical pathway allows the amygdala to detect environmental stimuli relevant to survival very rapidly. This constitutes a significant evolutionary advantage—woe to the person who has to engage in a fine-grained, time-consuming cognitive analysis when faced with a hungry predator.

Affective response priming

The essence of LeDoux's dual-pathway model is that humans are equipped to respond automatically to certain positively and negatively valenced stimuli before consciously knowing what these stimuli actually are. In a similar vein, Bradley and Lang (2000) suggest that emotions evolved from simple reflexive reactions. These primitive affective responses can be organised into two broad classes: approach movements towards positive, appetitive stimuli and avoidance movements away from negative, aversive stimuli (see also Bradley, Codispoti, Cuthbert, & Lang, 2001). An experiment conducted by Chen and Bargh (1999), Experiment 1; see also Solarz, 1960) suggested indeed that affective stimuli automatically activate corresponding action tendencies. Chen and Bargh instructed participants to evaluate a target word by moving a lever either toward their body or away from it, depending on the valence of the word. Participants were faster to respond to positively valenced words when pulling a lever toward them (which the authors interpreted as approach) than when pushing it away (avoidance). For negatively valenced words, the pattern was reversed: participants were faster to respond when pushing the lever than when pulling it. This suggests that positively valenced stimuli prime approach responses whereas negatively valenced stimuli prime avoidance responses.[1]

Even though Chen and Bargh's observations seemed to support the assumption of a fully automatic impact of affective stimuli on behaviour, later studies have suggested that this impact might be mediated by the intentions and goals of the acting individual. For instance, Klauer and Musch (2002) compared the effects of affective and nonaffective priming under evaluative and nonevaluative task goals. Affective decisions were primed by affective prime words and nonaffective decisions (e.g., colour judgements or letter-case comparisons) were primed by nonaffective primes (same colour or case). However, there was no evidence of affective priming across tasks, hence, nonaffective decisions were not primed by affective relations between the target word and a previous prime word. This observation suggests that the valence of words may not be processed as automatically as previously thought. One may object that processing words draws on rather higher cognitive processes, which are unlikely to tap into the fast and frugal low-level routes envisioned by Zajonc or LeDoux. Hence, verbal material may not be ideal for testing the automatic route from affect to behaviour. This argument also applies to a recent study by Markman and Brendl (2005). These authors demonstrated that people are faster to move positive words towards their name than away from their name, regardless of whether this response required a movement away from their body or towards their body. Even though this finding undermines Chen and Bargh's (1999) claim that positive and negative words activate particular movements automatically, the use of verbal material may well have biased the processing towards higher-level mechanisms. If the low route treats music from the Beatles and the Stones alike (to use an example of LeDoux, 1996), there is little reason to believe that it can discriminate between displays of the words "good" and "bad". Hence, the available evidence points to a critical role of goals and intentions, but the stimulus material used may have been inappropriate to allow for a fair test of the automaticity hypothesis.

---

[1] While some authors interpret stimulus–response mapping effects as reported by Chen and Bargh (1999) in terms of response conflict (Klinger, Burton, & Pitts, 2000), others have challenged this interpretation (Neumann, Förster, & Strack, 2003). We will get back to this issue below and suggest a solution to this apparent disagreement.

Better suited than words would seem stimuli with high ecological significance, such as human faces. Consistent with this reasoning, Rotteveel and Phaf (2004) presented subjects with facial expressions of positive and negative emotions and had them respond to either the valence of the expressed emotion (evaluative goal) or to the gender of the depicted person (nonevaluative goal) by flexing or extending their arms. As in studies with verbal material, response priming was found under the evaluative goal (where positive and negative emotions primed arm flexions and extensions, respectively) but not under the nonevaluative goal. However, even though this is encouraging, faces may not be ideal stimuli either. Indeed, while they are certainly of high ecological significance, it makes little evolutionary sense to approach or avoid the faces expressing particular emotions, rather than the events these emotions refer to. If so, it seems unlikely that dedicated processing routes developed for the fast translation of face information into manual action.

To summarise, preliminary evidence suggests that affective stimuli may prime approach and avoidance tendencies but that these priming effects might be less automatic than originally thought. However, it remains to be seen whether intentional modulation of affect–response coupling can be demonstrated with stimuli that are more plausibly related to approach and avoidance tendencies than those used hitherto.

Multiple routes in affective and nonaffective processing

Zajonc (1980), LeDoux (1996) and others have treated the processing of affective information as fundamentally different from the processing of other, nonaffective information, such as shape, colour, or location. On the one hand, this distinction might be taken to have some intuitive plausibility, as the dangerousness of a snake seems so much more important than whether it is green or yellow, apart from the fact that dangerousness just feels so different from green. On the other hand, however, it is interesting to realise that the models of affective and nonaffective processing share quite a number of architectural features. In particular, the way researchers have characterised the relation between affect and action closely resembles the way (non-affective) perception and action have been related in recent approaches (see Prinz & Hommel, 2002, for an overview). Let us consider the three most pertinent similarities.

First, the distinction between a slow, consciously and/or intentionally mediated processing stream that takes care of the controlled translation of stimulus information into appropriate actions and a fast (more or less) unmediated processing stream that activates response tendencies linked to, or congruent with, the present stimulus is not restricted to models of affective processing (such as those of Damasio, 1994; LeDoux, 1996;

Zajonc, 1980) but commonplace in approaches of perception–action coupling (e.g., De Jong, Liang, & Lauber, 1994; Hommel, 1993a; Kornblum, Hasbroucq, & Osman, 1990; Milner & Goodale, 1995; see Hommel, 2000, for an overview). As in affective theories, cognitive theories assume that the latter processing stream is more stimulus dependent and more difficult to control than the former.

Second, with respect to both affective and nonaffective processing, the available evidence suggests that the fast routes are (1) automatic in the sense that they process information that is not necessary for performing the task at hand but at the same time (2) intentional in the sense that they seem to be enabled by the current task goal. As indicated earlier, one may argue that the stimulus material used up to now does not provide a fair test of the automaticity hypothesis, but there are a number of preliminary indications that the fast route from affect to action is modulated by goals. A good example for the nonaffective processing domain is the Simon effect (Simon, 1969). This effect is observed if people give spatial responses to a nonspatial feature of a stimulus that varies randomly in location. For instance, assume that left and right key presses are carried out in response to the red or green colour of a stimulus that appears on the left or right of a display. Even though stimulus location is irrelevant to the task, subjects are commonly faster if stimulus and response spatially correspond, hence, if the stimulus appears on the side where the correct response key is located. Almost all models assume that stimulus location automatically primes the spatially corresponding response, which is beneficial if this is the correct response but interfering if this response is incorrect. Consistent with this assumption, presenting a stimulus has been demonstrated to activate the corresponding response up to the level of an (electrophysiologically measured) lateralised readiness potential, even if (in noncorresponding trials) this potential is later replaced by the potential of the actually correct response (Sommer, Leuthold, & Hermanutz, 1993). Even though this may be taken to demonstrate a strong form of automaticity, the priming of the corresponding response is only observed if subjects have implemented the instructed stimulus–response rules and are ready to go, but not if they are presented with a lateralised stimulus while awaiting the presentation of these rules (Valle-Inclán & Redondo, 1998). These observations seem to fit with the claims of Klauer and Musch (2002), Rotteveel and Phaf (2004), and Markman and Brendl (2005), that "automatic" stimulus–response translation is not independent of intentions. Thus, studies of both affective and nonaffective processing suggest that intentional processes set the stage for automatic stimulus–response translation (Bargh, 1989): The translation as such is automatic, but this automaticity is achieved only by virtue of the intentional implementation of the relevant task set—a kind of cognitively prepared reflex (Hommel, 2000).

Third, affective and nonaffective codes have been attributed very similar roles in decision making and action control (Hommel & Elsner, in press). According to the ideomotor principle developed by Lotze (1852), James (1890), and others (see Stock & Stock, 2004, for an overview), actions are represented by codes of their anticipated effects. Considering the human brain's preference for coding events in a distributed, feature-based fashion, this means that action plans are cognitively represented in terms of distributed codes of their perceived features (Hommel, 1997, 2006). The idea is that movement patterns and the perceptual (i.e., re-afferent) effects it produces are integrated and stored automatically as an infant develops or an adult gains expertise. For instance, an infant may at first grasp an object by accident but then store the grasping movement together with the feel and sight of the object. If it later wants to grasp the object again, it only needs to "think of" the intended action effect (the haptic feeling of the grasped object, say) and thereby primes the now associated movement pattern (Elsner & Hommel, 2001). This means that the perceptual representation of the action effect has now become a retrieval cue for the action and thus can be used to select the currently most appropriate or effective action, that is, the action effect that matches the action goal best. The same function has been attributed to affective codes only recently by Damasio (1994). He claims that the affective consequences of actions are stored together with the actions that produced them. This renders the representations of these consequences "somatic markers" of the action, so that actions can be selected on the basis of what affective state they are likely to create. Obviously, this is a mere extension of Jamesian ideomotor theorising, and one may indeed ask whether there is any logical or conceptual reason to separate perceptual and affective action effects.

In sum, recent research on human affect–action relationships leads to very similar conclusions as research on perception–action coupling. We suggest that this is no coincidence and more surprising from the common phenomenological point of view (focusing on perceptual vs. affective experience) than from an evolutionary approach. That is, even though perceptual experiences may "feel" very different from affective experiences, the processes underlying these experiences may be comparable. Indeed, the brain architectures for processing perceptual stimuli and affective stimuli are likely to have emerged from the same selection pressure: (1) in both cases general information about a new event (such as an approaching animal) needs to be available very quickly, so that the organism can decide in time whether approach or avoidance is more appropriate; this requires information about both affective significance (e.g., does the animal represent a threat?) and perceivable action implications or affordances (where can I go to approach or escape it?); (2) in both cases the information can be coarse, as it is only the general class of action that needs to be decided upon very quickly—more subtle behavioural strategies (e.g., in which way to approach) can take more time; (3) what counts in both cases is overt action rather than mental experience (escaping a threat is more important for survival than feeling bad), which suggests that, if there is automatic processing, it should access action control directly.

All these shared processing characteristics (fast, coarse, and action related) are important only for a very basic form of survival, however, and may well become partly dysfunctional in more socially organised societies and artificial environments. Accordingly, what is needed is another type of information processing, one that considers more subtle, context-dependent attributes (e.g., is this snake real or made of rubber?) and that allows for preplanning actions rather than relying on external stimuli. Again, however, this selection pressure towards another, more "reflecting" type of processing should affect perceptual and affective stimuli in comparable ways. Hence, from an evolutionary approach developing a dual-route processing architecture makes sense for both affective and nonaffective stimuli.

Affect as feature: An event-coding approach

If it is true that the affective coding of events and actions follows more or less the same principles as the nonaffective coding of perceptual and action events, it should be possible to account for affective and nonaffective stimulus–response interactions in comparable ways. Here we suggest extending the currently probably most comprehensive representational theory of perception and action, the theory of event coding (TEC; Hommel, Müsseler, Aschersleben, & Prinz, 2001), to the processing of affective events. We admit that our theorising is unlikely to account for the rich phenomenal flavour of true emotions, but we do think that it explains how the affective valence of events is computed and how affective codings of stimuli and responses interact to produce mapping effects of the type reported by Chen and Bargh (1999), Markman and Brendl (2005) and others.

TEC assumes that all stimuli and responses are coded in terms of their perceivable features, and that these features are associated with the motor patterns producing them. The basic building blocks of TEC thus consist of sensorimotor units, that can be further integrated into "event files" (Hommel, 1998). For instance, carrying out a speeded key press with the index finger of the right hand may lead to the coding of this action in terms of the features <right>, <right hand>, <index finger>, <fast>, and so on, with all these features being connected to the motor pattern moving the finger. If a stimulus is processed, this would also activate all the codes representing this stimulus' features, such as <red>, <circular>, <fruit>, etc., in the case of a cherry. This provides a natural explanation for the Simon effect: If a stimulus appears on the right, it activates, among other things, the code <right>, which is also shared by one of the possible responses. In other words, processing the stimulus leads to the priming (i.e., partial activation) of any other stimulus and response it shares features with. If this happens to include the correct response, which is true for corresponding trials, it can be carried out faster but if the incorrect response is primed, response conflict is created, the solution of which prolongs the eventual selection of the correct response (Hommel, 1997).

Even though TEC has been developed to account for all sorts of interactions between nonaffective stimulus and response events, its ideomotor heritage makes it easy to extend it to affective coding. According to ideomotor theorising a particular action is cognitively represented by codes that refer to how it feels to carry out that action, that is, to whatever perceptual experiences one has while performing it. Perceptual experiences by no means exclude experiences relating to the affective value of action-produced events. Indeed, James' (1884) own theory of emotion claims that emotions derive from the perceptual experiences one has while acting them out. Even though James' approach has often been interpreted as "peripheral" (cf. Cornelius, 1996)—only because it considers visceral and bodily processes as possible (peripheral) *sources* of affective experiences—close reading reveals that James is more concerned with the (central) *perception* of these processes rather than the processes themselves (see Barbalet, 1999; Ellsworth, 1994). Along these lines, an approach action might be represented not only by the kinaesthetic feeling of one's hand moving forward, the visual perception that it is the right hand and that it reaches towards an object, and the tactile experience when contact with the object is being made, but also by the positive feeling one has when processing the reward that commonly follows approach actions. This "feeling" is just another perception coded by a particular cell assembly, and there is no reason why this particular code (a "somatic marker" in the sense of Damasio, 1994) should not become part of the action's long-term representation.

Figure 1 shows how ideomotor theorising along the lines of TEC works in general and how it extends to affective codes (cf. Eder & Klauer, 2007 this issue). Let us begin with spatial compatibility, such as is operative in the Simon effect. Assume you are responding to a positively valenced picture that is rotated to the right by performing an approach movement with your right hand. The depicted little rabbit is coded as <white>, <furry>, and <small>, among other things. Given the picture's orientation the stimulus will also be coded as <right> and, given the heart-warming content, as positive (depicted as a smiley). The approach action might be coded as <towards>, as carried out by the <right hand>, which is a <body part>. Assuming hand-relative spatial coding (an issue we will get back to in a moment), the movement will also be coded as <right> and, given the frequent positive experience after carrying out approach movements, as positive. As shown in the figure, this stimulus–response combination creates

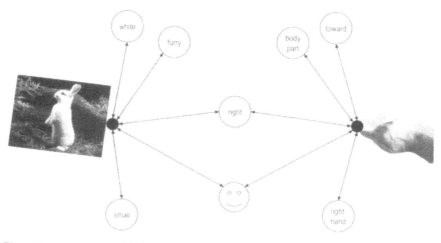

Figure 1. A cartoon model demonstrating how feature overlap between stimulus and response representations can mediate stimulus-induced response priming. The example shows a positively valenced, rightward rotated stimulus and a forward (approach) movement with the right hand. The smiley represents positive affect.

overlap with respect to two features: a spatial feature and the "affective" feature. Accordingly, processing the picture will prime the action in two ways, which should lead to benefit in comparison to a picture with negative valence and/or a left orientation. Along these lines, we cannot only account for Simon-type or other spatial or nonspatial stimulus–response compatibility effects, we can also account for the findings of Chen and Bargh (1999) and others.

Note that TEC attributes performance benefits and costs to conflict between cognitive representations of actions but not to interactions at the motor level. This has several theoretical advantages. First, it can explain why conflict can arise in tasks that comprise of only one response alternative (as in Chen & Bargh's Experiment 2). As Neumann, Förster, and Strack (2003) have argued, response conflict at a motor level is not plausible to account for stimulus–response interactions in such tasks. However, even if an approach action is the only alternative in a given task, its features may still overlap with the features of the stimulus and thus can be primed as a consequence of that. Indeed, spatial stimulus–response compatibility effects have also been demonstrated with simple go responses and accounted for in terms of feature overlap (Hommel, 1996a).

Second, referring to cognitive response representations instead of the response's physical realisation allows for considering top-down influences on these representations, that is, for interpretation. Consider, for instance, Chen and Bargh's (1999) definition of approach and avoidance as lever pulling and pushing, respectively. Pulling a lever involves flexing one's arm, which has been interpreted as typical for avoidance movements by other authors (Neumann et al., 2003). Hence, arm movements as such are ambiguous behavioural measures, since they can be defined either relative to the body of the actor or relative to an external object (cf. Markman & Brendl, 2005). Only the cognitive embedding into a particular frame of reference determines whether a given muscle movement is coded as approach or avoidance. Obviously, the same is true for spatial coding, which may refer to retinal, egocentric, allocentric, object- or effector-relative coding (cf. Hommel & Lippa, 1995).

Third, allowing for top-down influences on event representations also makes it easier to understand how action goals may modulate affective and nonaffective stimulus–response compatibility. TEC holds that perceiving a stimulus and planning an action does not involve all feature codes associated with that event to the same degree but mainly those codes that are related to the current action goal. Hence, the contribution of feature codes is "intentionally weighted" (Hommel et al., 2001). Intentional weighting is necessary to account for intentional effects, as demonstrated by Hommel (1993b). In his Simon study, subjects responded to the pitch of lateralised tones by pressing a left or right key. Each key flashed a light on the opposite side, that is, the left key flashed a light on the right side and the right key a light on the left side. When subjects were given a standard, key-related instruction (press left key to low pitch and right key to high pitch), a standard Simon effect was obtained: Subjects were faster if tone and key spatially corresponded. However, when subjects were instructed in terms of the visual action effects (flash right light to low pitch and left light to high pitch), the Simon effect completely reversed: Now subjects were faster if tone and key did not correspond! This means that the instruction must have changed the way the actions were cognitively represented. Along the lines of TEC, one can assume that each action was coded in terms of at least two opposite spatial codes: for instance, the left key press as <left>, because of the left hand and the left key involved, *and* as <right>, as it produced a light on the right. Receiving a key-related instruction was likely to weight the key-related codes more strongly, so that the two actions were more strongly represented in terms of key locations. In contrast, receiving a light-related instruction must have weighted light-related codes more strongly, so that the actions were coded in terms of light locations. In the former case, left key presses were thus primed by left stimuli but in the latter case the same left stimuli primed right key presses (Hommel, 1993b, 1996b). Along the same lines, it is easy to account for the stronger impact of features from goal-related stimulus dimensions as observed by Klauer and Musch (2002), Rotteveel and Phaf (2004), and others. Note that according to TEC, the activation of task-irrelevant codes, and thus action priming, is both automatic and modulated by task goals at the same time.

To summarise, we suggest modelling affective and nonaffective stimulus–response compatibility effects in comparable ways and consider TEC a useful framework for that purpose. To further explore whether and how TEC-inspired theorising can be applied to affective and nonaffective compatibility, and to the impact of action goals on the behavioural expression of compatibility, we carried out a study that directly compared these two types of effects. To avoid biasing our task towards higher cognitive processes, we used nonverbal stimuli of high ecological relevance: pictures of attracting and threatening animals and scenes.

Experimental design and hypotheses

To investigate the goal-dependency of affectively and nonaffectively induced response priming, we asked participants to respond as quickly as possible to pictures on a computer screen by moving a little doll either toward the screen (approach) or away from the screen (avoidance). Note that approach movements as we defined them required arm extensions, while avoidance movements required arm flexions. This allowed us to pit hypothetical biologically hardwired stimulus–response tendencies (which would predict faster extensions to negative stimuli and faster flexions to positive stimuli) against cognitively penetrated, goal-related tendencies (which would predict the opposite outcome)—similar to the rationale of Markman and Brendl (2005). In the following, our terminology will be based on the actions' goals and thus consider the combinations of positive stimuli and movements towards the screen and of negative stimuli and movements away from the screen as *compatible*. As approach movements require arm extensions and the avoidance movements arm flexions, our terminology is exactly opposite to that used by Chen and Bargh (1999) and Rotteveel and Phaf (2004). This means that finding a *negative* compatibility effect would replicate previous findings (and suggest a strong role of muscle movements), whereas finding a *positive* compatibility effect would imply a non-replication of previous findings (and suggest a strong role for cognitive interpretations).

Each stimulus picture had either a positive or a negative valence and was rotated slightly either to the left or to the right. Half of the participants were asked to judge the affective valence of each picture (*affective instruction*), whereas the other half were asked to judge the spatial orientation of each picture (*spatial instruction*). In the affective instruction condition, the *affective mapping* varied between subjects: half of the subjects were instructed to make an approach movement in response to a positive picture and an avoidance movement in response to a negative picture; for the other half, instructions were reversed. As sketched in Figure 2, approach

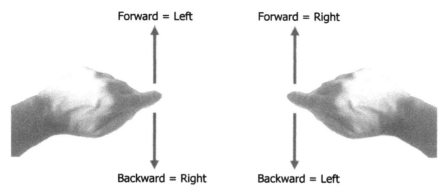

Forward = Left   Forward = Right

Backward = Right   Backward = Left

Figure 2.   Illustration of hand-relative coding for the left and right hand.

movements should be associated with a <positive> feature code (indicated by the smiley), while avoidance movements should be associated with a <negative> code. Positive codes should overlap with those of the positive pictures and negative codes should overlap with those of negative pictures, so that we expected faster responses for the positive-approach/negative-avoid mapping than for the positive-avoid/negative-approach mapping.

In the spatial instruction condition, the *spatial mapping* varied between subjects: half of the subjects were asked to make an approach movement in response to a right-oriented picture and an avoidance movement in response to a left-oriented picture; for the other half, instructions were reversed. This manipulation was intended to introduce spatial stimulus–response compatibility relations. Bauer and Miller (1982) have shown that, for movements with the left hand, the mapping of forward movements upon left stimuli and backward movements upon right stimuli is preferred over the forward-right/backward-left mapping, whereas movements with the right hand are associated with the opposite preference. In other words, the left hand prefers the left-forward (approach)/right-backward (avoidance) mapping while the right hand prefers the right-forward (approach)/left-backward (avoidance) mapping. According to Lippa (1996), this interaction could be due to the effector-relative coding of movements, hence, for coding relative to the intrinsic hand axis, especially if the hands are held in an angle to the body axis. For the left hand, moving forward implies a hand- or wrist-relative displacement to the left and moving backward a displacement to the right (see Figure 3). If so, the cognitive representation of a forward (approach) movement with the left hand shares a spatial feature with left stimuli and the representation of a backward (avoidance) movement with the left hand a spatial feature with right stimuli. The opposite is true for right-hand actions: moving forward implies a displacement to the hand-relative right (see Figure 2) and moving backward a displacement to the left.

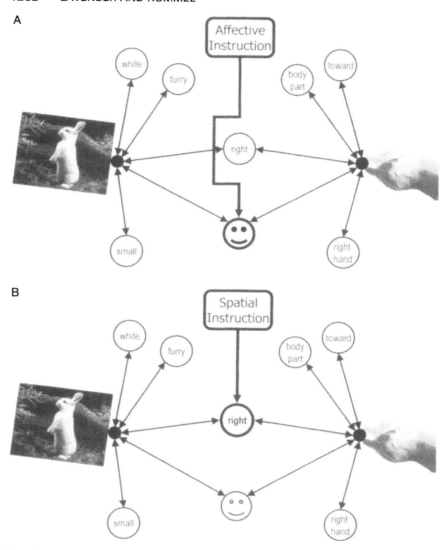

Figure 3. An adaptation of Figure 1 to demonstrate the impact of task relevance (instruction) on the "intentional weighting" of task-related features. (A) Affective instructions lead to a stronger weighting of affective codes. (B) Spatial instructions lead to a stronger weighting of spatial codes (for simplicity restricted to the <right> code).

Feature overlap between stimuli and responses should induce response priming, so that the interaction between hand and stimulus-movement mapping is likely to be just another example of a general "overlap = compatibility" principle. In the present study, we measured this hand-relative stimulus–response compatibility effect by having participants carry out their responses with the left or the right hand, in different blocks. This allowed us to compare effects of affective and spatial stimulus–response compatibility with exactly the same stimuli and responses by varying the task instructions only.

Given the findings of previous experiments, we expected the task goal to determine how much weight each feature dimension would receive, which again should affect the size of the compatibility effect each dimension would create. As sketched in Figure 2, we expected affective instructions to weight affective features more strongly, so that affective feature overlap should show a strong compatibility effect (i.e., a main effect of affective stimulus–response mapping). Likewise, we expected that spatial instructions would weight spatial features more strongly, thus creating a strong spatial compatibility effect (i.e., an interaction of spatial stimulus–response mapping and response hand). These effects would demonstrate that our manipulations worked and that stimulus–response relations matter if they are task relevant. However, we were also interested to see whether task-irrelevant feature dimensions would create stimulus–response compatibility effects, which would point to a strong form of automaticity. To test these effects, we varied stimulus valence and stimulus orientation under both instruction conditions.

In the affective instruction condition, this meant that some stimuli were spatially response compatible (left-oriented stimuli for approach movements with the left and avoidance movements with the right hand; right-oriented stimuli for avoidance movements with the left and approach movements with the right hand) and others were spatially response incompatible. Given that only stimulus valence was relevant and that valence and orientation varied independently, finding a substantial interaction between stimulus orientation, movement, and hand (i.e., a spatial compatibility effect) would point to automatic response activation induced by spatial stimulus attributes. In the spatial instruction condition, irrelevant affective stimulus–response compatibility was manipulated along the same lines. Given that stimulus valence varied randomly, some stimuli were affectively response compatible (positive stimuli for approach movements and negative stimuli for avoidance movements, irrespective of the hand) and others were affectively response incompatible. Finding a substantial interaction between stimulus valence and movement would point to automatic response activation induced by affective stimulus attributes.

To summarise, we varied relevant affective and spatial stimulus–response compatibility *between* subjects by manipulating the task instruction and the stimulus–response mapping, that is, by making either stimulus valence or stimulus orientation task relevant. We also varied irrelevant affective and spatial stimulus–response compatibility *within* subjects by randomly varying spatial compatibility relations in the affective task and affective compatibility relations in the spatial task. Effects of the between-subjects manipulation of mapping were intended to tap into voluntary, goal-related stimulus–response translation, whereas effects of the within-subjects manipulation of compatibility relations were intended to tap into automatic response priming.

METHOD

Participants

Fifty-six students (40 females, 16 males) volunteered on an informed-consent basis to participate in the experiment, either for partial fulfilment of course requirements or in exchange for a monetary reward. All participants had normal or corrected-to-normal vision, and were unaware of the purpose of the experiment. Their age ranged from 17 to 38 years with a mean of 21 years. All but one participant were right-handed.

Materials and apparatus

Pictures were selected from the International Affective Picture System (IAPS) developed by Lang and colleagues at the University of Florida (Lang, Bradley, & Cuthbert, 1996). Ten IAPS pictures depicting pleasant objects or events were used and 10 IAPS pictures depicting unpleasant objects or events. Digitalised versions of the IAPS pictures (117 × 84 mm) were displayed on a VGA monitor in a degraded colour palette (256 colours). All pictures were rotated slightly, either clockwise (right-oriented pictures) or counter clockwise (left-oriented pictures).[2]

Three square metal plates (10 × 10 cm) were positioned in front of the computer screen, as shown in Figure 4. Each plate had a tiny light-emitting diode (LED) attached to its upper-left corner. The LED (light bulb, LB) sent a light beam to the lower right corner, where a small light sensor (LS) was attached to the plate. When an object was placed in the middle of the plate, the beam was blocked, so that activation of the sensor served to indicate the presence or absence of an object on the plate.

At the beginning of each trial, a little doll was positioned on the middle plate, which is labelled "home plate" in Figure 4. The doll was faced towards the computer screen. Responses were made by moving the doll either

---

[2] Our manipulation of the spatial stimulus feature through orientation deviates from previous studies, where stimulus location was varied (e.g., Bauer & Miller, 1982). However, stimuli presented left and right from fixation are processed by different cortical hemispheres, which given the evidence of lateralised emotional systems (e.g., Davidson, 1995) might lead to unforeseeable interactions between stimulus location and affective processing.

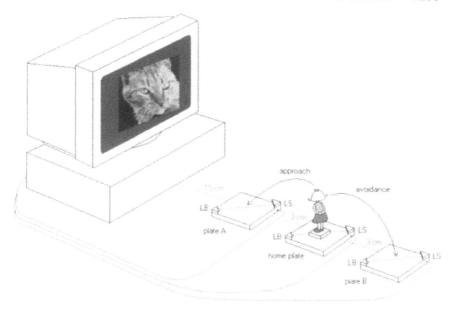

Figure 4.   Equipment used to measure approach and avoidance movements.

forward onto the plate that was nearer to the computer screen (approach movement) or backwards onto the plate that was farther away from the screen (avoidance movement). Picking up the doll unblocked the light beam and triggered the measurement of reaction time (RT) from stimulus presentation. Placing the doll onto one of the other plates blocked the corresponding light beam, which triggered the measurement of movement time (MT) and completed the trial.

Procedure

Participants were seated in front of the computer screen with the three plates aligned with their sagittal body plane. Participants were assigned randomly to one of the four experimental conditions, each with its own response instructions. In all conditions, participants were instructed to pick up the doll as quickly as possible when a picture appeared on the screen and move it onto the appropriate target plate. Each picture was preceded by a small fixation cross for 1200 ms, which allowed participants to prepare a response by taking hold of the doll (without picking it up already). The picture appeared at the centre of the screen after a blank interval of 800 ms and remained visible until the response was completed (that is, until the doll was displaced onto one of the other plates). At the end of each trial, participants were asked to return the doll to the home plate. The experimenter initiated a new trial by pressing the space bar on a keyboard that was interfaced with the computer.

The experiment consisted of 80 trials, divided into 2 blocks of 40 trials. In one of the two blocks, participants were asked to displace the doll with their right hand, and in the other block, with their left hand. Block order was balanced across participants. Each block was preceded by 6 practice trials. Each of the 20 pictures selected from the IAPS (of which 10 negative and 10 positive) was presented 4 times, twice with a left orientation and twice with a right orientation. The order of stimulus pictures was randomised within each block.

After the final trial, participants were handed a booklet containing coloured printouts of the 20 pictures used in the experiment, and were asked to evaluate them on a 9-category Likert scale (-4 = very negative/unpleasant; 0 = neutral; $+4$ = very positive/pleasant).[3] The results are provided in the Appendix.

RESULTS AND DISCUSSION

Because possible effects of affective and spatial compatibility may be distributed over RT and MT data (i.e., people may lift the doll before having decided where to put it), total response time ($TT = RT + MT$) was chosen as the primary measure. Mean TTs and percentages of errors (PEs) were calculated as a function of affective mapping or compatibility relation (positive-approach/negative-avoid vs. positive-avoid/negative-approach), spatial mapping or compatibility relation (left-approach/right-avoid vs. left-avoid/right-approach) and response hand (left vs. right). A first omnibus analysis showed that the two instruction groups were roughly comparable, $F(1, 54) = 1.81$, $p = .18$. To test our hypotheses, separate analyses were conducted for the affective and the spatial instruction condition.

Affective instruction

Total response times. Trials on which an incorrect response was given (1.8%) and trials on which at least one of the response measures (RT, MT, and/or TT) qualified as outliers with $p < .001$ (1.6%) were excluded from analysis. In total, then, 3.4% of trials were excluded. TTs were analysed by means of a mixed $2 \times 2 \times 2$ ANOVA with Affective Mapping (positive-approach/negative-avoid vs. positive-avoid/negative-approach) as between-subjects factor, and Spatial Stimulus–Response Relation

---

[3] The IAPS manual (Lang, Bradley, & Cuthbert, 1996) lists affective ratings for all pictures, but since we used a degraded colour palette we deemed it appropriate to let participants evaluate the degraded IAPS pictures (in random order).

(left-approach/right-avoid vs. left-avoid/right-approach) and Response Hand (left vs. right) as within-subjects factors.

As expected, the ANOVA revealed a main effect of affective mapping, $F(1, 26) = 5.27$, $p < .05$, see Figure 5A: The (presumably compatible) positive-approach/negative-avoid mapping ($M = 824$ ms, $SE = 33$ ms) yielded shorter TTs than the (presumably incompatible) positive-avoid/negative-approach mapping ($M = 977$ ms, $SE = 58$ ms). Note that the pattern of this effect points to a cognitively based compatibility effect: positive pictures facilitated approach actions carried out by extending the arm while negative pictures facilitated avoidance actions carried out by flexing the arm. With regard to the arm movements, this is the exact opposite of what Chen and Bargh (1999) and Rotteveel and Phaf (2004) observed. As is obvious from Figure 5B, main effects of the spatial stimulus–response relation, $F(1, 26) = 2.52$, $p = .12$, and response hand, $F(1, 26) = 0.99$, $p = .33$, as well as their interaction, $F(1, 26) = 0.44$, $p = .51$, failed to reach significance.

We also assessed whether stimulus valence and/or the degree of valence moderated the effect of affective mapping. Based on a median split of the mean affective ratings (see Appendix), we classified the valence of stimulus pictures as either moderate or strong. We then conducted an additional 2 × 2 × 2 ANOVA with Affective Mapping as between-subjects factor, and Valence (positive vs. negative) and Valence Strength (moderate vs. strong) as within-subjects factors. This analysis showed that response times were shorter for negative pictures ($M = 888$ ms, $SE = 33$ ms) than for positive

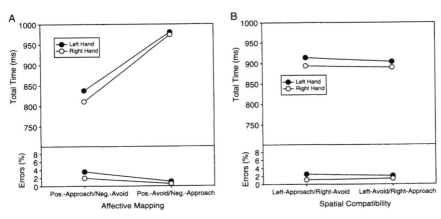

Figure 5. (A) Mean TTs (in ms) and PEs (in%) in the affective instruction mode condition as a function of affective mapping (positive-approach/negative-avoid vs. positive-avoid/negative-approach) and response hand (left vs. right). (B) Mean TTs (in ms) and PEs (in%) in the affective instruction mode condition as a function of spatial compatibility (left-approach/right-avoid vs. left-avoid/right-approach) and response hand (left vs. right).

pictures ($M = 913$ ms, $SE = 34$ ms), $F(1, 26) = 9.79$, $p < .01$. This finding is consistent with other studies showing a greater sensitivity toward negative stimuli (see Taylor, 1991, for an overview). However, as our stimulus material was not controlled for its impact on arousal, it may also be that negative stimuli were more arousing (Robinson, Storbeck, Meier, & Kirkeby, 2004). The ANOVA also revealed an interaction effect of affective mapping and valence, $F(1, 26) = 9.13$, $p < .01$, indicating that the effect of affective mapping was larger for positive pictures ($M = 825$ ms, $SE = 48$ ms vs. $M = 1002$ ms, $SE = 48$ ms) than for negative pictures ($M = 824$ ms, $SE = 47$ ms vs. $M = 953$ ms, $SE = 47$ ms). Valence strength did not moderate the effect of affective mapping.

Errors. Only the main effect of affective mapping approached significance, $F(1, 26) = 3.47$, $p < .08$, indicating that responses with the positive-approach/negative-avoid mapping ($M = 2.8\%$, $SE = 1.0\%$) were more error prone than responses with the positive-avoid/negative-approach mapping ($M = 0.8\%$, $SE = 0.4\%$). As this effect points in the opposite direction as the TT effect, we checked whether a speed–accuracy trade-off may be involved. The correlation between TTs and error rates was indeed negative, $r = -.29$, but not particularly pronounced and not reliable, $p = .13$.

Spatial instruction

Total response times. Trials on which an incorrect response was given (3.3%) and trials on which at least one of the response measures (RT, MT, and/or TT) qualified as outliers with $p < .001$ (2.4%) were excluded from analysis. In total, then, 5.7% of trials were excluded. A mixed $2 \times 2 \times 2$ ANOVA with Spatial Mapping (left-approach/right-avoid vs. left-avoid/right-approach) as between-subjects factor, and Affective Compatibility (positive-approach/negative-avoid vs. positive-avoid/negative-approach) and Response Hand (left vs. right) as within-subjects factors was conducted on the TT data.

The ANOVA revealed that response times were shorter for the left-approach/right-avoid mapping ($M = 770$ ms, $SE = 35$ ms) than for the left-avoid/right-approach mapping ($M = 912$ ms, $SE = 35$ ms), $F(1, 26) = 9.40$, $p < .01$. More importantly, the interaction effect of spatial mapping and response hand was highly significant, $F(1, 26) = 9.79$, $p < .01$. As shown in Figure 6A, the left-approach/right-avoid mapping was particularly beneficial for the left hand, whereas the left-avoid/right-approach mapping benefited the right hand. Note that due to the main effect of mapping, the interaction with hand did not yield a symmetric pattern.[4] A comparable asymmetry has

---

[4] Another factor that is likely to contribute to the asymmetry is the slight (numerical, but not statistically significant) advantage for the right hand, which is visible in all reaction-time graphs.

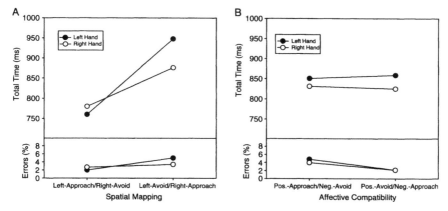

Figure 6. (A) Mean TTs (in ms) and PEs (in%) in the spatial instruction mode condition as a function of spatial mapping (left-approach/right-avoid vs. left-avoid/right-approach) and response hand (left vs. right). (B) Mean TTs (in ms) and PEs (in%) in the spatial instruction mode condition as a function of affective compatibility (positive-approach/negative-avoid vs. positive-avoid/negative-approach) and response hand (left vs. right).

been observed in the original study of Bauer and Miller (1982). However, given that Lippa (1996) found symmetric effects and Weeks and Proctor (1990) reported an overall benefit for the left-avoid/right-approach mapping, the main effect of spatial mapping should be interpreted with caution, the more so as our present manipulation of the spatial stimulus feature (i.e., by means of stimulus orientation) differs from previous manipulations (where stimulus location was varied). What is important, however, is that the interaction between mapping and hand fully replicated previous findings (Bauer & Miller, 1982; Lippa, 1996) and thus demonstrates that the manipulation of spatial stimulus–response compatibility had worked as expected. As obvious from Figure 6B, the manipulation of affective stimulus–response relation did not yield any effect ($F < 1$).

Errors. The interaction of spatial mapping and response hand approached significance, $F(1, 26) = 3.13$, $p < .09$, and the result pattern was comparable to that found in the TTs. The main effect of affective relation also approached significance, $F(1, 26) = 3.01$, $p < .10$. As in the affective task, the pattern was opposite to that obtained in the TTs of the affective task, indicating that responses with the positive-approach/ negative-avoid mapping ($M = 4.4\%$, $SE = 1.1\%$) were *more* error prone than responses with the positive-avoid/negative-approach mapping ($M = 2.1\%$, $SE = 0.7\%$). However, given that the correlation between TTs and error rates was positive, $r = .18$, and far from significance, $p = .37$, a speed–accuracy trade-off does not seem to be involved.

GENERAL DISCUSSION

The empirical outcome of our study is consistent with some, but not all, of the previous findings on affect–action compatibility. First, we were able to replicate previous observations that manual approach and avoidance reactions interact with the valence of visual stimuli. Some have attributed such interactions to the facilitation of arm flexions and extensions by positive and negative stimuli, respectively (Chen & Bargh, 1999; Rotteveel & Phaf, 2004), suggesting that it is the arm movement rather than its purpose that matters for the direction of compatibility effects. This assumption, however, is inconsistent with our results, which show the exact opposite outcome pattern of that obtained by Chen and Bargh (1999) and Rotteveel and Phaf (2004): Positive stimuli facilitated arm extensions while negative stimuli facilitated arm flexions. This observation supports the claim of Markman and Brendl (2005), that it is the cognitive representation of an action that matters for compatibility effects but not its physical realisation. At the same time, it also questions the strong anti-cognitivist view of Zajonc (1980) and does not seem to fit with LeDoux's (1996) assumption of an evolutionary old, hardwired route from affect action—at least to the degree that these accounts are taken to speak to the affect–action compatibility effects under investigation.

A second interesting observation is that no effect of affective compatibility occurred in participants who focused on the spatial orientation of pictures, supporting the conclusion of Klauer and Muscher (2002) and Rotteveel and Phaf (2004) that valence-induced priming of approach and avoidance tendencies is not sufficiently automatic to operate in the absence of an affective evaluation goal. Given that one may doubt that Klauer and Muscher's verbal material and the faces used by Rotteveel and Phaf allowed for tapping into phylogenetically old mechanisms that are thought to be triggered by the visual features of rewarding and threatening events (LeDoux, 1996), confirming these previous findings with arguably more appropriate stimuli provides important converging evidence. That is, direct affective visuo-motor links either do not exist or are more cognitively mediated than previously held.

Not only did we find affective compatibility to be restricted to affective task goals, but we also saw a comparable result pattern for nonaffective compatibility: Spatial compatibility had a strong impact under spatial instruction but not under affective instruction. This mirror-symmetric pattern replicates the observation of Klauer and Musch (2002) and extends it to nonverbal material. Both affective and nonaffective stimulus–response compatibility thus seem to be much stronger if the stimulus dimension on which stimulus and response features overlap is task relevant. Even though in the present study, compatibility was actually *only* obtained for the task-relevant dimension, we believe that contributions from relevant and irrelevant dimensions may sometimes differ more quantitatively than qualitatively—mainly because task relevance is often not a dichotomous variable.

Consider the standard Simon effect: It is produced by overlap between stimulus location and response location, even though stimulus location is nominally irrelevant to the task. However, while it is true that a Simon task can logically be performed without considering stimulus location, people need to attend to the location to process the critical nonspatial stimulus attribute and they need to carry out responses that are defined by their location in space. Hence, location is task relevant in a way, and even stimulus location is relevant in some sense. Accordingly, the location dimension may not be subject to heavy intentional weighting but depending on the task, the circumstances, and their interpretation by the subject, location codes may still have some impact. The same goes for the so-called affective Simon effect (De Houwer & Eelen, 1998). In tasks demonstrating this effect, participants respond to nonaffective stimulus features, such as the letter case, or grammatical or semantic attributes of words, by performing affectively charged actions, such as saying "good" or "bad", or moving a manikin towards or away from the stimulus (e.g., De Houwer, Crombez, Baeyens, & Eelen, 2001). Importantly, the stimuli also have affective features that can be compatible or incompatible with the response. Similar to the spatial Simon effect, such a setup produces faster responses with affective stimulus–response compatibility, such as if one is to say "good" to the letter case of the word "sunshine". Again, the affective valence of the stimulus words is nominally irrelevant to the task and need not be processed. And yet, given that the response set is, or at least can be, defined with regard to its affective implications, valence is task relevant to some degree, so that affective feature overlap can impact behaviour. We therefore claim that task-relevant feature dimensions are likely to receive high intentional weights, thereby boosting effects of feature overlap on these dimensions, but we do not assume that the weights for nominally task-irrelevant feature dimensions are necessarily zero. The more a dimension is directly or indirectly related to the task goal, or its interpretation by the subject, the more weight its codes will carry.

We have seen quite a number of similarities between affective and nonaffective compatibility effects. Even though this does not prove that the mechanisms underlying them are the same, it at least raises the possibility that they might be. This provides a solid basis for models that account for both affective and nonaffective effects—such the proposed affectively extended version of TEC. A number of recent observations are consistent with the extended TEC. For instance, Beckers, De Houwer, and Eelen (2002) showed that rendering a manual response "unpleasant" by having it consistently followed by a mild electric shock makes it compatible with word stimuli that refer to negative object and events. Apparently, the action acquired the valence of its consequences and sharing this valence with a stimulus facilitated performance. This supports our interpretation of affective stimulus–response compatibility effects and demonstrates that actions are indeed represented through codes of both their affective and their nonaffective consequences. The affective quality of actions is thus not fixed but sensitive to reward and punishment, and probably to other consequences resulting in more differentiated affective experiences. An interesting implication of the affective version of TEC is that it can easily account not only for stimulus-induced response priming but also for effects from action preparation on perception. Numerous studies have revealed that planning and/or executing affect-related actions, such as manual approach or avoidance movements or smiling, facilitates the processing of affectively compatible stimulus events and colours their emotional experience (see Neumann et al., 2003, for an overview). A particularly nice demonstration stems from Strack, Martin, and Stepper (1988), who showed that having subjects contract facial muscles involved in smiling makes them judge cartoons to be funnier. Likewise, Neumann and Strack (2000) observed that subjects who were asked to flex their arm categorised positive words faster than negative words. Even though one may object that smiling and arm flexing, and their negative counterparts, might have hardwired associations with the corresponding affect, recent work suggests that any action that is associated with positive (or negative) consequences might do the trick. Indeed, Eder and Klauer (2007 this issue) demonstrated that associating left or right key presses with positive and negative stimuli is sufficient to render the representations of these actions affective enough to modulate the processing of corresponding stimuli. Again, this suggests that stimuli and responses interact with each other if they are associated with the same affective state. This means that codes of those states must be part the cognitive representations of the stimuli and responses involved.

Up to now, we have emphasised the function and purpose of actions, which apparently are of higher importance for action coding and action control than are the motoric details (Hommel et al., 2001). However, this is not meant to say that the way actions are motorically realised cannot be cognitively represented in principle. TEC does not assume that concrete motoric parameters are stored, not the least because these would be too variable to be of use for action control (Schmidt, 1975). However, whether an action is realised through flexing or extending one's arm is no doubt perceivable and may thus be considered in the action's representation. Accordingly, if approaching objects were always associated with the same kind of movement (e.g., flexion of arm muscles), a perceptual (e.g., visual and kinaesthetic) representation of that movement might well become coded into the long-term representation of the action. If so, the respective codes might well mediate stimulus–response compatibility effects, for instance, when responding to arm movements of a human model. And yet, given the strong context dependency of the relationship between object valence and action (e.g., reaching for the same object involves flexing or extending of the arm, depending on whether the hand or the object is closer of the body) information about arm flexion or extension is unlikely to play an important role in the processing of affective information.

Taken together, we think that there are strong reasons to consider a common functional basis for representations of affective and nonaffective events. In particular, affective and nonaffective stimulus–response compatibility phenomena seem to follow comparable rules and show remarkably similar characteristics. Following the principle of Occam's razor, it thus seems to be a good idea to explore more extensively the possibility of explaining all compatibility phenomena within the same theoretical framework—and only construct separate models if this attempt turns out to fail. As we have argued, a minor extension of the theory of event coding seems sufficient to account for the bulk of the empirical phenomena, which raises doubts in the often assumed but rarely defended conceptual distinction between cognition and affect. Indeed, at this point it makes sense to us to consider the absence of this distinction as the null hypothesis that awaits empirical disproving.

REFERENCES

Barbalet, J. M. (1999). William James' theory of emotions: Filling in the picture. *Journal for the Theory of Social Behaviour, 29*, 251–266.

Bargh, J. A. (1989). Conditional automaticity: Varieties of automatic influence in social perception and cognition. In J. S. Uleman & J. A. Bargh (Eds.), *Unintended thought* (pp. 3–51). London: Guilford Press.

Bauer, D. W., & Miller, J. (1982). Stimulus–response compatibility and the motor system. *Quarterly Journal of Experimental Psychology, 34A*, 367–380.

Beckers, T., De Houwer, J., & Eelen, P. (2002). Automatic integration of non-perceptual action effect features: The case of the associative affective Simon effect. *Psychological Research, 66*, 166–173.

Bradley, M. M., Codispoti, M., Cuthbert, B. N., & Lang, P. J. (2001). Emotion and motivation I: Defensive and appetitive reactions in picture processing. *Emotion, 1*, 276–298.

Bradley, M. M., & Lang, P. J. (2000). Measuring emotion: Behavior, feeling, and physiology. In R. D. Lane & L. Nadel (Eds.), *Cognitive neuroscience of emotion* (pp. 242–276). Oxford, UK: Oxford University Press.

Chen, M., & Bargh, J. A. (1999). Consequences of automatic evaluation: Immediate behavioral predispositions to approach or avoid the stimulus. *Personality and Social Psychology Bulletin, 25*, 215–224.

Cornelius, R. (1996). *The science of emotion*. Upper Saddle River, NJ: Prentice Hall.

Damasio, A. (1994). *Descartes' error*. New York: G. P. Putnam's Sons.

Damasio, A. (1999). *The feeling of what happens: Body, emotion and the making of consciousness*. London: Vintage Books.

Davidson, R. J. (1995). Cerebral asymmetry, emotion and affective style. In R. J. Davidson & K. Hugdahl (Eds.), *Brain asymmetry* (pp. 361–387). Cambridge, MA: MIT Press.

De Houwer, J., Crombez, G., Baeyens, F., & Eelen, P. (2001). On the generality of the affective Simon effect. *Cognition and Emotion, 15*, 189–206.

De Houwer, J., & Eelen, P. (1998). An affective variant of the Simon paradigm. *Cognition and Emotion, 12*, 45–61.

De Jong, R., Liang, C.-C., & Lauber, E. (1994). Conditional and unconditional automaticity: A dual-process model of effects of spatial stimulus–response correspondence. *Journal of Experimental Psychology: Human Perception and Performance, 20*, 731–750.

Eder, A. B., & Klauer, K. (2007). Common valence coding in action and evaluation: Affective blindness towards response-compatible stimuli. *Cognition and Emotion, 21*, 1297–1322.

Ellsworth, P. C. (1994). William James and emotion: Is a century of fame worth a century of misunderstanding? *Psychological Review, 101*, 222–229.

Elsner, B., & Hommel, B. (2001). Effect anticipation and action control. *Journal of Experimental Psychology: Human Perception and Performance, 27*, 229–240.

Hommel, B. (1993a). The relationship between stimulus processing and response selection in the Simon task: Evidence for a temporal overlap. *Psychological Research, 55*, 280–290.

Hommel, B. (1993b). Inverting the Simon effect by intention: Determinants of direction and extent of effects of irrelevant spatial information. *Psychological Research, 55*, 270–279.

Hommel, B. (1996a). S–R compatibility effects without response uncertainty. *Quarterly Journal of Experimental Psychology, 49A*, 546–571.

Hommel, B. (1996b). The cognitive representation of action: Automatic integration of perceived action effects. *Psychological Research, 59*, 176–186.

Hommel, B. (1997). Toward an action–concept model of stimulus–response compatibility. In B. Hommel & W. Prinz (Eds.), *Theoretical issues in stimulus–response compatibility* (pp. 281–320). Amsterdam: North-Holland.

Hommel, B. (1998). Event files: Evidence for automatic integration of stimulus response episodes. *Visual Cognition, 5*, 183–216.

Hommel, B. (2000). The prepared reflex: Automaticity and control in stimulus–response translation. In S. Monsell & J. Driver (Eds.), *Control of cognitive processes. Attention and performance XVIII* (pp. 247–273). Cambridge, MA: MIT Press.

Hommel, B. (2006). How we do what we want: A neuro-cognitive perspective on human action planning. In R. J. Jorna, W. van Wezel, & A. Meystel (Eds.), *Planning in intelligent systems: Aspects, motivations and methods* (pp. 27–56). Hoboken, NJ: Wiley.

Hommel, B., & Elsner, B. (in press). Acquisition, representation, and control of action. In: E. Morsella, J. A. Bargh, & P. M. Gollwitzer (Eds.), *The psychology of action* (Vol. 2). Oxford, UK: Oxford University Press.

Hommel, B., & Lippa, Y. (1995). S–R compatibility effects due to context-dependent spatial stimulus coding. *Psychonomic Bulletin & Review, 2*, 370–374.

Hommel, B., Müsseler, J., Aschersleben, G., & Prinz, W. (2001). The theory of event coding (TEC): A framework for perception and action planning. *Behavioral and Brain Sciences, 24*, 849–878.

James, W. (1884). What is an emotion? *Mind, 9*, 188–205.

James, W. (1890). *The principles of psychology.* New York: Dover Publications.

Klauer, K. C., & Musch, J. (2002). Goal-dependent and goal-independent effects of irrelevant evaluations. *Personality and Social Psychology Bulletin, 28*, 802–814.

Klinger, M. R., Burton, P. C., & Pitts, G. S. (2000). Mechanisms of unconscious priming I: Response competition not spreading activation. *Journal of Experimental Psychology: Learning, Memory, and Cognition, 26*, 441–455.

Kornblum, S., Hasbroucq, T., & Osman, A. (1990). Dimensional overlap: Cognitive basis for stimulus–response compatibility—a model and taxonomy. *Psychological Review, 97*, 253–270.

Lang, P. J., Bradley, M. M., & Cuthbert, B. N. (1996). *International Affective Picture System (IAPS): Technical manual and affective ratings.* Gainesville, FL: The Center for Research in Psychophysiology, University of Florida.

Lazarus, R. S. (1982). Thoughts on the relations between emotion and cognition. *American Psychologist, 37*, 1019–1024.

Lazarus, R. S. (1984). On the primacy of cognition. *American Psychologist, 39*, 124–129.

LeDoux, J. (1996). *The emotional brain: The mysterious underpinnings of emotional life.* New York: Touchstone.

Lippa, Y. (1996). A referential-coding explanation for compatibility effects of physically orthogonal stimulus and response dimensions. *Quarterly Journal of Experimental Psychology, 49A*, 950–971.

Lotze, R. H. (1852). *Medicinische Psychologie oder die Physiologie der Seele.* Leipzig, Germany: Weidmann'sche Buchhandlung.

Markman, A. B., & Brendl, C. M. (2005). Constraining theories of embodied cognition. *Psychological Science, 16*, 6–10.

Milner, A. D., & Goodale, M. A. (1995). *The visual brain in action.* Oxford, UK: Oxford University Press.

Neumann, R., Förster, J., & Strack, F. (2003). Motor compatibility: The bidirectional link between behavior and evaluation. In J. Musch & K. C. Klauer (Eds.), *The psychology of evaluation: Affective processes in cognition and emotion* (pp. 371–391). Mahwah, NJ: Lawrence Erlbaum Associates, Inc.

Neumann, R., & Strack, F. (2000). Approach and avoidance: The influence of proprioceptive and exteroceptive encoding of affective information. *Journal of Personality and Social Psychology, 79*, 39–48.

Öhman, A., Flykt, A., & Lundqvist, D. (2000). Unconscious emotion: Evolutionary perspectives, psychophysiological data, and neuropsychological mechanisms. In R. D. Lane & L. Nadel (Eds.), *Cognitive neuroscience of emotion* (pp. 296–327). Oxford, UK: Oxford University Press.

Prinz, W., & Hommel, B. (Eds.). (2002) *Common mechanisms in perception and action: Attention & performance XIX.* Oxford, UK: Oxford University Press.

Robinson, M., D., Storbeck, J., Meier, B. P., & Kirkeby, B. S. (2004). Watch out! That could be dangerous: Valence-arousal interactions in evaluative processing. *Personality and Social Psychology Bulletin, 30*, 1472–1484.

Rotteveel, M., & Phaf, R. H. (2004). Automatic affective evaluation does not automatically predispose for arm flexion and extension. *Emotion, 4*, 156–172.

Schmidt, R. A. (1975). A schema theory of discrete motor skill learning. *Psychological Review, 82*, 225–260.

Simon, J. R. (1969). Reactions toward the source of stimulation. *Journal of Experimental Psychology, 81*, 174–176.

Solarz, A. K. (1960). Latency of instrumental responses as a function of compatibility. *Journal of Experimental Psychology, 59*, 239–245.

Sommer, W., Leuthold, H., & Hermanutz, M. (1993). Covert effects of alcohol revealed by event-related potentials. *Perception & Psychophysics, 54*, 127–135.

Stock, A., & Stock, C. (2004). A short history of ideo-motor action. *Psychological Research, 68*, 176–188.

Strack, F., Martin, L. L., & Stepper, S. (1988). Inhibiting and facilitating conditions of the human smile: A nonobtrusive test of the facial feedback hypothesis. *Journal of Personality and Social Psychology, 54*, 768–777.

Taylor, S. E. (1991). Asymmetrical effects of positive and negative events: The mobilization–minimization hypothesis. *Psychological Bulletin, 110,* 67–85.

Valle-Inclán, F., & Redondo, M. (1998). On the automaticity of ipsilateral response activation in the Simon effect. *Psychophysiology, 35,* 366–371.

Weeks, D. J., & Proctor, R. W. (1990). Salient-features coding in the translation between orthogonal stimulus and response dimensions. *Journal of Experimental Psychology: General, 119,* 355–366.

Zajonc, R. B. (1980). Feeling and thinking: Preferences need no inferences. *American Psychologist, 35,* 151–175.

Zajonc, R. B. (1984). On the primacy of affect. *American Psychologist, 39,* 117–123.

APPENDIX
Affective ratings of stimulus pictures

	M	*SD*
Extremely positive/pleasant		
Mother and child (2311)	3.0	1.1
Puppies (1710)	2.7	1.2
Butterfly (1603)	2.6	1.1
Rabbit (1610)	2.4	1.1
Sexy woman (4250)	2.3	1.1
Moderately positive/pleasant		
Happy couple (2352)	2.1	1.1
Smiling woman (2030)	2.1	1.0
Mickey mouse (1999)	1.9	1.2
Smiling man (4532)	1.6	1.2
Hamburger (7540)	0.8	1.3
Extremely negative/unpleasant		
Mutilated body (3120)	−3.5	0.8
Injured man (3550)	−3.4	0.7
Growling terrier (1300)	−3.2	0.9
Man with gun (6260)	−2.9	1.1
Man with knife (6510)	−2.8	1.0
Moderately negative/unpleasant		
Skulls (9440)	−2.6	1.3
Shark (1930)	−2.5	1.0
Snake (1120)	−2.4	1.2
Angry man (2120)	−2.1	1.1
Growling German shepherd (1302)	−1.8	1.1

Note: −4 =*very negative/unpleasant;* 0 =*neutral;* +4 =*very positive/pleasant. Numbers of IAPS pictures are indicated in parentheses.*

COGNITION AND EMOTION
2007, 21 (6), 1297–1322

Common valence coding in action and evaluation: Affective blindness towards response-compatible stimuli

Andreas B. Eder

Friedrich-Schiller-Universität, Jena, Germany

Karl Christoph Klauer

Albert-Ludwigs-Universität, Freiburg, Germany

A common coding account of bidirectional evaluation–behaviour interactions proposes that evaluative attributes of stimuli and responses are coded in a common representational format. This assumption was tested in two experiments that required evaluations of positive and negative stimuli during the generation of a positively or negatively charged motor response. The results of both experiments revealed a reduced evaluative sensitivity (d') towards response-compatible stimulus valences. This action–valence blindness supports the notion of a common valence coding in action and evaluation.

Much evidence for a bidirectional relationship between perception and action has accrued in cognitive psychology. On the one hand, feature correspondence between stimuli and responses affects action-planning processes. On the other hand, characteristics of action-control processes have a selective influence on basic perceptual processes. This perception–action crosstalk is paralleled by a research tradition in emotion psychology: An evaluative match between stimuli and responses can affect action preparation as well as stimulus evaluations. The purpose of this article is to bridge both research lines within a more general perspective on perception–action crosstalks. Specifically, a common coding account of bidirectional evaluation–action relationships is tested that proposes a coding of evaluative attributes of stimuli and responses in a common representational format.

Correspondence should be addressed to: Andreas B. Eder, Department of Psychology, University of Jena, Am Steiger 3/Haus 1, D-07743 Jena, Germany. E-mail: andreas.eder@uni-jena.de

© 2007 Psychology Press, an imprint of the Taylor & Francis Group, an Informa business
www.psypress.com/cogemotion   DOI: 10.1080/02699930701438277

Influence of stimulus processing on action preparation

In behaviour research the observation that some reactions are performed more efficiently in response to specific stimuli than other assigned reactions is captured by the notion of *stimulus–response (S–R) compatibility*: Reaction planning benefits from a perceptual, conceptual, or structural similarity between the response set and the stimulus set, and the greater this similarity the greater is the size of the S–R compatibility effect supposed to be (Eimer, Hommel, & Prinz, 1995; Kornblum, Hasbroucq, & Osman, 1990). For example, a left key is typically pressed faster in response to an arrow pointing to the left than to the right, and the reverse pattern is typically obtained with right-button presses. Such a feature correspondence of stimulus and response representations is in no way restricted to "natural" response dimensions like spatial orientation. Basically, any conceptual, structural, or perceptual similarity between stimulus and response sets can form the basis for S–R compatibility effects (Kornblum et al., 1990). A particular interesting type of conceptual S–R overlap is created in *affective S–R compatibility* paradigms (e.g., Chen & Bargh, 1999; De Houwer & Eelen, 1998; Fazio, Sanbonmatsu, Powell, & Kardes, 1986). Here stimulus and response sets vary in their positive and negative meaning, and response assignments establish either valence-compatible (same valence) or valence-incompatible (different valence) S–R relations. In affective variants of the so-called Simon task, for example, response selection is affected by a task-irrelevant correspondence between stimuli and responses on the evaluative dimension (e.g., De Houwer & Eelen, 1998). Evaluative responses (e.g., the pronunciation of "good" and "bad") are selected on the basis of a nonevaluative feature (e.g., the grammatical category of words) of clearly valenced stimuli (e.g., words with positive and negative meaning). A typical finding is an improved response selection when the response valence matches the stimulus valence, whereas response planning is hampered by a valence mismatch. Like other types of compatibility effects, affective S–R compatibility effects are predicted by cognitive coding accounts that assume that both stimuli and responses are cognitively represented by means of codes (e.g., by the affective codes "positive" and "negative"), and that response selection is facilitated by a code match and misled by a code mismatch (e.g., Eimer et al., 1995; Kornblum et al., 1990).

Influence of action preparation on stimulus perception

Compatibility effects between stimuli and responses reveal a selective influence of stimulus processing on subsequent action preparation. However, recent research has also shown a reverse influence of action preparation on perceptual processes that challenges linear stage models of stimulus–response translations. In an experiment by Wohlschläger (2000; see also Ishimura & Shimojo, 1994), for example, participants were to turn a knob either in a clockwise or counter clockwise direction. During the turning movement a circular motion display was continuously shifted about a constant angle, so that the motion direction (clockwise vs. counter clockwise) of the display was ambiguous to the perceiver. The results showed that unseen rotational hand movements primed the perception of rotational motion in the direction of the hand movement. Importantly, this effect was even obtained when movements were merely planned during the display presentation rather than executed, showing that action planning is sufficient for visual motion priming. Converging evidence for a crosstalk between action and perception on a common, cognitively specified dimension (e.g., spatial direction or amplitude) was found in several studies that differed in the specifics of perceptual and motor requirements (e.g., Müsseler & Hommel, 1997a, 1997b; Schubö, Prinz, & Aschersleben, 2004; Viviani & Stucci, 1992).

This cognitive research is paralleled by a long-standing interest of emotion psychologists in influences of motor patterns on basic evaluative processes that can be traced back to early ideas of the James–Lange theory on the groundings of emotional experience in physiological and bodily patterns (James, 1884), and to experimental research examining the facial feedback hypothesis that posits an influence of facial expressions on emotional experiences and judgements (Adelman & Zajonc, 1989). An intriguing line of research employed isometric movements of arm extension and flexion that are presumed to be associated with negative and positive outcomes, respectively (e.g., Cacioppo, Priester, & Berntson, 1993; Neumann & Strack, 2000). In several experiments arm flexion induced a positive shift in evaluative judgements of stimuli and arm extension a negative shift in stimulus ratings. Experiments employing arm postures and other types of body movements (e.g., Tom, Pettersen, Lau, Burton, & Cook, 1991; see also Centerbar & Clore, 2006; Cretenet & Dru, 2004) corroborate the claim that actions and their representations can impact on basic evaluative processes.

Common valence coding in action and evaluation

Cognitive research into the influence of action preparation on perception on the one side and affective research into the impact of body movements on evaluations on the other side converge on the conclusion that mental representations of actions and motor movements can influence basic processes of stimulus elaboration. Both lines of research developed fairly independently of each other, and different models were proposed to account for the bidirectionality between stimulus and motor processing in both research areas (e.g., Hommel, Müsseler, Aschersleben, & Prinz, 2001; Neumann, Förster, & Strack, 2003). In the present research we intend to bridge both research traditions within a more general framework on perception–action interactions. Specifically, a common coding assumption is tested that proposes a coding of stimulus and response features in a common representational format.

The assumption of a common coding of stimulus and response features is a key principle of the theory of event coding (TEC; Hommel et al., 2001). The TEC is designed to explain interactions between products of perceptual processes and the first steps of action planning, and rests on three core assumptions. First, an *ideo-motor* or *effect-based view of action control* proposes that motor responses become activated through the anticipation of the responses' sensory consequences (e.g., Beckers, De Houwer, & Eelen, 2002; Elsner & Hommel, 2001; Greenwald, 1970). Second, this effect-based view of action coding is further specified by the *common coding assumption* that suggests that perceived events and anticipated action events are coded in a common representational format (Prinz, 1997). Third, in line with the common coding hypothesis the TEC rejects the assumption of separate sensory and motor codes at the perception–action interface, and replaces it with the notion of *event coding*: Perceived features of objects and planned features of motor actions are cognitively represented through structurally identical event codes, with the effect that stimulus and action features may prime each other on the basis of their overlap in the common representational domain. In consequence the TEC not only predicts biases in action preparation as a consequence of stimulus processing (with S–R compatibility effects serving as prime examples), but it also predicts a reverse influence of action planning on perceptual processes.

How can we test the assumption that affective attributes of stimuli and responses are coded in a common representation format? Assumptions about representation can only be tested in conjunction with assumptions about processes operating on these representations. The TEC incorporates a two-stage model of the dynamics of event coding that allows for specific predictions of a common coding account. In a first *activation stage* distributed stored feature codes of perceived or to-be-produced events are activated, with the effect that they become *more* accessible for other temporally overlapping events. For example, the planning of a left-button press may benefit from the prolonged activation of the feature code "left" in the perceptual encoding of a left-pointing arrow, thus explaining spatial S–R compatibility effects. However, code activation alone is not sufficient for event coding because an additional mechanism is needed to "bind" the information to the relevant events and to distinguish it from information pertaining to other events (Hommel, 2004; Treisman, 1996). This binding is accomplished in a subsequent *integration stage* in which the activated features codes are bound together into a coherent (but not unitary) event code, with the effect that they become *less* accessible to temporally overlapping events. Accordingly, benefits of code or feature overlap are expected only for the activation phase, whereas costs of code compatibility are predicted for the integration phase of event coding. This prediction of compatibility costs (i.e., better task performance in incompatible trials) due to feature encapsulation in action planning was extensively tested in a series of studies conducted by Müsseler and colleagues (see Müsseler, 1999, for an overview).

In their studies Müsseler and colleagues (e.g., Müsseler & Hommel, 1997a) were specifically interested in the influence of action planning upon perceptual processes. The basic procedure involves two temporally over-lapping tasks that have a conceptual correspondence on the spatial dimension: A primary *reaction task* requires left and right button presses and a secondary *identification task* demands the identification of the spatial direction of an arrow. Starting with the reaction task participants had unlimited time to prepare a left or right button press (R_1) to a response-specifying stimulus (S_1). The self-paced planning time was to ensure that the integration of (spatial) action features was completed at the time when the to-be-identified arrow was presented. When the participant felt ready for the execution of the response, he or she first performed an initiatory double key press that was immediately followed by the speeded execution of the well-prepared button press (R_1). Importantly, the double press additionally initiated the identification task with the brief presentation of a to-be-identified arrow (S_2) whose direction (left vs. right) was indicated after a fixed delay with another left or right button press (R_2). The crucial manipulation consisted in the R_1-S_2 relation on the spatial dimension that was either compatible (i.e., left–left, right–right) or incompatible (i.e., left–right, right–left). As predicted the results revealed poorer identification of response-compatible arrows than of response-incompatible arrows. This *action–effect blindness* was attributed to an impaired access of perceptual encoding processes to (spatial) feature codes that were already occupied by well-prepared action plans. Furthermore, the very finding that a feature overlap between actions and perceptions produces selective impairments strongly suggests that the coding of percepts and acts draw on commensurably formatted representations.

Subsequent studies corroborated the basic finding and extended it to other variants of the paradigm. Impaired identification of response-compatible stimulus features was found in detection tasks (Müsseler & Hommel, 1997b), with timed-responses (Wühr & Müsseler, 2001), or with speeded responses (Wühr & Müsseler, 2002). These studies investigated the time course of the blindness effect and showed that the effect is somewhat weaker in the planning phase, greatest at the beginning of the response execution, and absent after the execution of the response. Furthermore, blindness effects of equal size were obtained with spatial reactions performed with crossed and uncrossed arms (Kunde & Wühr, 2004), strengthening the assumption of a distal coding of spatial action features in this task. A particularly strong case for the top-down control of action–effect blindness was made in an experiment by Stevanovski, Oriet, and Jolicoeur (2002) who introduced the same arrow (<) as a left-pointing arrow in one condition and as a right-beaming headlight in another condition. Even though the identical stimulus was presented, left key presses selectively impaired the identification of "arrows" pointing to the left but not the identification of "headlights" beaming to the right. Cost-benefit analyses (Müsseler & Wühr, 2002; Oriet, Stevanovski, & Jolicoeur, 2003) showed that the action-induced blindness effect is indeed caused by costs of feature overlap and not by a benefit of code incompatibility. Finally, Kunde and Wühr (2004) generalised action–effect blindness to the colour domain, showing that the pronunciation of colour words (e.g., "red") selectively impaired the identification of corresponding (e.g., red) colour patches.

Extensive research was also done to rule out alternative accounts of action–effect blindness that may arise from $S_1 - S_2$ and $R_1 - R_2$ relationships. Stevanovski, Oriet, and Jolicoeur (2003), for example, obtained a symbolic blindness effect without any action planning with the mere repeated presentation of an arrow within a short time range. This finding is reminiscent of perceptual impairments that became known as repetition blindness effects (e.g., Park & Kanwisher, 1994), and is well within the explanatory scope of event coding that encompasses S–S interactions as well as S–R and R–R couplings (e.g., Stoet & Hommel, 1999; see also Hommel, 2004). However, a particular rigorous exclusion of an $S_1 - S_2$ contribution to action-induced blindness effects was done in an experiment (Müsseler, Wühr, & Prinz, 2000) that included no presentation of a response-imperative S_1 at all. In this experiment participants were to select a left or right button press on their own in a predefined order; nevertheless a blindness effect emerged. Another alternative account of action–effect blindness is that action planning induced a judgement bias (i.e., R_1-R_2 relationship) that biases the selection of the arrow pointing in the direction opposite to that of the planned spatial response. Such a contrasting judgemental strategy mimics a worse identification of response-compatible attributes but does not reflect a perceptual impairment. Müsseler, Steininger, and Wühr (2001) subjected action–effect blindness to signal detection analyses, however, and found a genuine perceptual impairment in the discrimination indices (d') but no judgement bias. In sum, action–effect blindness describes a decreased perceptibility of overlapping stimulus features during the maintenance of a (nearly) completed central movement command. This specific perceptual impairment is assumed to originate from feature coding of action and perception in a common representational domain.

EXPERIMENT 1

On the basis of the TEC we hypothesised that evaluative attributes of stimuli and responses might be also coded in a commensurable representational format. If the planning of affectively charged actions like saying "good" or "bad" encapsulates valence codes, simultaneous evaluations of stimuli with the same valence should be impaired. Accordingly, we predicted an affective variant of the action–effect blindness in a dual task situation that requires evaluations of clearly positive and negative stimuli right before the execution of affectively charged actions. In a first experiment, participants had unlimited time to prepare a left or right button press (R_1) according to the positive or negative meaning of a word (S_1). In line with previous research on affective S–R relations (e.g., De Houwer, 2003), we assumed that this evaluative S–R assignment would impose a positive meaning on the positive classification response (e.g., a right button press) and a negative meaning on the negative classification response (e.g., a left button press). Right before the execution of the well-prepared evaluative response, a target word (S_2) was presented on the screen whose valence was either compatible (i.e., the same valence) or incompatible (i.e., a different valence) with the meaning of the classification response (R_1). In analogy to the findings of action–effect blindness we expected a worse identification of response-compatible stimulus valence than of response-incompatible valence (an effect further referred to as *action–valence blindness*).

Judging the valence of target words under ambiguous presentation conditions is a two-alternative decisional process that might be affected by the strength of evidence as well as by decision rules. We used a signal detection model to disentangle effects on participants' ability to discriminate stimulus valence from possible shifts in response criteria induced by the action planning. The response frequencies from the action planning conditions and targets were analysed jointly by means of the signal detection model shown in Figure 1. For estimation of the response bias measure c we added noise trials to the evaluative signal trials in our experimental design that involved the presentation of meaningless consonant strings instead of words with positive and negative meaning (cf. Müsseler et al., 2001). We selected consonant strings because of the profound difficulties of finding words consistently rated as neutral in valence.

For each response planning condition a response criterion was calculated to model the possibility that the planning of evaluative responses differentially biases the judgements "positive" or "negative" (see Figure 1). The relative position of the response criteria $c_{positive}$ and $c_{negative}$ on the strength-of-evidence axis can be used to determine which judgement strategies are used by the decision maker (cf. Müsseler et al., 2001). First, decision makers might adopt a *contrast strategy* when uncertain about the valence of stimuli,

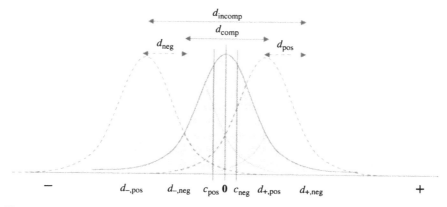

Figure 1.   Graphical representation of the signal detection model and its parameters. The shaded distribution in the middle indicates the noise distribution. Positive and negative action planning conditions are indicated by the subscripts $_{pos}$ and $_{neg}$, respectively. Positive and negative target signals are specified by the subscripts $_+$ and $_-$, respectively.

that is, they might prefer the valence opposite to that of the response valence (i.e., a judgemental bias for "positive" after a negative button press and vice versa). A contrast bias increases the hit rate for target words with response-incompatible valence and the miss rate for target words with response-compatible valence without any concomitant changes in perceptibility, thus overestimating action–valence blindness in percent correct measures. Second, and exactly the opposite of a contrast strategy, is an *assimilation strategy* that is reflected in the tendency to choose the valence that is congruent with the response valence (i.e., more judgements of "negative" and "positive" in conditions with the planning of negative and positive button presses, respectively). In percent correct measures an assimilation bias underestimates action–valence blindness with more hits in response-compatible trials and more misses in the response-incompatible trials. In sum, the proportion of correct valence identification might result in a systematic overestimation (contrast bias) or underestimation (assimilation bias) of action–valence blindness, necessitating signal detection analyses to separate perceptual sensitivity (d') from judgement preferences (c).

Following standard scaling assumptions of signal detection analyses (Wickens & Hirshman, 2000) six model parameters were defined by crossing target valence (S_2: positive vs. neutral vs. negative) and evaluative action (R_1: positive vs. negative): Two response criteria, $c_{positive}$ and $c_{negative}$, and four d'-values for the means of the distributions of positive and negative targets $(+, -)$ preceded by the two evaluative classification responses (positive, negative), $d_{-, \, negative}$, $d_{-, \, positive}$, $d_{+, \, negative}$, $d_{+, \, positive}$. The distribution of neutral targets, shown as the shaded area in Figure 1, was given a zero mean, independently of the kind of prior response planning. Parameter values were estimated from each participant's data, using an iterative search algorithm that maximised the likelihood of the observed data. The effects of evaluative action planning on target valence perception are modelled by shifts of the target distributions: Negative classification responses (R_1) are assumed to induce a small shift of negative targets to the right of average size $d_{negative}$ thereby making an erroneous positive response somewhat more likely. This shift is measured relative to the distribution of negative targets preceded by positive responses. Analogously, positive classification responses are assumed to produce a small shift of each positive target to the left of average size $d_{positive}$ making an erroneous negative response more likely. This shift is measured relative to the distribution of positive targets preceded by negative responses. Action–valence blindness can be assessed for each kind of target valence on the basis of these parameters by computing $d_{negative} = d_{-, \text{ negative}} - d_{-, \text{ positive}}$ and $d_{positive} = d_{+, \text{ negative}} - d_{+, \text{ positive}}$, or alternatively by the aggregation of discrimination estimates to perceptibility indices of the valence of response-compatible targets ($d_{compatible} = d_{+, \text{ positive}} - d_{-, \text{ negative}}$) and response-incompatible target words ($d_{incompatible} = d_{+, \text{ negative}} - d_{-, \text{ positive}}$). Finally, an overall index of action–valence blindness is computed by the subtraction of response-compatible target perceptibility from the sensitivity index for response-incompatible targets (i.e., action–valence blindness $= d_{incompatible} - d_{compatible}$).

Method

Participants. A total of 20 students (7 men, 13 women) with different majors participated in fulfilment of course requirement or for payment. All participants had normal or corrected-to-normal vision and were fluent in German. Two participants were dropped from data analyses because their percentages of correct R_1 within the time limit ($M = 61.5\%$ and $M = 62.1\%$, respectively) was several standard deviations below the mean correct rate of the rest of the sample ($M = 91.9\%$, $SD = 5.1$; $n = 18$).

Apparatus and stimuli. In a dimly lit experimental chamber participants were seated at a distance of 50 cm from a 17-inch VGA colour monitor with 70 Hz refresh rate. Stimulus presentation and measurement of response latencies were controlled by a software timer with video synchronisation (Haussmann, 1992). To respond, the participants had to press the two buttons of a computer mouse with the index and middle fingers of the dominant hand (15 right-handed, 3 left-handed).

As response-specifying stimuli (S_1) served 72 strongly positive ($M = 1.1$, $SD = 0.22$) and 72 strongly negative nouns ($M = -1.4$, $SD = 0.29$) selected from a standardised word pool on the basis of their evaluative norms (Schwibbe, Röder, Schwibbe, Borchardt, & Geiken-Pophanken, 1981). Twenty additional nouns (10 positive, 10 negative) served as practice stimuli. All nouns comprised between 3 and 12 letters and were presented in upper case in white-on-black at the centre of the computer screen. Target stimuli (S_2) were 48 clearly positive ($M = 2.1$, $SD = 0.45$) and 48 clearly negative adjectives ($M = -2.1$, $SD = 0.53$) taken from the same standardisation study as the nouns were. The subsets of positive and negative adjectives did not differ in valence extremity, frequency of usage, or number of letters (range: 4–9), with all $Fs < 1$. Ten additional positive and ten negative adjectives were selected for practice trials. All adjectives were presented in lower case letters in grey-on-black at the centre of the computer screen. Finally, 6 consonant strings (e.g., "ysvw") of ascending length (range: 4–9) were constructed as "noise" stimuli that shared no letter with the test or practice adjectives on a specific letter position.

Design. The experimental design was a crossed 2 (R_1 planning: positive vs. negative) × 3 (S_2 target: positive vs. neutral vs. negative) factorial design. Each block consisted of three trials from each of the six conditions of the design, resulting in 18 trials per block that were presented in random order. Each participant worked through 16 experimental blocks. In total there were 96 response-compatible, 96 response-incompatible, and 96 response-neutral assignments.

Procedure. Each experimental session consisted of an adjustment phase and an experimental phase. In the adjustment phase the presentation duration of the target words was individually adjusted to avoid ceiling or floor effects in the identification task of the test phase. Participants performed 8 blocks with 12 trials each that involved the presentation of a positive or negative adjective with equal probability. Target words were the same adjectives that were later used as targets in the experimental phase, and they were randomly drawn from the word pool without replacement. Each trial started with the brief presentation (100 ms) of an asterisk (∗) as a fixation mark in the middle of the screen. After an additional interval of 100 ms, a white premask (XXXXXXXXX) was presented for one refresh cycle (14 ms), immediately followed by the adjective that stayed on the screen for an individually set presentation time (starting with 114 ms in the first block). The target word was followed by a white postmask (XXXXXXXXX) for 1 s, followed by a blank screen for 257 ms. An identification screen then appeared that asked the participant for his or her valence judgement with a corresponding left or right mouse button press. An arbitrary time limit of two seconds was set for the judgement but no emphasis was put on the speed of the response. To counteract systematic valence–response associations, the assignment of the classification response to the mouse button was random, and each of the two assignments appeared with equal probability in each block. At the end of each trial participants were informed about false valence judgements or time-limit violations if any. The next trial started after one second.

After each block the word presentation time was adjusted using a staircase procedure to achieve a correct valence identification rate between 59% and 84% (cf. Müsseler & Hommel, 1997a). The presentation time was decreased by 14 ms when the error rate was equal or lower than 16%. It was increased by 14 ms when the error rate was equal or above 41%. The final presentation time was computed by averaging across presentation times of the last three blocks (rounded up or down to the next multiple of the refresh cycle).

After the adjustment phase participants were informed that the valence identification task would now become more complicated with the simultaneous handling of an additional simple "reaction task." The sequence of events in the test phase is shown in Figure 2. For the reaction task a single mouse button press (R_1) was prepared according to the valence of a noun (S_1) presented at the beginning of each trial for 500 ms. A negative noun dictated a left button press and a positive noun a right button press. In the

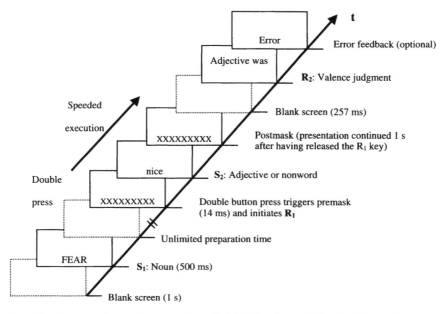

Figure 2. Sequence of events in an experimental trial of Experiment 1. The subscripts $_1$ and $_2$ refer to Task 1 (reaction task) and Task 2 (identification task), respectively.

instructions strong emphasis was put on the unlimited planning time of the mouse button response that was purported to greatly improve the task performance. When the participant felt ready for the execution of the left or right button press, he or she first pressed both mouse buttons simultaneously and then the appropriate single mouse button (R_1) as quickly as possible. A time limit of 600 ms was set for the execution of the single button press after the double press to ensure a thorough planning of the response. The double button press additionally initiated the valence identification task the sequence of events of which paralleled that of the identification task in the adjustment phase, except for the omission of a fixation mark and the presentation of neutral target stimuli. The presentation time of neutral targets was fixed to a brief 42 ms, and a wrong S_2 identification was reported in half of the noise trials in each block to maintain the illusion of word presentations. The postmask stayed on the screen for one second after the release of the R_1 button, adding up to a minimum R_1–R_2 delay of 1257 ms. A single trial ended with an optional error feedback that reported a wrong R_1, a false identification of S_2, and violations of the time limits of R_1 and R_2. In addition, a detailed performance summary was given at the end of each block.

Participants worked first through 20 practice trials with 10 response-compatible and 10 response-incompatible assignments (i.e., no neutral stimuli were presented in the practice block), followed by the 288 experimental trials. The final S_2 presentation time of the adjustment phase set the presentation duration of S_2 in the practice block, but was still adjusted (if necessary) after each experimental block according to the staircase procedure detailed above.

Results

The mean adjusted presentation duration for S_2 across all participants was 67 ms ($SD = 21$ ms). Trials with wrong R_1 (4.8% of all trials) and/or R_1 exceeding the time limit of 600 ms (4.3% of all trials) were excluded from further data analyses, thereby eliminating 8.1% of all trials. Error rates did not interact with the compatibility factor nor did the number of valid trials, all $Fs < 1$.

Proportion correct identification. The percentages of correct valence identifications were separately calculated for each condition of the 2 (R_1: positive vs. negative) × 2 (S_2: positive vs. negative) matrix, as listed in Table 1, and subjected to a repeated measures analysis of variance (ANOVA) with Valence (positive vs. negative) and Compatibility (compatible vs. incompatible) as within-participants factors. The analysis revealed a better valence identification of response-compatible words ($M = 73.6\%$, $SE = 0.6$)

than of response-incompatible words ($M = 68.1\%$, $SE = 1.5$), $F(1, 17) = 10.3$, $p < .01$, but as indicated by a significant interaction, $F(1, 17) = 14.5$, $p < .01$, the effect was restricted to negative words. The identification rate of negative words was, however, not different from that of positive words across both planning conditions ($M = 70.4\%$ vs. $M = 71.2\%$, $F < 1$). The presence of a response bias was tested in an additional repeated-measures ANOVA of the "negative" judgement rates in each cell of the 2 (R_1: positive vs. negative) $\times$ 3 (S_2: positive vs. neutral vs. negative) design. Beside the trivial main effect of the S_2-factor with more frequent negative-judgements after negative adjective presentations than after nonword and positive word presentations, $F(2, 34) = 226.2$, $p < .001$, the main effect of the planning condition R_1 became significant showing more frequent negative judgements after negative planning ($M = 57.2\%$, $SE = 1.3$) than after positive response planning ($M = 49.1\%$, $SE = 1.2$), $F(1, 17) = 20.1$, $p < .001$. The interaction between both factors was also significant, $F(2, 34) = 11.7$, $p < .001$. The joint impact of action planning and S_2 valence on response bias and identification rates that is expressed in this interaction is disentangled in the signal detection analyses presented next.

Signal detection analyses. Table 1 shows mean perceptual sensitivity d' for each cell of the 2 (R_1) $\times$ 2 (S_2) matrix, and the estimates of the response criterion c for each action-planning condition. The positive scores of the response bias indices c reveal that participants did generally prefer to choose "negative" over "positive" when uncertain about stimulus valence.

TABLE 1

Mean percent correct, sensitivity d', and response criterion c for affectively charged words in evaluative action planning conditions of Experiments 1 and 2 (Standard Deviations in parentheses)

	Percent correct			Sensitivity d'		
Action plan	Positive S_2	Neutral S_2	Negative S_2	Positive S_2	Negative S_2	Response criterion c
Experiment 1						
Positive R_1	70.0 (5.2)	53.6 (10.5)[a]	63.6 (8.4)	0.63 (0.27)	−0.51 (0.26)	0.10 (0.28)
Negative R_1	72.4 (7.5)	66.9 (12.2)[a]	77.3 (6.2)	0.82 (0.37)	−0.30 (0.31)	0.47 (0.37)
Experiment 2						
Positive R_1	70.2 (6.3)	49.8 (9.4)[a]	68.6 (7.8)	0.53 (0.23)	−0.62 (0.37)	0.00 (0.24)
Negative R_1	72.3 (8.2)	61.6 (10.5)[a]	74.6 (7.4)	0.80 (0.23)	−0.37 (0.27)	0.31 (0.30)

Note. Positive values on the response criterion c signify an inclination towards the decision "negative" and negative values a tendency to decide "positive". For the sensitivity index d' greater deviations from zero indicate a better discrimination performance. Sensitivity indices were estimated relative to neutral S_2-judgement distributions in each planning condition.
[a]Proportion of judgement "negative" in percent.

More importantly, this judgement preference was significantly influenced by the prior action-planning condition. Participants were more inclined to decide "negative" after the planning of a negative button press ($c = 0.47$, $SE = 0.09$) and less so after the planning of a positive button press ($c = 0.10$, $SE = 0.07$), $t(17) = 4.31$, $p < .001$, revealing a strong assimilation bias in evaluative decisions. To test for action–valence blindness, mean scores of perceptual sensitivity d' were analysed that were uncontaminated by the assimilation bias in valence judgements. As predicted, perceptual sensitivity (d') to the valence of response-compatible words ($d'_{comp} = 0.92$, $SE = 0.09$) was on average significantly lower than the sensitivity to the valence of response-incompatible words ($d'_{incomp} = 1.34$, $SE = 0.10$), $t(17) = 2.54$, $p < .05$. This action–valence blindness was of moderate size ($\Delta\ d' = 0.42$) and equally strong for positive and negative R_1–S_2 compatibility relations, as there was no interaction with the valence factor, $F < 1$ (see Table 1).

Reaction times.   Reaction times of R_1 were measured from the onset of the double button press to the onset of the single mouse button press. An overall t-test revealed that reactions overlapping with neutral S_2 ($M = 304$ ms, $SE = 16.7$) were executed significantly faster than reactions that concurred with the presentation of evaluative S_2 words ($M = 307$ ms, $SE = 17.4$), $t(17) = -2.45$, $p < .05$. This small difference was not due to a trade-off in the accuracy of the reactions, $F < 1$. To our surprise, the execution of R_1 was also selectively affected by an evaluative overlap with the S_2 word. In signal trials S_2-compatible button presses ($M = 306$ ms, $SE = 17.4$) were performed significantly faster than affectively incompatible button presses ($M = 309$ ms, $SE = 17.5$), $t(17) = -2.12$, $p < .05$. A further decomposition of R_1 latencies in release times for the double button press and single button press latencies revealed that the compatibility effect is mainly located in the latencies of the R_1 button presses [compatible: $M = 113$ ms, $SE = 10.3$, vs. incompatible: $M = 115$ ms, $SE = 10.4$, $t(17) = -1.86$, $p < .05$], whereas the release times of the buttons after the double button press did not differ with compatible ($M = 193$ ms, $SE = 11.9$) and incompatible R_1–S_2 assignments ($M = 194$ ms, $SE = 12.1$), $t(17) = -1.14$, $p = .27$. Of course, the performance difference of 3 ms is very small but it is significant and it cannot be explained by a trade-off in response accuracy or time-limit violations (all Fs < 1). Finally, latencies of the unspeeded valence judgements (R_2) were measured from the onset of the identification screen to the onset of the classification response. For reaction time analysis, latencies exceeding the time limit of 2000 ms were dropped from analysis (0.3% of all trials). There were no differences in judgement speed between noise ($M = 640$ ms, $SE = 32.7$) and signal trials ($M = 636$ ms, $SE = 31.1$), $F < 1$. Furthermore, a compatibility effect approached significance with faster response-compatible judgements ($M = 629$ ms, $SE = 30.7$) than incompatible decisions ($M = 643$ ms, $SE = 31.9$) in signal trials, $t(17) = -1.71$, $p = .11$, presumably reflecting an assimilation bias in judgement latencies.

Discussion

The central finding of Experiment 1 is a decreased evaluative sensitivity (d') towards response-compatible stimuli that are presented during the generation of an evaluative classification response. A positive meaning of words was harder to detect when a positive classification response was planned than when a negative response was prepared. An analogous impairment was found for evaluations of negative words that overlapped with negative action plans. The impairment in valence discrimination (d') is likely to reflect a genuine perceptual impairment, as strategic factors like a contrast bias can be ruled out as an alternative explanation.

Proportion correct measures that exclusively consider hit-rates in valence identification proved not to be sensitive to perceptual impairments. These measures were contaminated by participants' tendency to align uncertain evaluative decisions to the valence of the foregoing action plan (and/or response-specifying S_1 noun), inflating the hit-rate (and false alarm rate) in response-compatible trials. Signal detection analyses revealed that the improved identification of response-compatible valences in percent correct measures reflect a strong assimilation bias and not a change in valence perceptibility. The assimilation bias itself comes as no surprise as many experimental studies have shown an affective priming of evaluative judgements on a conceptual level (e.g., Murphy & Zajonc, 1993). Valence becomes strongly activated in the course of S_1 elaboration and R_1 planning, and it is reasonable to assume that a residual activation survives the rather long R_1–R_2 delay, priming evaluative decisions in ambiguous judgemental situations in a subtle way. In addition, one might also construe the assimilation bias as a sort of manipulation check that reveals the effectiveness of the S_1–R_1 mapping to impose a positive and negative meaning on button presses.

The effects of S_2 processing on the execution times of the well-prepared button presses (R_1) were unexpected, especially in view of the short reaction times (range of mean latencies: 221–454 ms). The finding of slower button presses with the simultaneous processing of evaluative information points to mental capacity restrictions that are typical of dual task situations (e.g., Jolicoeur, 1999). The faster execution of S_2-compatible button presses, however, poses an explanatory challenge because it is very unlikely that response-selection processes are still affected after the long response preparation time ($M = 1322$ ms, $SD = 459$). Note, however, that this small-sized compatibility benefit was not replicated in Experiment 2 despite only minor task changes.

EXPERIMENT 2

In Experiment 1 we obtained first evidence that the planning of affectively charged actions like negative and positive button presses (R_1) selectively impairs simultaneous evaluations of stimuli (S_2) with the same valence. However, one can doubt this interpretation of an action-induced blindness in view of the perfect confounding of the action valence with the valence of the response-imperative noun (S_1). The mere presentation of the valenced words S_1 and S_2 in succession might be already sufficient to produce an impaired identification of stimuli with the same valence (Silvert, Naveteur, Honoré, Sequeira, & Boucart, 2004; Stevanovski, Oriet, & Jolicoeur, 2003). Therefore, we conducted a second experiment to rule out any remaining doubts that it is indeed the planning of evaluative actions that selectively interferes with evaluations of same-valenced stimuli. In Experiment 2 affectively neutral letters were used as response-imperative stimuli (S_1) to instruct the planning of positive and negative button presses (R_1). If action–valence blindness is still observed despite the use of affectively neutral S_1, emotional repetition blindness arising from the S_1–S_2 relationship can be ruled out as an alternative explanation.

Method

Participants. Twenty students (6 men, 14 women) with different majors participated in fulfilment of course requirement or for payment. All participants had normal or corrected-to-normal vision and were fluent in German. Six participants out of 20 reported left-handedness. None of the subjects had participated in Experiment 1.

Stimuli, design, and procedure. Experiment 2 was identical in design and procedure to Experiment 1 except for the following changes. Positive and negative nouns were now replaced by the letters *P*, *O*, or *S* specifying a positive (right) button press and the letters *N*, *E*, or *G* requiring a negative (left) button press. The letters (S_1) appeared in white-on-black on the centre of the screen for 500 ms. To ensure a positive and negative coding of the button presses, participants were additionally required to pronounce "positive" at the time of the positive button press and "negative" at the time of the negative button press. A female experimenter blind to the hypotheses was sitting beside the participant and controlled on-line timing and accuracy of the vocal responses. The pronunciations of the response valence were additionally recorded with an audio tape recorder. To avoid an intrusion of the vocal responses into the valence judgement phase, the R_1–R_2 delay was increased by extending the presentation of the postmask for additional

500 ms. The valence judgement screen thereby followed R_1-offset no sooner than 1757 ms.

Results

The mean adjusted presentation duration for S_2 was 63 ms ($SD = 27$ ms). Trials with wrong R_1 (1.6% of all trials) and/or R_1 exceeding the time limit of 600 ms (3.4% of all trials) were excluded from further data analyses, thereby eliminating 4.8% of all trials. Error rates did not interact with the compatibility factor (both $ps > .15$) nor did the total number of valid trials, $F < 1$.

Proportion correct identification. Table 1 shows the mean percentage of correct valence identifications in each condition of the 2 (R_1: positive vs. negative) × 2 (S_2: positive vs. negative) design. A repeated-measures ANOVA with Valence (positive vs. negative) and Compatibility (compatible vs. incompatible) as within-participants factors showed neither a main effect of valence ($M = 71.2$, $SE = 1.2$ vs. $M = 71.6$, $SE = 0.9$, for positive and negative words, $F < 1$) nor differences in the valence identification of response-compatible ($M = 72.4$, $SE = 0.8$) and response-incompatible adjectives ($M = 70.4$, $SE = 1.2$), $F(1, 19) = 1.19$, $p = .29$. The interaction between the factors valence and compatibility was, however, significant with a compatibility advantage in the discrimination of negative words and a compatibility disadvantage in the identification of positive words, $F(1, 19) = 4.7$, $p < .05$. An additional repeated-measures ANOVA of the "negative" judgement rates in each cell of the 2 (R_1: positive vs. negative) × 3 (S_2: positive vs. neutral vs. negative) design showed a main effect of the S_2 factor with more frequent negative judgements after negative adjective presentations than after nonword and positive word presentations, $F(2, 38) = 314.2$, $p < .001$, a significant main effect of the planning condition R_1 showing more frequent negative judgements after negative ($M = 54.6\%$, $SE = 1.4$) than positive response planning ($M = 49.4\%$, $SE = 1.0$), $F(1, 19) = 10.6$, $p < .01$, and a significant interaction between both factors, $F(2, 38) = 7.71$, $p < .01$. The joint impact of response planning and S_2 valence on response bias and identification rates that is expressed in this interaction is disentangled in the signal detection analyses presented next.

Signal detection analyses. Indices for evaluative sensitivity d' and response strategies c were separately calculated for positive and negative targets in each planning condition (see Table 1). Inspection of the response criteria applied by the decision makers revealed a strong assimilation of uncertain valence judgements (R_2) to the valence of the foregoing action plan (R_1), $t(19) = -4.15$, $p < .001$. Thus, after the planning of negative button presses participants were more inclined to judge "negative" than "positive" (mean $c = 0.31$, $SE = 0.07$). In contrast, the planning of a positive button press exerted no priming influence on valence judgements across all participants (mean $c = 0.00$, $SE = 0.05$). Most importantly, mean evaluative sensitivity d' was lower for response-compatible words ($d'_{comp} = 0.90$, $SE = 0.07$) than for response-incompatible words, $d'_{incomp} = 1.42$, $SE = 0.10$, $t(19) = -3.13$, $p < .01$, replicating action–valence blindness observed in Experiment 1. The perceptual impairment was of moderate size ($\Delta\, d' = 0.52$), and equally pronounced for the identification of positive and negative targets as was revealed by a lack of interaction between target valence and compatibility, $F(1, 19) = 0.4$.

Reaction times.   Reaction times of R_1 (speeded evaluative button presses) and R_2 (unspeeded valence judgements) were measured in the same way as was done in Experiment 1. There were no differences in R_1 execution times between signal ($M = 325$ ms, $SE = 23.8$) and noise trials ($M = 325$ ms, $SE = 24.3$), $p = .64$. Furthermore, S_2-compatible button presses ($M = 325$ ms, $SE = 24.1$) were executed on average with identical speed as S_2-incompatible button presses ($M = 325$ ms, $SE = 24.5$), $p = .97$. Valence judgement (R_2) latencies exceeding the time limit of 2000 ms were dropped from reaction-time analysis (0.1% of all trials). Evaluative decisions were made significantly faster for noise trials ($M = 555$ ms, $SE = 27.5$) than for signal trials, $M = 593$ ms, $SE = 30.5$, $t(19) = -2.49$, $p < .05$. There was only a tendency for response-compatible S_2 ($M = 590$ ms, $SE = 31.2$) to elicit faster judgements than response-incompatible S_2 ($M = 598$ ms, $SE = 30$), $t(19) = -1.48$, $p = .16$.

Discussion

Experiment 2 replicated action–valence blindness despite the use of affectively neutral letters (S_1) to instruct positive and negative action planning. Emotional repetition blindness due to the mere repeated presentation of valenced words (S_1–S_2) is consequently no longer a viable alternative explanation for action–valence blindness in this experiment, strengthening the attribution of action–valence blindness to the compatibility of the R_1–S_2 relationship. However, one might still uphold an S_1–S_2 interference account assuming that originally neutral letter symbols might have acquired a weak positive and negative valence due to consistent pairings with pronunciations of "positive" and "negative". In this case action–valence blindness should grow in size with the number of S_1–R_1 pairings as evaluative conditioning trials; we observed, however, no differences in the size of the specific evaluation impairment in the first and second half of the experimental blocks ($F < 1$). Furthermore, very long time intervals between the presentations of S_1 and S_2 (range of mean planning time: 522–2301 ms in Exp. 1 and 377–1687 ms in Exp. 2) are known to eliminate repetition blindness effects at a symbolic and perceptual level (Park & Kanwisher, 1994; Silvert et al., 2004; Stevanovski et al., 2003). Accordingly, we view a symbolic repetition blindness effect arising from the $S_1–S_2$ relationship as an implausible explanation of the blindness effects observed in our experiments.

For Experiment 2 we cannot decide whether evaluative sensitivity (d') was selectively reduced by the planning of positive and negative button presses, by the preparation of the pronunciation of their valence, or by the grouped planning of both responses. But whatever $R_1–S_2$ combination might have been responsible for the identification impairment, the conclusion is upheld that the planning of affectively charged *actions* is sufficient to produce selective impairments in evaluations of same-valenced stimuli.

GENERAL DISCUSSION

Two experiments consistently showed reduced sensitivity (d') for the valence of positive and negative stimuli during the execution of compatible positive and negative actions. This action–valence blindness was masked in proportion correct measures by a strong assimilation bias in valence judgements, presumably reflecting affective judgement priming on a conceptual level (e.g., Murphy & Zajonc, 1993). Nevertheless, in the d' metric of signal-detection models the mean magnitude of action–valence blindness observed in Experiment 1 ($\Delta d' = 0.42$) and Experiment 2 ($\Delta d' = 0.51$) are close to the mean effect sizes found in spatial variants of action–effect blindness (e.g., $\Delta d' = 0.46$ and $\Delta d' = 0.49$ in Experiment 1 and 2 of Müsseler et al., 2001). Furthermore, alternative accounts of action–valence blindness that arise from confoundings with $S_1–S_2$ and $R_1–R_2$ relationships were ruled out through the use of signal detection measures in both experiments and through the use of affectively neutral S_1 in Experiment 2. These experimental and data-analytic controls strengthen the assumption that the planning of positively and negatively charged actions interfered with simultaneous evaluations of same-valenced stimuli.

The empirical finding of action–valence blindness is of theoretical importance in several respects. First, it provides first evidence for an influence of discrete motor movements on evaluative processes. Previous research into action-evaluation influences mainly employed isometric arm positions (arm flexion and extension) that were manipulated between participants. The present research extends findings of action-evaluation interactions to trial-to-trial variations of valenced actions. Second, the impact of task-induced action valences on evaluations extends previous work on the influence of intrinsically valenced movements on evaluations. The bidirectional evaluation–behaviour link is accordingly not restricted to approach and avoidance movements but does also operate with rather artificially valenced actions like positive and negative button presses. In this respect it is interesting to note that Eder and Klauer (2004) also observed a reduced evaluative sensitivity towards positive and negative stimuli during the generation of (positive) arm flexing and (negative) arm extending lever movements, respectively. This finding suggests that similar processes might be involved in the control of explicitly valenced button presses and more implicitly valenced approach and avoidance movements (cf. Lavender & Hommel, 2007 this issue). Third, on the basis of the dynamic model of the TEC (Hommel et al., 2001) we predicted worse evaluation performance with affective code match than with code mismatch. Costs of affective compatibility pose a challenge to existing theories on the evaluation–behaviour link that uniformly expect a processing advantage given an affective or motivational correspondence between stimuli and responses (e.g., Lang, Bradley, & Cuthbert, 1998; Neumann et al., 2003). Moreover, findings of action–evaluation interactions are also beyond the explanatory scope of cognitive compatibility models commonly used in the explanation of affective S–R compatibility effects (e.g., the dimensional overlap model; Kornblum et al., 1990). The TEC makes the novel prediction of affective compatibility costs in action-evaluation interactions and is thereby capable of explaining the present data. Fourth, action–valence blindness clearly shows that a conceptual correspondence between action and stimulus features on the evaluative dimension is sufficient for the emergence of blindness effects. This and other findings of conceptually based blindness effects (e.g., Kunde & Wühr, 2004; Stevanovski et al., 2002) support the conclusion that blindness towards response-compatible stimuli is not restricted to perceptual or perceptually derived feature overlaps (see also Hommel & Müsseler, 2006), although this distinction between "perceptual" and "conceptual" features is blurred in the assumption of recent embodiment views that even abstract word-referents are grounded in concrete somatosensory states (see Duncan & Barrett, 2007 this issue).

Another consistent finding in both experiments is the strong assimilation bias in valence judgements (R_2) that was estimated from the trials with nonword presentations. Participants were more inclined to choose "negative" after planning a negative response than after the preparation of a positive button press. Note that peripheral R_1–R_2 associations cannot explain this judgement bias because the assignment of the valence to the mouse buttons was balanced in each block. A more plausible explanation offers a conceptual variant of affective priming that shows up in congruent shifts in preference ratings of neutrally valenced stimuli after presentations of positive and negative prime stimuli (e.g., Murphy & Zajonc, 1993). In one study (Rotteveel & Phaf, 2004) participants evaluated the connotation of Japanese ideographs with button presses labelled "positive" and "negative", and results revealed more frequent positive ideograph evaluations after presentations of happy facial expressions and more frequent negative judgements after presentations of angry facial expressions in conditions of working memory load. The similarity of this preference judgement task to the evaluative identification task of our experiments is obvious because in both tasks information about the target valence is missing or only weakly activated, opening irrelevant evaluative activations a gate to shift the weights in the decision process. It is remarkable, however, that participants were generally more inclined to judge "negative" in uncertainty about the word valence; in fact, collapsed across both planning conditions a response bias favouring "negative" was observed in both experiments. The bias was significant in Experiment 1 (mean $c = 0.28$, $SD = 0.27$), $t(17) = 4.47$, $p < .001$, and in Experiment 2 (mean $c = 0.15$, $SD = 0.21$), $t(19) = 3.2$, $p < .01$. This negativity bias in judgemental tendencies suggests that better hit rates for negative stimuli (e.g., Dijksterhuis & Aarts, 2003; see also Labiouse, 2004) can reflect judgemental bias rather than enhanced perceptual discriminability.

The present research adds a further piece to the puzzle of the bidirectional evaluation–behaviour link in suggesting that the valence of stimuli and responses is coded in a common representational format. The empirical finding that a valence overlap between stimuli and responses is detrimental to evaluation performance argues strongly for the assumption that valence coding of stimuli and responses draws on common resources. For the response selection stage common valence coding rejects a translation of "perceptual" valence codes in "motor" valence codes, or some sort of automatic spreading activation between distinctively coded valence repre-sentations; instead, it is assumed that actions are selected by their affective consequences, which are commensurably coded with the valence of perceived events (cf. Lavender & Hommel, 2007 this issue).

The TEC (Hommel et al., 2001) suggests a two-stage model of the dynamics of perceptual and action coding processes that can be easily adapted to explain well-established findings of affective compatibility benefits (e.g., sequential affective priming effects; Fazio et al., 1986; see Klauer & Musch, 2003, for a review) as well as novel findings of affective compatibility costs (e.g., action–valence blindness). Benefits of affective code match are attributed to valence activation in a common coding domain that "primes" access to matching feature compounds in response planning (e.g., S–R compatibility effects in affective priming) and target categorisation (e.g., S–S compatibility effects in affective priming; see Klauer, Musch, & Eder, 2005). Costs of affective code match are instead attributed to a feature integration process that binds (activated) feature codes belonging to perceptual objects and actions together to an event file so that single feature codes cannot be addressed anymore without activating the whole event file. It is assumed that valence codes once integrated are occupied by their respective feature compounds, rendering them less accessible for other event codes that need to bind the very same valence code (Hommel & Müsseler, 2006; Müsseler & Hommel, 1997a, 1997b). According to this view action–valence blindness is explained by an encapsulation of valence codes in affective action planning that impairs code access or code integration in overlapping evaluations of same-valenced stimuli. Similarly, valence-specific negative priming observed in sequential affective priming (Wentura, 1999) and in modified affective Simon tasks (De Houwer, Rothermund, & Wentura, 2001) can be explained by a time-consuming dissolution and rebinding process of automatically retrieved S–R episodes in ignored-repetition trials (cf. Rothermund, Wentura, & De Houwer, 2005). Note that the mere temporal co-occurrence of stimulus features, and of stimuli and responses, is considered to be sufficient to bind their codes (Hommel, 2005). However, which features are activated and integrated is assumed to depend heavily on their task-relevance and on the attentional set imposed by the specific task setting (Hommel & Colzato, 2004), explaining the evaluative task goal-dependency of affective S–R compatibility effects (e.g., Klauer & Musch, 2002; Lavender & Hommel, 2007 this issue).

Given the similar findings in cognitive and affective variants of blindness towards response-compatible stimuli one might ask whether we do not deprive affective meaning of its distinctiveness in deliberate evaluative classifications, treating valence just like any other semantic category in this specific experimental setup. First, note that the scope of the present research is restricted to (bidirectional) interactions between evaluation and action that are typical of affective S–R compatibility paradigms (e.g., sequential affective priming, affective Simon task) and to motor compatibility paradigms showing an influence of motor states on evaluations (e.g., Neumann & Strack, 2000). Accordingly, the fuzzy concept "affect" refers here to categorical evaluations in positive and negative that should not be confused with emotional and mood states. Just like many other researchers interested in affect and emotion we do however think that investigations of evaluative processing effects reveal important processes underlying many "hot" phenomena including feelings and emotions. Cacioppo, Larsen, Smith, and Berntson (2004), for example, claim fast and frugal evaluative categorisations as the operating system driving affect, emotion, and feeling. Duncan and Barrett (2007 this issue) similarly view hedonic valence (pleasure/displeasure) besides arousal as constituents of "core affect" that determines phenomenological outcomes including feeling states. In addition, many appraisal-theorists of emotion regard an evaluative categorisation stage as a separate and critical determinant in emotion generation (e.g., the *intrinsic pleasantness check* of Scherer, 1984). In sum, there is a broad consensus that evaluations are implicated in various "hot" processing functions including attitudes, emotional feelings and valenced action generation. The latter point is particularly well made in a study by Beckers and colleagues (2002) in which one of two movements of a throttle-like response key was consistently paired with an aversive electrocutaneous stimulus, thereby acquiring a negative valence. The throttle-movements were later on required as grammatical categorisation responses in an affective Simon task (without any shock applications), and the results showed faster responding to negative words than to positive words with the previously shock-followed movement. This finding that aversively conditioned responses interact with word valence in a similar manner like responses instructed to be "positive" and "negative" points to the generality of the principles involved in affective S–R compatibility paradigms.

To conclude, two experiments showed that evaluative attributes of stimuli and responses are coded in a common representational format. Theories drawing on approach and avoidance motivations to account for the bidirectional evaluation–behaviour link are not suitable to explain costs of affective compatibility and paralleling findings of action–effect blindness in cognitive research. Instead the TEC receives empirical support that is well-equipped to explain close interactions between evaluations and actions (cf. Lavender & Hommel, 2007 this issue). The cognitive modelling of the evaluation–behaviour link entails that evaluative information is treated in a similar manner as other types of information, arguing against a distinctive processing route of evaluative information in action preparation. However, a common architecture of cognitive and affective S–R interactions does not imply that there are no differences at all between different types of S–R bindings. The systematic exploration of such differences might be an exciting avenue for future research.

REFERENCES

Adelman, P. K., & Zajonc, R. B. (1989). Facial efference and the experience of emotion. *Annual Review of Psychology, 40*, 249–280.

Beckers, T., De Houwer, J., & Eelen, P. (2002). Automatic integration of non-perceptual action effect features: The case of the associative Simon effect. *Psychological Research, 66*, 166–173.

Cacioppo, J. T., Larsen, J. T., Smith, K. N., & Berntson, G. G. (2004). The affect system: What lurks beyond the surface of feelings? In A. S. R. Manstead, N. Frijda, & A. Fischer (Eds.), *Feelings and emotions: The Amsterdam symposium* (pp. 223–242). Cambridge, UK: Cambridge University Press.

Cacioppo, J. T., Priester, J. R., & Berntson, G. G. (1993). Rudimentary determinants of attitudes. II: Arm flexion and extension have differential effects on attitudes. *Journal of Personality and Social Psychology*, 65, 5–17.

Centerbar, D. B., & Clore, G. L. (2006). Do approach–avoidance actions create attitudes? *Psychological Science*, 17, 22–29.

Chen, M., & Bargh, J. A. (1999). Consequences of automatic evaluation: Immediate behavioral predispositions to approach or avoid the stimulus. *Personality and Social Psychology Bulletin*, 25, 215–224.

Cretenet, J. I., & Dru, V. (2004). The influence of unilateral and bilateral arm flexion versus extension on judgments: An explanatory case of motor congruence. *Emotion*, 4, 282–294.

De Houwer, J. (2003). The extrinsic affective Simon task. *Experimental Psychology*, 50, 77–85.

De Houwer, J., & Eelen, P. (1998). An affective variant of the Simon paradigm. *Cognition and Emotion*, 12, 45–61.

De Houwer, J., Rothermund, K., & Wentura, D. (2001). Stimulus-feature specific negative priming. *Memory and Cognition*, 29, 931–939.

Dijksterhuis, A., & Aarts, H. (2003). On wildebeests and humans: The preferential detection of negative stimuli. *Psychological Science*, 14, 14–18.

Duncan, S., & Barrett, L. F. (2007). Affect is a form of cognition: A neurobiological analysis. *Cognition and Emotion*, 21, 1184–1211.

Eder, A. B., & Klauer, K. C. (2004, December). *Control of approach and avoidance movements by common affect codes*. Poster session presented at the Seminar on Neurosciences and Cognitive Control, Ghent, Belgium.

Eimer, M., Hommel, B., & Prinz, W. (1995). S–R compatibility and response selection. *Acta Psychologica*, 90, 301–313.

Elsner, B., & Hommel, B. (2001). Effect anticipation and action control. *Journal of Experimental Psychology: Human Perception and Performance*, 27, 229–240.

Fazio, R. H., Sanbonmatsu, D. M., Powell, M. C., & Kardes, F. R. (1986). On the automatic activation of attitudes. *Journal of Personality and Social Psychology*, 50, 229–238.

Greenwald, A. G. (1970). Sensory feedback mechanisms in performance control: With special reference to the ideomotor mechanism. *Psychological Review*, 77, 73–99.

Haussmann, R. E. (1992). Tachistoscopic presentation and millisecond timing on the IBM PC/XT/AT and PS/2: A Turbo Pascal unit to provide general-purpose routines for CGA, Hercules, EGA, and VGA monitors. *Behavior Research Methods, Instruments, Computers*, 24, 303–310.

Hommel, B. (2004). Event files: Feature binding in and across perception and action. *Trends in Cognitive Sciences*, 8, 494–500.

Hommel, B. (2005). How much attention does an event file need? *Journal of Experimental Psychology: Human Perception and Performance*, 31, 1067–1082.

Hommel, B., & Colzato, L. (2004). Visual attention and the temporal dynamics of feature integration. *Visual Cognition*, 11, 483–521.

Hommel, B., & Müsseler, J. (2006). Action-feature integration blinds to feature-overlapping perceptual events: Evidence from manual and vocal actions. *Quarterly Journal of Experimental Psychology*, 59, 509–523.

Hommel, B., Müsseler, J., Aschersleben, G., & Prinz, W. (2001). The theory of event coding (TEC): A framework for perception and action. *Behavioral and Brain Sciences*, 24, 849–878.

Ishimura, G., & Shimojo, S. (1994). Voluntary action captures visual motion. *Investigative Ophthalmology and Visual Sciences*, 35, 1275.

James, W. (1884). What is an emotion? *Mind*, 9, 188–205.

Jolicoeur, P. (1999). Dual-task interference and visual encoding. *Journal of Experimental Psychology: Human Perception and Performance*, 25, 596–616.

Klauer, K. C., & Musch, J. (2002). Goal-dependent and goal-independent effects of irrelevant evaluations. *Personality and Social Psychology Bulletin, 28*, 802–814.

Klauer, K. C., & Musch, J. (2003). Affective priming: Findings and theories. In J. Musch & K. C. Klauer (Eds.), *The psychology of evaluation: Affective processes in cognition and emotion* (pp. 7–49). Mahwah, NJ: Lawrence Erlbaum Associates, Inc.

Klauer, K. C., Musch, J., & Eder, A. B. (2005). Priming of semantic classifications: Late and response-related, or earlier and more central? *Psychonomic Bulletin & Review, 12*, 897–903.

Kornblum, S., Hasbroucq, T., & Osman, A. (1990). Dimensional overlap: Cognitive basis for stimulus–response compatibility—A model and taxonomy. *Psychological Review, 97*, 253–270.

Kunde, W., & Wühr, P. (2004). Actions blind to conceptually overlapping stimuli. *Psychological Research, 68*, 199–207.

Labiouse, C. L. (2004). Is there a real preferential detection of negative stimuli? A comment on Dijksterhuis and Aarts (2003). *Psychological Science, 15*, 364–365.

Lang, P. J., Bradley, M. M., & Cuthbert, B. N. (1998). Emotion and attention: Stop, look, and listen. *Cahiers de Psychologie Cognitive/Current Psychology of Cognition, 17*, 997–1020.

Lavender, T., & Hommel, B. (2007). Affect and action: Towards an event-coding account. *Cognition and Emotion, 21*, 1270–1296

Murphy, S. T., & Zajonc, R. B. (1993). Affect, cognition, and awareness: Affective priming with optimal and suboptimal stimulus exposure. *Journal of Personality and Social Psychology, 64*, 723–739.

Müsseler, J. (1999). How independent from action control is perception? An event-coding account for more equally ranked crosstalks. In G. Aschersleben, T. Bachmann, & J. Müsseler (Eds.), *Cognitive contributions to the perception of spatial and temporal events* (Advances in Psychology, Vol. 129, pp. 121–147). Amsterdam: Elsevier.

Müsseler, J., & Hommel, B. (1997a). Blindness to response-compatible stimuli. *Journal of Experimental Psychology: Human Perception and Performance, 23*, 861–872.

Müsseler, J., & Hommel, B. (1997b). Detecting and identifying response-compatible stimuli. *Psychonomic Bulletin & Review, 4*, 125–129.

Müsseler, J., Steininger, S., & Wühr, P. (2001). Can actions affect perceptual processing? *The Quarterly Journal of Experimental Psychology, 54A*, 137–154.

Müsseler, J., & Wühr, P. (2002). Response-evoked interference in visual encoding. In W. Prinz & B. Hommel (Eds.), *Common mechanisms in perception and action: Attention and Performance* (Vol. XIX, pp. 520–537). Oxford: Oxford University Press.

Müsseler, J., Wühr, P., & Prinz, W. (2000). Varying the response code in the blindness to response-compatible stimuli. *Visual Cognition, 7*, 743–767.

Neumann, R., Förster, J., & Strack, F. (2003). Motor compatibility: The bidirectional link between behavior and evaluation. In J. Musch & K. C. Klauer (Eds.), *The psychology of evaluation: Affective processes in cognition and emotion* (pp. 371–391). Mahwah, NJ: Lawrence Erlbaum Associates, Inc.

Neumann, R., & Strack, F. (2000). Approach and avoidance: The influence of proprioceptive and exteroceptive cues on encoding of affective information. *Journal of Personality and Social Psychology, 79*, 39–48.

Oriet, C., Stevanovski, B., & Jolicoeur, P. (2003). Congruency-induced blindness: A cost-benefit analysis. *Acta Psychologica, 112*, 243–258.

Park, J., & Kanwisher, N. (1994). Determinants of repetition blindness. *Journal of Experimental Psychology: Human Perception and Performance, 20*, 500–519.

Prinz, W. (1997). Perception and action planning. *European Journal of Cognitive Psychology, 9*, 129–154.

Rothermund, K., Wentura, D., & De Houwer, J. (2005). Retrieval of incidental stimulus–response associations as a source of negative priming. *Journal of Experimental Psychology: Learning, Memory, and Cognition, 31*, 482–495.

Rotteveel, M., & Phaf, R. H. (2004). Loading working memory enhances affective priming. *Psychonomic Bulletin & Review, 11*, 326–331.

Scherer, K. R. (1984). On the nature and function of emotion: A component process approach. In K. R. Scherer & P. Ekman (Eds.), *Approaches to emotion* (pp. 293–318). Hillsdale, NJ: Lawrence Erlbaum Associates, Inc.

Schubö, A., Prinz, W., & Aschersleben, G. (2004). Perceiving while acting: Action affects perception. *Psychological Research, 68*, 208–215.

Schwibbe, M., Röder, K., Schwibbe, G., Borchardt, M., & Geiken-Pophanken, G. (1981). Zum emotionalen Gehalt von Substantiven, Adjektiven und Verben [The emotional contents of nouns, adjectives and verbs]. *Zeitschrift für experimentelle und angewandte Psychologie, 28*, 486–501.

Silvert, L., Naveteur, J., Honoré, J., Sequeira, H., & Boucart, M. (2004). Emotional stimuli in rapid serial visual presentation. *Visual Cognition, 11*, 433–460.

Stevanovski, B., Oriet, C., & Jolicoeur, P. (2002). Blinded by headlights. *Canadian Journal of Experimental Psychology, 56*, 65–74.

Stevanovski, B., Oriet, C., & Jolicoeur, P. (2003). Can blindness to response-compatible stimuli be observed in the absence of a response? *Journal of Experimental Psychology: Human Perception and Performance, 29*, 431–440.

Stoet, G., & Hommel, B. (1999). Action planning and the temporal binding of response codes. *Journal of Experimental Psychology: Human Perception and Performance, 25*, 1625–1640.

Tom, G., Petterson, P., Lau, T., Burton, T., & Cook, J. (1991). The role of overt head movements in the formation of affect. *Basic and Applied Social Psychology, 12*, 281–289.

Treisman, A. (1996). The binding problem. *Current Opinion in Neurobiology, 6*, 171–178.

Viviani, P., & Stucchi, N. (1992). Biological movements look uniform: Evidence of motor-perceputal interactions. *Journal of Experimental Psychology: Human Perception and Performance, 18*, 603–623.

Wentura, D. (1999). Activation and inhibition of affective information: Evidence for negative priming in the evaluation task. *Cognition and Emotion, 13*, 65–91.

Wickens, T. D., & Hirshman, E. (2000). False memories and statistical decision theory: Comment on Miller and Wolford (1999) and Roediger and McDermott (1999). *Psychological Review, 107*, 377–383.

Wohlschläger, A. (2000). Visual motion priming by invisible actions. *Vision Research, 40*, 925–930.

Wühr, P., & Müsseler, J. (2001). Time course of the blindness to response-compatible stimuli. *Journal of Experimental Psychology: Human Perception and Performance, 27*, 1260–1270.

Wühr, P., & Müsseler, J. (2002). Blindness to response-compatible stimuli in the psychological refractory period paradigm. *Visual Cognition, 9*, 421–457.

COGNITION AND EMOTION
2007, 21 (6), 1323–1346

Mere exposure in reverse: Mood and motion modulate memory bias

Mark Rotteveel and R. Hans Phaf

University of Amsterdam, Amsterdam, The Netherlands

Mere exposure, generally, entails influences of familiarity manipulations on affective dependent variables. Previously (Phaf & Rotteveel, 2005), we have argued that familiarity corresponds intrinsically to positive affect, and have extended the correspondence to novelty and negative affect. Here, we present two experiments that show reverse effects of affective manipulations on perceived familiarity. In Experiment 1 affectively valenced exteroceptive cues of approach and avoidance (e.g., apparent movement) modulated recognition bias of neutral targets. This finding suggests that our correspondence hypotheses can be generalised to an important aspect of emotion, namely approach and avoidance tendencies. In Experiment 2 participants' emotional mood was manipulated within the Jacoby–Whitehouse paradigm and a pattern of results was obtained as if consciousness was manipulated. We interpret the latter results within the affective modulation framework (AMF), which postulates facilitation of nonconscious processing by positive affect and an enhancement of conscious processing by negative affect.

If affect and cognition can be distinguished, they, at least, interact at many different levels. The distinction has been an issue of longstanding debate and has been surrounded by several controversies in the literature (see Storbeck & Clore, this issue). One of the most prominent debates concerned "affective primacy", which was proposed by Zajonc in his seminal paper entitled "Feeling and thinking. Preferences need no inferences" (1980, see also 1981, and 1984). Zajonc argued that affect could precede *and* operate independently of cognition and based his position also on his findings with mere exposure that preferences shifts due to previous presentation could occur without conscious recognition. Affective primacy was opposed by Lazarus (1981, 1982; but see also Baars, 1981), who argued that feeling and emotion, and by definition affect, depends on, and is completely intertwined with,

Correspondence should be addressed to: Mark Rotteveel, University of Amsterdam, Department of Psychology, NL-1018 WB Amsterdam, The Netherlands. E-mail: m.rotteveel@uva.nl

We thank Sumit Mehra and Floris van der Hoek for their assistance in collecting the data.

© 2007 Psychology Press, an imprint of the Taylor & Francis Group, an Informa business
DOI: 10.1080/02699930701438319

cognition, which in his theory is embodied by the concept of "appraisal" or "cognitive appraisal". Although this debate could easily be reduced to semantics and variable definitions of "cognition", there seems to be at least one matter of substance in the debate. As Baars pointed out, Zajonc's definition of cognition is defined by *conscious* judgement and inference by *conscious* inference, whereas Lazarus' definition of cognition incorporates both conscious and nonconscious cognition (see Lazarus, 1981). Zajonc may have been led into this definition of cognition by the research method of subjective (i.e., conscious) report (e.g., Frijda, Kuipers & ter Schure, 1989; Shaver, Schwartz, Kirson, & O'Connor, 1987; Smith & Ellsworth, 1985) that is predominantly used to investigate the structure of appraisals. This method, implicitly or explicitly, adheres to an identity position (e.g., Mandler, 1996), which assumes that conscious and nonconscious processes do not differ qualitatively, and that conscious report can, thus, be used to probe the structure of nonconscious appraisal (this "vexing" problem was later even acknowledged by Lazarus, 1995). In our opinion, the main gain of the Zajonc–Lazarus debate was that the conscious–nonconscious distinction was again put on the map in emotion research. In this paper we will argue that the conscious–nonconscious distinction is much more useful to emotion research than the affect–cognition distinction and that the latter distinction is further contradicted by shifts in general modes of information processing due to different affective states, as proposed in our affective modulation framework (AMF). In two experiments we conceptually reversed mere exposure by investigating the influence of affective manipulations on perceived familiarity.

The experimental paradigm of "mere exposure" on which Zajonc (1980) built his "affective primacy" hypothesis shows the effect of a non-affective, presumably "cognitive" (according to Lazarus), manipulation (i.e., repetition) on an affective dependent variable (i.e., preference). Classically, mere exposure is the finding of a preference for previously presented stimuli above novel stimuli (Kunst-Wilson & Zajonc, 1980). The primarily nonconscious nature of mere exposure was underlined by a meta-analysis (Bornstein, 1989), which showed that preference shifts for previously presented stimuli were larger when they were unavailable for consciousness at initial presentation. Though some theorists hold that mere exposure is merely a non-affective implicit memory effect (e.g., Mandler, Nakamura, & Van Zandt, 1987; Seamon, Marsh, & Brody, 1984; Whittlesea & Price, 2001), there is now sufficient evidence to show that genuine affect is involved in mere exposure. Repeated exposures were, for instance, shown to increase liking of unrelated and even dissimilar stimuli, and elevate, moreover, general mood (Monahan, Murphy, & Zajonc, 2000). Perhaps the strongest evidence comes from a facial electromyography study (Harmon-Jones & Allen, 2001) showing that mere exposure is also accompanied by facial muscle contractions (i.e., of the musculus zygomaticus major) indicative of positive affect (see also Winkielman & Cacioppo, 2001). The finding of stronger effects in predominantly nonconscious conditions itself may also be taken as evidence for affective processing (see also Murphy & Zajonc, 1993; Rotteveel, de Groot, Geutskens, & Phaf, 2001). It appears that particularly affective processes can be evoked at the earliest stages of information processing and in subcortical brain centres (Liddell et al., 2005; see Elliot & Dolan, 1998, for a neuroimaging study of mere exposure).

An integrative (i.e., of affect and cognition) account of mere exposure was first proposed by Reber, Winkielman, and Schwarz (1998) and extended by Phaf and Rotteveel (2005). Reber et al. postulated that perceptual fluency corresponds to positive affect. In three experiments perceptual fluency was manipulated by means other than repetition as with classic mere exposure. In their first experiment a target picture was preceded by a matching or a nonmatching prime. Targets preceded by matching primes were judged as prettier than when they were preceded by nonmatching primes. Higher contrast, and therefore more fluency, between stimuli filled with different grey tones with respect to their background evoked, moreover, more "pretty" *and* less "ugly" responses in Experiment 2. In the third experiment longer stimulus presentation was accompanied by higher liking *and* lower disliking. The authors concluded that fluency, and, therefore, also previous exposure, evokes the experience of processing ease that *itself* is positively valenced and is subsequently interpreted as a stimulus quality. Particularly, the finding of a positively valenced preference shift in positively and negatively framed questions (Experiments 2 and 3; see also Seamon, McKenna, & Binder, 1998), led Reber et al. to this hypothesis. The correspondence between fluency and positive affect was further strengthened by findings that ease of processing also induced musculus zygomaticus major activity (similar to Harmon-Jones & Allen, 2001) that is indicative of positive affect (Winkielman & Cacioppo, 2001).

The theoretical account of Reber et al. (1998), in which memory- (i.e., cognitively) and affect-oriented accounts of mere exposure were integrated, was not only extended by Phaf and Rotteveel (2005) with regard to negative affect but also implications for memory performance were formulated. We proposed an intrinsic relationship between subjective familiarity (which can, though not exclusively, be induced by fluency) and affect by proposing that not only the early processing of positive affect and familiarity corresponds but also of novelty and negative affect. This theoretical point of view reflects our *correspondence hypothesis* that was initially supported by two experiments. The first experiment was similar to the experimental design of Jacoby and Whitehouse (1989), but affectively valenced word primes were added. After first presenting a study list, Jacoby and Whitehouse measured recognition of old as well as new words that were immediately preceded by either the same (matching) or by a new (nonmatching) context word (i.e., prime). In addition, the primes were either presented so briefly that there was no later prime recognition, or sufficiently long to allow for conscious perception of the context words. Short exposure to matching primes raised overall test word familiarity, irrespective of their memory status (i.e., old or new). Matching primes increased both false alarm rates ("old" responses to new words) and, to a lesser degree, hit rates ("old" responses to studied words). With long presentations participants could consciously distinguish sources of familiarity (i.e., studied or primed) and discount inappropriate (i.e., due to the primes) feelings of familiarity. In optimal conditions familiarity of the test words was now even smaller with matching than with nonmatching primes. Phaf and Rotteveel added positive and negative words to the experimental design (Experiment 1) and a similar pattern of results was obtained as in suboptimal conditions with matching and nonmatching context words, respectively. In other words, positively valenced context words increased test word familiarity, as with suboptimal matching context words, whereas negatively valenced context words decreased test word familiarity as with suboptimal nonmatching context words.

Facial muscles (and hand muscles in the control condition) were non-obtrusively manipulated in Experiment 2 of Phaf and Rotteveel (2005), see Strack, Martin, & Stepper, 1988; Strack & Neumann, 2000, for a similar method) to induce either a positive, negative or affectively neutral state (i.e., the control condition). Again, familiarity was higher with positive affect than with negative affect, whereas familiarity in the control condition was at an intermediate level. The results of Experiment 1 were, therefore, replicated conceptually. It is important to note that in signal-detection terms only bias but not sensitivity (i.e., recognition accuracy) was influenced by the affective manipulations in both experiments. Subjective familiarity is primarily reflected in how liberal or conservative participants are in making their recognition judgements. The results supported the correspondence hypothesis and indicated, moreover, that affective modulation of recognition bias can be extended from a trial-based priming effect to a more general influence of affective state. In Experiment 2 of this study we will further expand this to general mood effects.

Our correspondence hypothesis can be embedded in the framework of dual-process theories in the domains of memory (e.g., Jacoby, 1983; Jacoby & Dallas, 1981; Jacoby & Whitehouse, 1989) and of emotion (LeDoux, 1986, 1996; Oatley & Johnson-Laird, 1987, 1995). Oatley and Johnson-Laird, for instance, proposed two kinds of internal signals accompanying an emotional event, a control and an informational signal. The informational signal contains information about what caused the emotion and to whom it is directed. The evolutionary older control signal sets the brain in a particular mode of organisation and has an emotional tone, but no other informational content. The control signal primarily prepares the system for action (i.e., action tendencies) by tuning particular modes of information processing (i.e., information processing tendencies) that belong to specific emotions (see also Gray, 2004). Fear is, for instance, characterised by tendencies to freeze and prepare for vigorous action and to carefully scrutinise the surroundings for signs of actual threat due to this control signal. Such global information-processing tendencies, or emotion modes, are particularly adaptive when there is a lack of information (e.g., with time pressure; LeDoux, 1996). According to the correspondence hypothesis, emotional modes of action and information processing are not exclusively evoked by emotionally significant stimuli, but also by classically "cognitive" features like memory status and also ease of information processing.

The control signal involves both action and information processing tendencies. The activation of action tendencies by affective stimuli has been reported in many experiments (Chen & Bargh, 1999; Duckworth, Bargh, Garcia, & Chaiken, 2002; Roelofs, Elzinga, & Rotteveel, 2005; Rotteveel & Phaf, 2004a; Rotteveel, van Ditzhuijzen, & Phaf, 2004; Solarz, 1960) showing that positive and negative valence can either facilitate or inhibit approach and avoidance action tendencies. Whereas the action tendencies may be activated directly by the control signal, these effects also seem mediated by the additional, more indirect, translation of these tendencies into specific actions (Lavender & Hommel, this issue; Markman & Brendl, 2005). In our experiments (Rotteveel & Phaf, 2004a, Experiments 1 and 3) the speed of arm flexion/extension was modulated by affective evaluation of emotional expressions. Arm flexion was faster with happy faces than with angry faces, whereas arm extension was faster with angry faces than with happy faces. The association, moreover, seems to be bi-directional because performing similar actions influences affective information processing. Affective evaluations of novel and neutral ideographs were, for instance, congruently influenced by isometric arm flexion and extension (Cacioppo, Priester, & Berntson, 1993; but see Centerbar & Clore, 2006, for results which can be interpreted as support for our correspondence hypothesis). Categorising positively valenced words was, moreover, easier with isometric arm flexion than with isometric arm extension, whereas, categorising negatively valenced words was easier with isometric arm extension than with isometric arm flexion (Neumann & Strack, 2000, Experiment 1).

The close association between affect and action tendencies is further supported by findings that monitoring consequences of these actions also induces affect. Neumann and Strack (2000, Experiment 2) showed that in the case of the illusion of movement with respect to the computer screen a similar impact was obtained on affective information processing as with proprioceptive cues from arm flexion or extension (Neumann & Strack, Experiment 1). The illusion of distance reduction (i.e., exteroceptive cue of approach) was accompanied by shorter latencies with affective evaluations of positively valenced words than with negatively valenced words, whereas, the illusion of increasing distance (i.e., exteroceptive cue of avoidance) was accompanied by the reversed pattern of results. Similar results were obtained by Rotteveel, Bonarius, and Phaf (2007) with arm flexion and extension as dependent variables when faces with emotional expressions moved away or approached the participant. The close association between affect and motion, either by the participant or by the stimulus, can easily be accommodated within the notion of mirror neurons (Rizzolatti & Arbib, 1998). Mirror neurons either become activated when action is performed or when that particular action is observed and thus link action and the observation of that action. Recently, the concept has been extended to the execution and observation of affective actions and expressions (Gallese, Keysers, & Rizzolatti, 2004).

Affective modulation by exteroceptive cues of approach and avoidance follows quite naturally from the combination of the theoretical framework of Oatley and Johnson-Laird (1987, 1995) with the notion of mirror neurons. In the next experiment we tested whether exteroceptive cues of approach and avoidance would bias recognition in a similar manner as positively valenced primes and states and negative valenced primes and states, respectively. If a neutral stimulus apparently moves towards participants, it should, according to the correspondence hypothesis, be judged more familiar than when it apparently moves away. Because no reference is made to affect or emotion, or approach or avoidance for that matter, either in the stimuli or in the response required, such a result would suggest that affective modulation by means of exteroceptive cues of approach and avoidance is implicit, and requires little or no conscious "cognitive" processing.

EXPERIMENT 1

We aim to show with this first experiment that exteroceptive cues of approach and avoidance influence recognition bias of neutral target words according to the correspondence hypothesis (Phaf & Rotteveel, 2005). Because actual approach and avoidance behaviour (e.g., by means of arm flexion or extension) results in decreased or increased visual angles in stimulus perception, motion was operationalised by the gradual manipulation of target size. A movement toward participants entails gradually increasing target sizes, whereas an apparent movement away entails gradually decreasing target sizes of both the horizontal and the vertical visual angles. A subsequent task served as a manipulation check of affect induction by apparent movement. The same paradigm was applied to (unfamiliar) Finnish words with affective evaluation as the dependent variable this time.

Method

Participants.   Eighty-six participants (average age = 22.2, $SD = 6.41$, 24 male) participated in the experiment, announced as a "Do you remember or not?" experiment for course credit or a financial compensation of €5. All participants had Dutch as their first language and were unfamiliar with the Finnish language and had normal or corrected to normal vision.

Design.   The experiment had a 2×2 factorial design for the memory test. Independent within-participant factors were Memory Status ("old" or "new" words) and Apparent Movement (toward or away) of the target words. The dependent variable was the proportion "old" responses. For the test of affect a one-factor design was used and the dependent measure was the proportion "positive" responses in the two-alternative-forced-choice affective evaluation task.

Material and apparatus.   For the targets and fillers in the memory test 252 affectively neutral Dutch nouns were collected. The words had two or three syllables, consisted of four to six letters and had a medium word frequency in the Dutch language (between 10 and 49 times per million words; according to the CELEX database; Burnage, 1990).

The study list contained 80 words that were actually tested in the test phase and were selected randomly from the set of 240 words. The study list was preceded by 3 fillers and concluded by 3 fillers to prevent primacy and recency effects. Fillers were picked randomly from an additional set of 12 affectively neutral Dutch nouns. These fillers were all used in practice trials that preceded the test phase. Target stimuli were presented in the study phase for 1500 ms in Tahoma font (upper case, 24 points) with an inter-stimulus-interval (ISI) of 1500 ms.

To obtain apparent motion in the subsequent test phase all studied and new words (Tahoma font, upper case) gradually increased or decreased in size from 8 to 104 points relative to monitor mid-point within a time frame of 500 ms using Authorware 7.0. The words were presented in the centre of the screen on a light-grey background. A total of 240 words were tested so that the formerly used old/new quotient of 1/3 was reached (see Phaf & Rotteveel, 2005). ISI was varied randomly from 1.5 to 2 seconds. There were no further restrictions other than that half of both categories (old and new) apparently moved towards or away from participants.

The experiment was carried out on eight PCs (Pentium II) with 17-inch CRT monitors (1024×768 pixel resolution). Responses ("old"/"new") could be made by means of the keyboard ("z"/"m" buttons) and labelling was counterbalanced fully across participants. Participants were seated approximately 60–70 cm from the monitors.

For the two-alternative forced-choice affective evaluation task 32 Finnish words were used that were randomly assigned to both movement conditions. Similar to the Dutch words all target words had two or three syllables and consisted of four to six letters. The test of affect was preceded by 6 practice trials using 6 words similar to the test words. Apparent motion was obtained similarly to the memory test. Affective evaluation ("positive" or "negative") responses could be given by pressing keyboard buttons ("a"/"l") and labelling was counterbalanced fully across participants.

Procedure. The participants were tested in eight cubicles. It was explained that the experiment consisted of two tests and that the first was about the influence of stimulus motion on memory performance. No reference was made with respect to the number of studied and new words, approach/avoidance or with respect to affective or emotional influences. After signing informed consent the study list was presented with the instruction to remember as much of it as possible, although it would probably be hard because of the large number of stimulus words. After completing the study phase, participants were instructed to complete a non-related puzzle for 5 minutes after which the test phase was started, which was preceded by 12 practice trials. After completing the memory test, the affective evaluation test was introduced. Participants were instructed to evaluate unknown Finnish words intuitively as representing something with a positive or negative meaning. This second test phase was preceded by 6 practice trials and after finishing this phase participants completed the exit interview and were subsequently thanked for their cooperation.

Results

Eighty-three percent of the participants indicated in the exit interview that they experienced stimulus movement, whereas 12% experienced self-motion. This difference did not influence recognition performance or the results in general. No participant reported any connection between apparent motion and affect or emotion, even when explicitly asked for.

Participants' overall correct recognitions ($M = 0.52$, $SD = 0.18$) surpassed their proportion false recognitions ($M = 0.24$, $SD = 0.17$) in the memory test, which indicated (see also Table 1) successful recognition, $F(1, 84) = 173.48$, $p < .0001$, $\eta_p^2 = .67$. As expected, motion modulated subjective familiarity. When words moved toward participants, the proportion of responses to both studied and nonstudied words ($M = 0.40$, $SD = 0.22$) surpassed the proportion of responses to words that moved away ($M = 0.37$, $SD = 0.22$); $F(1, 84) = 10.3$, $p < .01$, $\eta_p^2 = .11$. Interestingly, this main effect held both

TABLE 1
Proportions correct and false recognitions (standard deviations) as a function of apparent movement in Experiment 1

	Correct recognition	False recognition
Movement toward	0.54 (0.18)	0.25 (0.16)
Movement away	0.50 (0.18)	0.23 (0.16)

for correct and false recognitions as evidenced by the absence of the interaction between the factors apparent movement and memory status, $F(1, 84) = 2.26$, ns.

The comparable effects of apparent movement on studied and new words suggest a bias effect. To verify this recognition performance was also investigated (see Table 2) in terms of the signal-detection measures sensitivity (P_r) and bias (B_r) according to the two-high threshold model (Snodgrass & Corwin, 1988; see Phaf & Rotteveel, 2005, for a similar approach). Statistical analyses showed that the effect of apparent movement was due, specifically, to bias, $t(85) = 3.15$, $p < .01$, and not to sensitivity, $t(85) = 1.4$, ns. This finding indicated that in the approach condition participants were less conservative in "recognising" items, and may have experienced higher subjective familiarity, than in the avoidance condition.

Affective evaluation of the Finnish words in the second task indicated that movement towards participants resulted in more positive responses ($M = 0.51$, $SD = 0.17$) than movement away ($M = 0.48$, $SD = 0.15$), which, however, only approached significance, $t(85) = 1.33$, $p = .09$, in a one-tailed paired t-test. Interestingly, the effect of exteroceptive cues of approach and avoidance on affective evaluation (i.e., proportion "positive" responses in the movement toward minus the movement away condition) of the unfamiliar Finnish words correlated positively (one-tailed, $r = .21$, $p < .05$) with the effect of these cues in recognition performance (i.e., proportion "old" responses in the movement toward minus the movement away condition). This suggested that apparent movement had corresponding effects on affective evaluation and subjective familiarity.

TABLE 2
Sensitivity (P_r) and Bias (B_r) of recognition performance (standard deviations) in Experiment 1 according to the two-high threshold model

	P_r	B_r
Apparent movement towards	0.29 (0.21)	0.35 (0.17)
Apparent movement away	0.27 (0.21)	0.32 (0.18)

Discussion

Apparent movement of target stimuli clearly influenced subjective familiarity. The shift in recognition performance was due to bias instead of sensitivity and the results of Phaf and Rotteveel (2005) were conceptually replicated using exteroceptive cues of approach and avoidance, instead of explicit affective manipulations. Formerly studied, as well as new (i.e., nonstudied), neutral words that apparently moved toward participants were more often recognised as previously studied than neutral words that apparently moved away. In contrast to Neumann and Strack's (2000) apparent motion experiment (Experiment 2), moreover, our target stimuli had no explicit affective valence. It appears, therefore, that affective modulation by exteroceptive cues of approach and avoidance does not clearly depend on explicit affective evaluation. It should also be noted that the experimental manipulation (i.e., apparent movement) as well as the dependent measure (i.e., recognition performance) were considered, by the participants at least, as completely non-affective. Insofar as we were successful in manipulating affect by means of exteroceptive cues of approach and avoidance, both the induction and measurement of affect appeared to have been implicit entailing little or no conscious affective processing.

Affective modulation of recognition bias may appear somewhat paradoxical in the light of Bornstein's (1989) conclusion that mere exposure is strongest when there is no recognition of the previously presented stimuli. Primarily in less conscious conditions, the meta-analysis thus seems to show a lack of correspondence between affect and familiarity. Whittlesea and Price (2001) have already noted that Bornstein's conclusion seems inconsistent with dual-process theories of recognition (Mandler, 1980). If familiarity increases liking, it should similarly increase recognition performance, which, at least in part, also depends on familiarity (i.e., next to conscious recollection). No dissociation between liking and recognition should then be observed after mere exposure. These paradoxical findings can, however, be fitted in dual-process theory (see Whittlesea & Price, 2001) by assuming that in the setup of the classical mere-exposure paradigm different processing strategies are tapped by evaluation and recognition.

Whittlesea and Price (2001) argued that the instruction to recognise old stimuli among a set of very similar stimuli evokes the strategy to scrutinise each test item for distinctive, recognisable, features (i.e., analytic processing). When asked for an affective evaluation, however, there is no need to discriminate between similar test stimuli and to search for an episodic context. Participants can then rely on a more direct and intuitive "feeling" about the stimulus (i.e., non-analytic processing). In a series of experiments Whittlesea and Price demonstrated that preference and recognition effects of mere exposure could be made to appear and disappear by instructing non-analytic and analytic processing modes, respectively. Whittlesea and Price concluded, therefore, that the apparent dissociation in mere exposure does not follow from earlier or later stages for processing affect or familiarity, but from different processing strategies evoked by the task context in affective evaluation and recognition. Due to the long study lists, which apparently made it difficult to explicitly remember details of the presentation, participants in our experiments probably adopted a non-analytic retrieval strategy, which relies on feelings of familiarity. Both in Experiment 1 and in the experiments of Phaf and Rotteveel (2005) the processing strategy adopted by the participants thus enabled us to find corresponding effects of affect and familiarity. In the next experiment we will manipulate processing strategy by inducing different moods, which according to Oatley and Johnson-Laird (1987, 1995) evoke different processing modes.

The Jacoby–Whitehouse effect can also be interpreted in terms of processing modes (see Whittlesea & Price, 2001, for this suggestion). Long prime presentation induces detailed analytic processing, whereas short presentation leads to global non-analytic processing. With long presentation both sources of familiarity (i.e., context word and previously studied or not) are distinguished through analytic processing, whereas with short presentation insufficient information is available for this analysis. Conscious analytic processing may even result in discounting the additional familiarity due to the matching prime, leading to a recognition bias towards the test words primed by nonmatching context words. The crossover interaction characteristic of the Jacoby–Whitehouse effect may, thus, be a contrast between conscious, analytic, processing and nonconscious, non-analytic, processing. In our opinion, this account in terms of different processing modes can even be generalised to other contrast findings, such as affective priming (e.g., Murphy & Zajonc, 1993; Rotteveel et al., 2001; Rotteveel & Phaf, 2004b).

If one carries through these arguments to the reverse mere-exposure effect (i.e., affective modulation of recognition in the extended Jacoby–Whitehouse paradigm), one would expect similar processing-mode effects. In our view these modes of processing may even belong to the control signal of specific emotions (Oatley & Johnson-Laird, 1987, 1995). In particular we expect analytic processing to be evoked by a fearful mood and non-analytic processing by a happy mood. Fear motivates the careful scrutinisation of the environment for potential threats, whereas happiness allows for the indiscriminate intake of beneficial stimuli. If the control signal of these emotions and corresponding moods (emotions and moods are assumed to differ only in their information signal) indeed consists of these specific processing modes, the two moods could be used to emulate the effects of optimal (i.e., conscious) and suboptimal (i.e., less conscious) presentation in the extended Jacoby–Whitehouse paradigm. If the prime presentation time is chosen carefully between suboptimal and fully optimal conditions, mood may, thus, tip the balance either in the conscious and analytic direction, or in the nonconscious non-analytic direction.

There is very little research (but see Storbeck & Clore, this issue, for much new research into this issue) that explicitly investigates affective modulation of non-affective information processing, but recently it has been observed, for instance, that positive mood increases semantic priming (Corson, 2002) and also the incidence of false memories (Storbeck & Clore, 2005). The finding from our previous study (Phaf & Rotteveel, 2005, Experiment 1) that only suboptimally presented, negative primes could be recognised above chance after completing the Jacoby–Whitehouse task, also provides support for our view. The negative primes probably had a mood-inducing effect and thus evoked analytic processing of these primes, which enhanced subsequent explicit recollection. In the next experiment we aim to show that affective state not only influences priming of individual items, but can also lead to qualitative changes in the general pattern of priming due to different information-processing tendencies.

EXPERIMENT 2

To investigate whether positive mood favoured nonconscious modes of information processing, and negative mood conscious modes we set up an experiment in which a happy or a fearful mood was induced before the recognition test in an extended Jacoby–Whitehouse task (i.e., with matching, nonmatching, positive and negative primes). In a bogus "subliminal" study task (see Monin, 2003, Experiment 4, for a similar approach) it was suggested to participants that words were presented for study, while in fact they were not. All "old" responses represented, therefore, false recognition in this experiment (i.e., "old" words were absent). False alarms in a recognition task probably provide a purer measure of subjective familiarity induced by the context words than hits (see also Jacoby & Whitehouse, 1989).

Prime presentation duration was not varied but set at an intermediate level. Mood should bias processing of the matching and nonmatching primes either in the non-analytic or the analytic direction. It was expected that the effects of happy vs. fearful moods would mirror the effects of suboptimal vs. optimal stimulus presentation. If it is assumed that positive and negative primes have corresponding effects on familiarity as matching and nonmatching primes (see Phaf & Rotteveel, 2005), a similar crossover effect should be observed with both types of primes as a function of mood. Finally, a prime recognition task was conducted after the Jacoby–Whitehouse task to investigate whether negative affect favours conscious recollection relative to positive affect.

Method

Participants. Forty-one psychology students from the University of Amsterdam (average age = 21.76, $SD = 3.14$, 15 male) participated in the experiment, announced as a "Movie and Memory" experiment, for course credit or a financial compensation of €7. All participants had Dutch as their first language and normal or corrected-to-normal vision. They were divided in two groups for the happy (21) or the fearful induction (20).

Design. The experiment had a $2 \times 2 \times 2$ mixed-factorial design. Independent within-participants factors were Affectivity of the Prime (affective vs. non-affective) and Familiarity of the Primes (matching/positive vs. non-matching/negative). The independent between-participant factor was Mood (happy vs. fearful). The dependent variable was the proportion "old" responses on the test words. The coupling of primes to test words was counterbalanced. Four different test lists were created in which every test word was preceded equally often by each type of prime. The order of the test words was random and determined by the computer.

Material and apparatus. For the targets 120 affectively neutral Dutch nouns were collected. The words had two or three syllables, consisted of five to nine letters and had a medium word frequency in the Dutch language (between 10 and 49 times per million words; according to the CELEX database; Burnage, 1990). The prime words were selected along the same criteria as the targets, but the affective primes had a positive or negative valence, and the non-matching primes were neutral words that differed from the targets. Thirty words were selected for each affective valence that were categorised most consistently and fastest as positive, neutral, or negative in a perceptual clarification task (Phaf, van der Leij, Stienen, & Bierman, 2006). A participant in this task was instructed to categorise the word as quickly as possible while the mask over the word gradually disappears due to the "clarification" of randomly selected pixels. The task enabled the collection of emotion words that require the lowest level of stimulus presentation for their emotional categorisation.

The present experiment was carried out on a PC with a presentation monitor that was set at a refresh rate of 60 Hz. The words were presented at the centre of the screen on a light-grey background. The characters were black and approximately 2 cm in size. Participants were seated at approximately 70 cm from the display. In the study phase 60 bogus subliminal presentation trials were conducted. A trial started with the presentation of a mask for 83 ms, followed by an empty interval of 33 ms, and subsequently another mask appeared for 33 ms. The interval between trials was 4.83 s. The masks consisted of nonsense letter strings with only consonants (e.g., hJkRBsQm, dWtPZxYr). In the test phase, consisting of 120 trials, a prime appeared for 50 ms (three refreshes, resulting in an effective presentation of approximately 37 ms; see Bridgeman, 1998), and was preceded and followed by a mask, consisting of 10 @ characters, both for 249 ms. Subsequently, the test word appeared for 2.49 s. After the test word disappeared, 6.1 s remained for participants to respond before the next trial started The non-proportional Courier New font was used, so that all letters of the prime word would be masked by the @ characters. Participants operated the two-button response box with their preferred hand. The right button was labelled "OLD" and the left button "NEW".

For the prime recognition test after the Jacoby–Whitehouse task, 30 new distracters (10 from each valence) were selected that matched the primes. Also 10 positive, 10 negative, and 10 matching primes were selected that were presented in the Jacoby–Whitehouse task. The words were presented in random order for 3.32 s each. Subsequently, a participant had 4.15 s to indicate whether the word had been presented in the previous task.

Mood induction.   A number of different emotion induction techniques were combined. To induce a fearful mood a fragment from the movie "The Ring" was shown, and to induce a happy mood a fragment from the television serial "Friends". Before participants saw these fragments, they were asked to remember a fearful or happy episode from their own life and asked to relive the experience. After the fragment they were asked which technique worked best to instigate the desired mood. In the breaks of the Jacoby–Whitehouse recognition test they were instructed to think back to the induction technique that worked best for them. Mood was further maintained by playing positively (from the soundtrack of "Friends") or negatively (from the soundtracks of Hitchcock movies) charged music for the remainder of the experiment. The experimenter, moreover, behaved in a mood-congruent manner and smiled a lot with the positive induction, or acted more aloof with the negative induction. Mood was measured with a short self-report questionnaire, consisting of four items. The poles of the 7-point rating scales were Brave vs. Fearful, Happy vs. Sad, Contented vs. Angry, and Energetic vs. Tired. This questionnaire was filled out seven times: at arrival, after the film fragment, during the three breaks of the Jacoby–Whitehouse recognition test, after the recognition test, and after the prime recognition test.

Procedure.   The participants were first explained that they took part in an experiment investigating the influence of mood on memory and that they would be asked to get in an anxious or happy mood. After signing informed consent, the participants completed the first questionnaire. They were then told that 60 words would be presented one by one, but that it would be extremely difficult to see them. It was explained that it was known from previous research that even this "subliminal" presentation leaves a memory trace, and that they would later be tested on these words. After the bogus presentation trials the mood induction and the recognition test followed. The recognition test was first practised in six trials, which resembled the experimental test trials in every respect, except that no primes appeared between the masks (this was not divulged to the participants). The participants were then asked to write down briefly an episode in which they had experienced the desired emotion and subsequent to that they watched the fragment. The most effective induction technique was chosen and the mood questionnaire completed again. They were told that the actual recognition test would contain 60 new and 60 old words. The participants were instructed to use the @ characters as a fixation, and not to think too long about the answer but to take intuitive decisions. In the breaks and at the end of the recognition task the mood questionnaire was administered again. An unexpected recognition test of the primes in the first recognition test concluded the memory tests. After the last mood questionnaire was filled out, the music was turned off and an exit interview followed.

Results

Mood reports indicated successful mood induction. Before the start of the experiment there were no significant differences in mood reports on any of the items, but the reports of Brave–Fearful, interaction of mood with time: $F(6, 216) = 9.62$, $p < .0001$, $\eta_p^2 = .211$, Happy–Sad, $F(6, 216) = 8.01$, $p < .0001$, $\eta_p^2 = .182$, and Contented–Angry, $F(6, 216) = 4.48$, $p < .005$, $\eta_p^2 = .111$, were clearly influenced by the induction (see Figure 1). Only with the Energetic–Tired item did the development over time not reach significance, $F(6, 216) = 1.26$, ns, $\eta_p^2 = .182$, despite a significant overall effect of emotional state, $F(1, 36) = 4.95$, $p < .05$, $\eta_p^2 = .121$.

Mood effects were also obtained both in the non-affective and the affective priming task (see Table 3). In the exit interview none of the participants reported having noticed that no words were presented in the bogus subliminal presentation task and fairly high levels of illusory familiarity were attained. The classic Jacoby–Whitehouse crossover effect, $F(1, 39) = 11.36$, $p < .005$, $\eta_p^2 = .225$, of the matching and non-matching primes was replicated, this time not as a function of presentation time, which was held constant in the experiment, but as a function of induced mood. In a positive mood priming with matching context words relative to nonmatching words, $t(20) = 4.38$, $p < .0001$, was similar to the classic Jacoby–Whitehouse effect when comparing short and long prime presentation conditions, larger than the contrast (i.e., reversed priming) obtained with the negative mood, $t(19) = -0.31$, ns. Matching primes (0.535, $SD = 0.165$) thus led, irrespective

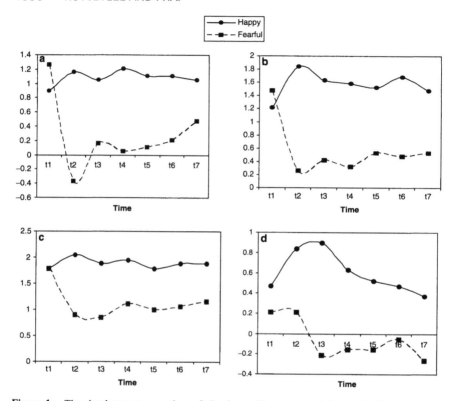

Figure 1. The development over time of the four self-report mood items: (a) Brave–Fearful; (b) Happy–Sad; (c) Contented–Angry; and (d) Energetic–Tired.

of mood induction, $F(1, 39) = 8.58$, $p < .01$, $\eta_p^2 = .180$, to a higher illusory familiarity than nonmatching primes (0.439, $SD = 0.128$). In the non-affective part of the priming task there also was an overall tendency, $F(1, 39) = 3.40$, $p = .073$, $\eta_p^2 = .080$, for target words to be judged more familiar in the happy (0.512, $SD = 0.134$) than in the fearful mood (0.460, $SD = 0.169$).

With affective priming (see Table 3) mood effects had the same direction as with non-affective priming, but they were weaker. The interaction between prime and mood was in the same direction as with non-affective priming, but reached only marginal significance, $F(1, 39) = 3.48$, $p = .070$, $\eta_p^2 = .082$. Here reversed priming, $t(19) = 2.00$, $p < .05$, in the negative mood (i.e., similar to long prime-presentation conditions) was larger than priming, $t(20) = 0.49$, ns, with the positive mood (i.e., similar to short prime-presentation conditions). Neither the main effect of emotional state ($F < 1$) or of prime type, $F(1, 39) = 1.48$, ns, were significant in the affective priming

TABLE 3
Proportions false recognitions (standard deviations) as a function of induced mood
and prime type in Experiment 2

Mood	Matching	Non-matching	Positive	Negative
Happy	0.61 (0.15)	0.41 (0.12)	0.42 (0.16)	0.41 (0.15)
Fearful	0.45 (0.14)	0.47 (0.13)	0.40 (0.13)	0.47 (0.13)

part of the task. In the prime-recognition task we found clear mood-congruency effects (see below), which may also have played a role in the affective priming results. Priming due to mood congruency may have made the affective words that were presented at intermediate presentation times more visible, so that the results shifted towards a more optimal pattern of results in the Jacoby–Whitehouse task.

Recognition in the prime-recognition task of both previously presented and new words was biased in a mood-congruent (cf. Bower, 1981) fashion, interaction between test word valence and mood: $F(2, 76) = 4.42$, $p = .05$, $\eta_p^2 = .104$. Mood congruency did not seem to depend on whether the prime word had previously been presented or not (three-way interaction between memory status, valence and mood: $F < 1$). In a happy mood both old and new positive words (0.513, $SD = 0.229$) were more often believed to be previously presented than (nonmatching) neutral (0.394, $SD = 0.208$) and negative words (0.423, $SD = 0.257$). In a fearful mood negative words (0.559, $SD = 0.213$) were more often labelled old than neutral (0.416, $SD = 0.168$) and positive words (0.405, $SD = 0.171$). Overall, the prime words presented at the intermediate duration could be recognised. Previously presented primes were more often called old than new words, $F(1, 38) = 10.15$, $p < .005$, $\eta_p^2 = .211$. Interestingly, the successful recognition did not seem to depend on mood ($F < 1$), but only on prime valence, $F(2, 76) = 4.21$, $p = .05$, $\eta_p^2 = .100$. We also calculated (see Joordens & Merikle, 1992) the two-high threshold model measure of sensitivity (P_r; see Snodgrass & Corwin, 1988) for the three prime types. Both negative (0.129), one-tailed $t(39) = 3.25$, $p < .005$, and positive (0.072), $t(39) = 2.21$, $p < .05$, words were successfully recognised. The recognition appeared to depend on word emotionality, because neutral nonmatching primes could not be recognised (-0.10), $t(39) = -0.338$, ns.

Discussion

Mood differentially modulated illusory familiarity in the extended Jacoby–Whitehouse paradigm, as if level of consciousness for the primes was manipulated. Successful mood induction was indicated by subjective mood reports and mood congruency effects in the prime-recognition task. Mood did not influence conscious recollection of the primes, but biased towards affect-congruent responses. Negative valence, and to a lesser extent also positive valence, however, enhanced conscious recollection of the primes. When mood is manipulated explicitly, affective primes have similar, but weaker, effects as matching and nonmatching primes. The affective primes are themselves, however, primed by mood, so that more conscious prime processing may take place. Both global affective modulation of illusory familiarity, and corresponding effects of matching/nonmatching and positive/negative primes (see Phaf & Rotteveel, 2005), thus, have been observed in the experiment. A positive mood may increase both familiarity directly and, indirectly, by raising susceptibility to feelings of familiarity. A negative mood, on the other hand, induces feelings of novelty and uncertainty that necessitate detailed and careful inspection (see also Pratto & John, 1991; Taylor, 1991) and reduce reliance on global impressions.

It remains to be tested, of course, whether instruction of non-analytic and analytic processing modes (see Whittlesea & Price, 2001) can also reverse priming effects in the Jacoby–Whitehouse paradigm similarly to mood. Interestingly, our assumption that moods and information processing mode are closely linked leads to the prediction that such an instruction also induces mood changes. This also implies that in many cases task design will interfere with mood due to the, implicit or explicit, instruction of particular processing strategies. If participants in a Jacoby–Whitehouse task are, for instance, asked to recognise meaningless (i.e., novel, even when presented for a second time) stimuli, this will evoke an analytic processing mode. It will then be very difficult to obtain a suboptimal priming pattern, even in a happy mood. The mood-inducing capability of non-affective instructions and the mood effects on non-affective material could illustrate further that affective and "cognitive" processes are so closely interwoven that they cannot really be distinguished.

GENERAL DISCUSSION

The correspondence hypothesis that we presented earlier (Phaf & Rotteveel, 2005) fits in a more general framework of affective modulation, and even in a broader view on emotions. Correspondence specifies, at least in part, the type of stimuli that may trigger the emotional control signal. Positive and negative valence, have similar modulatory consequences as such, at first sight non-affective, stimulus features as familiarity and novelty (i.e., memory status), fluent and laborious processing, and exteroceptive cues of approach and avoidance. We think that these features can be used to characterise affective valence, which in the past has stubbornly withstood further analysis (see also Frijda, 2007). Extending a Jamesian view, affect may emerge not only from the perception of bodily states (i.e., proprioceptive perception of, for instance, arm flexion), but also from exteroceptive cues of approach and avoidance (i.e., motion), and from the monitoring of internal states of information processing (see Frijda, 2007, for similar suggestions). If processing can proceed easily and without interruption, a positive state will be activated (see also Winkielman & Cacioppo, 2001). Similarly, a negative mode, and eventually emotional state, will arise when processing is slow, laborious, and obstructed. Such conditions require attention and careful deliberation, whereas positive conditions allow for free-flowing, so-called "automatic" processing and the acceptance and uptake of all beneficial stimulation that is coming in.

In our view, affect is only experienced afterwards when the information signal, action tendencies, and bodily states are interpreted through a process of appraisal. The primary step in appraisal is monitoring internal functioning and determining whether everything goes well or that there are difficulties. In most instances, emotion involves a dynamic interaction between action tendencies, information-processing tendencies and appraisal, but when a discrete emotional stimulus or event is first processed, appraisal follows the action tendencies, instead of preceding them (Frijda, 1986). Such appraisals can subsequently activate further action and processing tendencies, which may blur the initial order. Secondary appraisal processes may further differentiate emotional experience and shift the control signal in other directions. Our position, therefore, stresses the recursive nature of the interaction between the two qualitatively different processes of modulation and appraisal.

This view may also help clear up the affect–cognition and conscious–nonconscious distinctions in the Zajonc–Lazarus debate. The action and modulatory tendencies, which are initially triggered nonconsciously, should not be considered full emotions, but should be seen as inherent affective processes that contribute to the development of emotions. Full emotions only emerge when conscious affect is constructed from the information signal (Oatley & Johnson-Laird, 1987, 1995) and the perception of these tendencies. Appraisal is then considered a construction process (see Mandler, 1996; Phaf, Mul, & Wolters, 1994; Phaf & Wolters, 1997) that always results in conscious contents (i.e., feelings). Both nonconscious affective modulation and appraisal processes resulting in conscious feelings represent cognitive processes in this view. The appraisals may, however, not accurately reflect the underlying tendencies, because these tendencies also modulate and possibly even distort the construction process. Our view, therefore, does not adhere to an identity position (Mandler, 1996) with respect to conscious and nonconscious processes, as many cognitive emotion theorists, implicitly or explicitly, seem to do. The primary distinction that eventually emerges from the Zajonc–Lazarus debate, in our opinion, is thus the qualitative distinction between nonconscious modulatory tendencies and appraisals resulting in conscious emotional experience.

We propose here, in what we will call the affective modulation framework (AMF), that positive (i.e., happy) conditions shift processing towards global non-analytic and nonconscious modes, whereas negative (i.e., fearful) conditions evoke detailed analytic modes characteristic of conscious processing. In a positive mode suboptimally presented stimuli, irrespective of whether they are affective or non-affective, will show their strongest effect, but in a negative mood these effects are weakened or may even be absent. A negative mode will strengthen the effects of optimal stimulus presentation and could, for instance, evoke discounting and even contrast effects such as in affective priming (e.g., Berner & Maier, 2004; Murphy & Zajonc, 1993; Rotteveel et al., 2001; Rotteveel & Phaf, 2004b; Stapel, Koomen, & Ruys, 2002; Wong & Root, 2003), associative and repetition priming (e.g., Huber, Shiffrin, Lyle, & Ruys, 2001) and the Jacoby–Whitehouse effect (e.g., Jacoby & Whitehouse, 1989; Joordens & Merikle, 1992). Absence of control over emotional states may thus well be responsible for mixed findings in areas such as affective priming (e.g., Spruyt, Hermans, Pandelaere, De Houwer, & Eelen, 2004), particularly when level of consciousness is varied between participants. Within the domain of emotion, our theoretical position leads, moreover, to the interesting hypothesis that negative emotions will be appraised and consciously experienced to a higher degree than positive emotions, which to our knowledge has not yet been explicitly investigated.

The AMF has a bearing not only on emotion research but also on non-affective information processing research, particularly when conscious and nonconscious conditions are contrasted. A remarkable example of non-affective research, where affective modulation may present the key, are the conflicting findings of Berry, Shanks, and Henson (2006) and Merikle and Reingold (1991), in the field of implicit (i.e., indirect) and explicit (i.e., direct) memory. The latter authors obtained greater sensitivity to unattended presentation of neutral words in implicit than in explicit memory tasks, whereas the former authors found the opposite pattern of results. Berry et al. already cited Whittlesea and Price's (2001) analytic versus non-analytic processing strategies as a possible explanation of these strikingly different findings. We surmise here that uncontrolled emotional state or mood differences between the Canadian and British groups of participants may be responsible. Currently, research, explicitly inducing mood in the Merikle and Reingold paradigm, is underway in our laboratory to investigate this conjecture. We think that affective modulation can be applied to many other contrastive paradigms, in which the results sometimes appear to be variable.

There is already some evidence that analytic and non-analytic processing strategies (or "look" and "pop" strategies, respectively) modulate emotional processes (e.g., Snodgrass, Shevrin, & Kopka, 1993; Van Selst & Merikle, 1993; Whittlesea & Price, 2001), and we expect much further evidence that emotional state and mood modulate many kinds of non-affective information processing (see Corson, 2002; Storbeck & Clore, 2005; Storbeck & Clore, this issue; Experiment 2 in this study) in the future.

REFERENCES

Baars, B. J. (1981). Cognitive versus inference. *American Psychologist*, *36*, 223–224.

Berner, M. P., & Maier, M. A. (2004). The direction of affective priming as a function of trait anxiety when naming target words with regular and irregular pronunciation. *Experimental Psychology*, *51*, 180–190.

Berry, C. J., Shanks, D. R., & Henson, R. N. A. (2006). On the status of unconscious memory: Merikle and Reingold (1991) revisited. *Journal of Experimental Psychology: Learning, Memory, and Cognition*, *32*, 925–934.

Bornstein, R. F. (1989). Exposure and affect: Overview and meta-analysis of research, 1968–1987. *Psychological Bulletin*, *106*, 265–289.

Bower, G. H. (1981). Mood and memory. *American Psychologist*, *36*, 129–148.

Bridgeman, B. (1998). Durations of stimuli displayed on video display terminals: $(n-1)/f+$ persistence. *Psychological Science*, *9*, 232–233.

Burnage, G. (1990). *CELEX: A guide for users*. Nijmegen, The Netherlands: SSN.

Cacioppo, J. T., Priester, J. R., & Berntson, G. G. (1993). Rudimentary determinants of attitudes. II: Arm flexion and extension have differential effects on attitudes. *Journal of Personality and Social Psychology*, *65*, 5–17.

Centerbar, D. B., & Clore, G. L. (2006). Do approach–avoidance actions create attitudes? *Psychological Science*, *17*, 22–29.

Chen, M., & Bargh, J. A. (1999). Consequences of automatic evaluation: Immediate behavioral predispositions to approach or avoid the stimulus. *Personality and Social Psychology Bulletin*, *25*, 215–224.

Corson, Y. (2002). Effects of positive, negative, and neutral moods on associative and semantic priming. *Current Psychology of Cognition*, *21*, 33–62.

Duckworth, K. L., Bargh, J. A., Garcia, M., & Chaiken, S. (2002). The automatic evaluation of novel stimuli. *Psychological Science*, *13*, 513–519.

Elliot, R., & Dolan, R. J. (1998). Neural response during preference and memory judgments for subliminally presented stimuli: A functional neuroimaging study. *The Journal of Neuroscience*, *18*, 4697–4704.

Frijda, N. H. (1986). *The emotions*. Cambridge, UK: Cambridge University Press.

Frijda, N. H. (2007). *The laws of emotion*. Mahwah, NJ: Lawrence Erlbaum Associates, Inc.

Frijda, N. H., Kuipers, P., & ter Schure, E. (1989). Relations among emotion, appraisal, and emotional action readiness. *Journal of Personality and Social Psychology*, *57*, 212–228.

Gallese, V., Keysers, C., & Rizzolatti, G. (2004). A unifying view of the basis of social cognition. *Trends in Cognitive Sciences*, *8*, 396–403.

Gray, J. R. (2004). Integration of emotion and cognitive control. *Current Directions in Psychological Science*, *13*, 46–48.

Harmon-Jones, E., & Allen, J. J. B. (2001). The role of affect in the mere exposure effect: Evidence from psychophysiological and individual differences approaches. *Personality and Social Psychology Bulletin, 27,* 889–898.

Huber, D. E., Shiffrin, R. M., Lyle, K. B., & Ruys, K. I. (2001). Perception and preference in short-term word priming. *Psychological Review, 108,* 149–182.

Jacoby, L. L. (1983). Perceptual enhancement: Persistent effects of experience. *Journal of Experimental Psychology: Learning, Memory, and Cognition, 9,* 21–38.

Jacoby, L. L., & Dallas, M. (1981). On the relationship between autobiographical memory and perceptual learning. *Journal of Experimental Psychology: General, 110,* 306–340.

Jacoby, L. L., & Whitehouse, K. (1989). An illusion of memory: False recognition influenced by unconscious perception. *Journal of Experimental Psychology: General, 118,* 126–135.

Joordens, S., & Merikle, P. M. (1992). False recognition and perception without awareness. *Memory and Cognition, 20,* 151–159.

Kunst-Wilson, W. R., & Zajonc, R. B. (1980). Affective discrimination of stimuli that cannot be recognized. *Science, 207,* 557–558.

Lavender, T., & Hommel, B. (2007). Affect and action: Towards an event-coding account. *Cognition and Emotion, 21,* 1270–1296.

Lazarus, R. S. (1981). A cognitivist's reply to Zajonc on emotion and cognition. *American Psychologist, 36,* 222–223.

Lazarus, R. S. (1982). Thoughts on the relations between emotion and cognition. *American Psychologist, 37,* 1019–1024.

Lazarus, R. S. (1995). Vexing research problems inherent in cognitive-mediational theories of emotion—And some solutions. *Psychological Inquiry, 6,* 183–196.

LeDoux, J. E. (1986). Sensory systems and emotion: A model of affective processing. *Integrative Psychiatry, 4,* 237–243.

LeDoux, J. E. (1996). *The emotional brain.* New York: Simon & Schuster.

Liddell, B. J., Brown, K. J., Kemp, A. H., Barton, M. J., Das, P., Peduto, A., et al. (2005). A direct brainstem–amygdalacortical "alarm" system for subliminal signals of fear. *Neuro-Image, 24,* 235–243.

Mandler, G. (1980). Recognizing: The judgment of previous occurrence. *Psychological Review, 87,* 252–271.

Mandler, G. (1996). Consciousness redux. In J. C. Cohen & J. W. Schooler (Eds.), *Scientific approaches to consciousness: The twenty-fifth Carnegie symposium on cognition* (pp. 479–498). Hillsdale, NJ: Lawrence Erlbaum Associates, Inc.

Mandler, G., Nakamura, Y., & Van Zandt, B. J. S. (1987). Nonspecific effects of exposure on stimuli that cannot be recognized. *Journal of Experimental Psychology, 13,* 646–648.

Markman, A. B., & Brendl, C. M. (2005). Constraining theories of embodied cognition. *Psychological Science, 16,* 6–10.

Merikle, P. M., & Reingold, E. M. (1991). Comparing direct (explicit) and indirect (implicit) measures to study unconscious memory. *Journal of Experimental Psychology: Learning, Memory, and Cognition, 17,* 224–233.

Monahan, J. L., Murphy, S. T., & Zajonc, R. B. (2000). Subliminal mere exposure: Specific, general, and diffuse effects. *Psychological Science, 11,* 462–466.

Monin, B. (2003). The warm glow heuristic: When liking leads to familiarity. *Journal of Personality and Social Psychology, 85,* 1035–1048.

Murphy, S. T., & Zajonc, R. B. (1993). Affect, cognition and awareness: Affective priming with optimal and suboptimal stimulus exposures. *Journal of Personality and Social Psychology, 64,* 723–739.

Neumann, R., & Strack, F. (2000). Approach and avoidance: The influence of proprioceptive and exteroceptive cues on encoding of affective information. *Journal of Personality and Social Psychology, 79,* 39–48.

Oatley, K., & Johnson-Laird, P. N. (1987). Towards a cognitive theory of emotions. *Cognition and Emotion, 1,* 29–50.

Oatley, K., & Johnson-Laird, P. N. (1995). The communicative theory of emotions: Empirical tests, mental models, and implications for social interaction. In L. L. Martin & A. Tesser (Eds.), *Striving and feeling: Interactions among goals, affect, and self-regulation* (pp. 363–380). Mahwah, NJ: Lawrence Erlbaum Associates, Inc.

Phaf, R. H., Mul, N. M., & Wolters, G. (1994). A connectionist view on dissociations. In C. Umiltà & M. Moscovitch (Eds.), *Attention and performance: XV. Conscious and nonconscious information processing* (pp. 725–751). Cambridge MA: MIT Press.

Phaf, R. H., & Rotteveel, M. (2005). Affective modulation of recognition bias. *Emotion, 5,* 309–318.

Phaf, R. H., van der Leij, A. R., Stienen, B. M. C., & Bierman, D. (2006). *Positieve, neutrale en negatieve woorden bij minimale aanbieding: Een ordening door perceptuele clarificatie* [Positive, neutral, and negative words at minimal presentation levels: Ordering by perceptual clarification]. Amsterdam, The Netherlands: Technical Report, Universiteit van Amsterdam.

Phaf, R. H., & Wolters, G. (1997). A constructivist and connectionist view on conscious and nonconscious processes. *Philosophical Psychology, 10,* 287–307.

Pratto, F., & John, O. P. (1991). Automatic vigilance: The attention-grabbing power of negative social information. *Journal of Personality and Social Psychology, 61,* 380–391.

Reber, R., Winkielman, P., & Schwarz, N. (1998). Effects of perceptual fluency on affective judgments. *Psychological Science, 9,* 45–48.

Rizzolatti, G., & Arbib, M. (1998). Language within our grasp. *Trends in Neurosciences, 21,* 188–192.

Roelofs, K., Elzinga, B. M., & Rotteveel, M. (2005). The effects of stress-induced cortisol responses on approach–avoidance behavior. *Psychoneuroendocrinology, 30,* 665–677.

Rotteveel, M., Bonarius, H., & Phaf, R. H. (2007). *Avoiding the withdrawing angry face.* Manuscript in preparation, University of Amsterdam.

Rotteveel, M., de Groot, P., Geutskens, A., & Phaf, R. H. (2001). Stronger suboptimal than optimal affective priming? *Emotion, 1,* 348–364.

Rotteveel, M., & Phaf, R. H. (2004a). Automatic affective evaluation does not automatically predispose for arm flexion and extension. *Emotion, 4,* 156–172.

Rotteveel, M., & Phaf, R. H. (2004b). Loading working memory enhances affective priming. *Psychonomic Bulletin & Review, 11,* 326–331.

Rotteveel, M., van Ditzhuijzen, J., & Phaf, R. H. (2004). Loading working memory interferes with affect incongruent movements. In F. Columbus (Ed.), *Advances in psychology research* (Vol. 31, pp. 111–122). New York: Nova Publishers.

Seamon, J. G., Marsh, R. L., & Brody, N. (1984). Critical importance of exposure duration for affective discrimination of stimuli that are not recognized. *Journal of Experimental Psychology: Learning, Memory, and Cognition, 10,* 465–469.

Seamon, J. G., McKenna, P. A., & Binder, N. (1998). The mere exposure effect is differentially sensitive to different judgments tasks. *Consciousness and Cognition, 7,* 85–102.

Shaver, P., Schwartz, J., Kirson, D., & O'Connor, C. (1987). Emotion knowledge: Further exploration of a prototype approach. *Journal of Personality and Social Psychology, 52,* 1061–1086.

Smith, C. A., & Ellsworth, P. C. (1985). Patterns of cognitive appraisal in emotion. *Journal of Personality and Social Psychology, 48,* 813–838.

Snodgrass, J. G., & Corwin, J. (1988). Pragmatics of measuring recognition memory: Applications to dementia and amnesia. *Journal of Experimental Psychology: General, 117,* 34–50.

Snodgrass, M., Shevrin, H., & Kopka, M. (1993). The mediation of intentional judgments by unconscious perceptions: The influences of task strategy, task preference, word meaning, and motivation. *Consciousness and Cognition, 2,* 169–193.

Solarz, A. K. (1960). Latency of instrumental responses as a function of compatibility with the meaning of eliciting verbal signs. *Journal of Experimental Psychology, 59,* 239–245.

Spruyt, A., Hermans, D., Pandelaere, M., De Houwer, J., & Eelen, P. (2004). On the replicability of the affective priming effect in the pronunciation task. *Experimental Psychology, 51,* 109–115.

Stapel, D. A., Koomen, W., & Ruys, K. I. (2002). The effects of diffuse and distinct affect. *Journal of Personality and Social Psychology, 83,* 60–74.

Storbeck, J., & Clore, G. L. (2005). With sadness comes accuracy, with happiness, false memory: Mood and the false memory effect. *Psychological Science, 16,* 785–791.

Storbeck, J., & Clore, G. L. (2007). On the interdependence of cognition and emotion. *Cognition and Emotion, 21,* 1212–1237.

Strack, F., Martin, L. L., & Stepper, S. (1988). Inhibiting and facilitating conditions of the human smile: A nonobtrusive test of the facial feedback hypothesis. *Journal of Personality and Social Psychology, 54,* 768–777.

Strack, F., & Neumann, R. (2000). Furrowing the brow may undermine perceived fame: The role of facial feedback in judgments of celebrity. *Personality and Social Psychology Bulletin, 26,* 762–768.

Taylor, S. E. (1991). Asymmetrical effects of positive and negative events: The mobilization–minimization hypothesis. *Psychological Bulletin, 110,* 67–85.

Van Selst, M., & Merikle, P. M. (1993). Perception below the objective threshold? *Consciousness and Cognition, 2,* 194–203.

Whittlesea, B. W. A., & Price, J. R. (2001). Implicit/explicit memory versus analytic/non-analytic processing: Rethinking the mere exposure effect. *Memory & Cognition, 29,* 234–246.

Winkielman, P., & Cacioppo, J. T. (2001). Mind at ease puts a smile on the face: Psychophysiological evidence that processing facilitation elicits positive affect. *Journal of Personality and Social Psychology, 81,* 989–1000.

Wong, P. S., & Root, J. C. (2003). Dynamic variations in affective priming. *Consciousness and Cognition, 12,* 147–168.

Zajonc, R. B. (1980). Feeling and thinking: Preferences need no inferences. *American Psychologist, 35,* 151–175.

Zajonc, R. B. (1981). A one-factor mind about mind and emotion. *American Psychologist, 36,* 102–103.

Zajonc, R. B. (1984). On the primacy of affect. *American Psychologist, 39,* 117–123.

COGNITION AND EMOTION
2007, 21 (6), 1347–1359

Affective distinctiveness: Illusory or real?

John T. Cacioppo

University of Chicago, Chicago, IL, USA

Gary G. Berntson

Ohio State University, Columbus, OH, USA

The contributions to this special issue illustrate the value of cognitive methods and theory in the study of affect. Together, this work makes a compelling case that it is time to move beyond the question of whether human affect and cognition represent completely independent constructs, and that there is much yet to be gleaned about affect from the perspective of cognitive science. Evidence that aspects of affect can be conceived as cognition leaves open the question of whether *all* aspects of affect are a special case of cognition. We pose a series of questions about whether all aspects of affect can be subsumed within cognition; and if not what the fundamental distinctions might be between affect and cognition, where and on what basis the line might be drawn between affect and cognition, what is the nature of the interactions between affect and cognition, and how are these processes implemented in the human nervous system.

Imagine you attend a magic show and are dazzled and amazed by a magician who enters a closet on one side of the stage and nearly simultaneously exits an identical closet on the other side of the stage. Imagine, further, that you are so taken by this trick that you devote yourself to determining how the trick is performed. After extensive work, you are able to reverse engineer this feat by using a fast-moving conveyer belt that runs beneath the stage between the two closets. You are so delighted by your success, even if bruised by the transition between closets, that you show the trick to the magician who responds that he did not know you too had a twin.

The contributors to this special issue provide rich and thoughtful treatments of the value of cognitive methods and theory in the study of affect. A compelling case is made by the contributors to this special issue that cognitive processes are involved in many human emotions, specifically

---

Correspondence should be addressed to: John T. Cacioppo, Center for Cognitive and Social Neuroscience, University of Chicago, 5848 S. University Avenue, Chicago, IL 60637, USA. E-mail: Cacioppo@uchicago.edu

Preparation of this paper was supported by NIMH Grant No. P50 MH72850.

© 2007 Psychology Press, an imprint of the Taylor & Francis Group, an Informa business
DOI: 10.1080/02699930701502262

that cognition can cause affect (e.g., Moors, 2007 this issue; Storbeck & Clore, 2007 this issue) and can be influenced by affect (e.g., Rotteveel & Phaf, 2007 this issue). The stronger claim—that affect is simply a form of cognition—is also made in this special issue (e.g., Duncan & Barrett, 2007 this issue; Lavender & Hommel, 2007 this issue; cf. Barnard, Duke, Byrne, & Davidson, 2007 this issue).

Collectively, the contributors to this issue also leave little doubt that there is much yet to be gleaned about affect and emotion from the perspective of cognitive science and that it is time to move beyond the question of whether affect and cognition represent the outputs of completely independent systems. However, evidence that aspects of affect can be conceived as cognition leaves open the question of whether there is something distinctive about affect—that is, whether all aspects of affect are a special case of cognition. The contributors to this special issue differ in their response to this important question, and we seek here to encourage further thought and research on this topic.

THE COGNITIVE REVOLUTION

The cognitive revolution is an intellectual movement that was begun in the 1950s by psychologists, anthropologists, and linguists as a response to the claim by behaviourists that mental processes (including feelings and emotions) did not fall under the purview of science (e.g., see Chomsky, 1959). Mental representations and processes were rendered testable in these early years by virtue of reverse engineering: mathematical and computer models were created that specified stimulus inputs, information processing operations that acted on and transformed these inputs to produce and change representational structures, and information processing operations that led to observable responses. The cognitive revolution has profoundly changed how we think about and investigate mental processes and behaviour as well as the selection of methods we use to investigate these phenomena.

No less a god of psychological theory than William James (1884) presaged the notion that affective processes resemble sensory processes and needed no special conceptual status to be explained:

And yet it is even now certain that of two things concerning the emotions, one must be true. Either separate and special centres, affected to them alone, are their brain-seat, or else they correspond to processes occurring in the motor and sensory centres, already assigned, or in others like them, not yet mapped out ... If the latter be the case, we must ask whether the emotional "process" in the sensory or motor centre be an altogether peculiar one, or whether it resembles the ordinary perceptive processes of which those centres are already recognized to be the seat. (James, 1884, p. 188)

As valuable as the cognitive paradigm has been in advancing the scientific study of human affect, and as eminent a supporter as is William James, well over a century after James issued this proposition the theoretical question lingers. Scientific theory and research are fuelled by imagining what the alternative possibilities might be. In the spirit of promoting the imagination of what else might be theoretically possible, we raise the following questions about the dominion of cognition over affect.

Question 1

Are cognitive methods and theories the appropriate means to examine the non-cognitive, unique parts of affective processing? Or is evidence that affect can fruitfully be studied using cognitive theories and methods strong evidence that there are no unique parts to affective processing? The assumptions with which one begins a study and the theories and methods one employs in the study can dramatically alter what is found (Cacioppo & Berntson, 1994). Eder, Hommel, and De Houwer (2007 this issue) begin this special issue by noting that "recent research on affect and emotion relies heavily on cognitive methods and cognitive or cognitively inspired theorising" and they provide a compelling review that these developments have provided new insights into human affect and affective processes. The evidence that cognitive methods and theories can contribute to our understanding of affect leaves open the question of whether affect is nothing more than a form of cognition, perhaps a form of cognition that is focused on affairs inside rather than outside the body.

Zajonc's (1980) seminal paper on the topic, in which he argued that cognition and affect were distinctive, was also based on findings from cognitive paradigms (dichotic listening task and tachistoscopic presentations of visual stimuli). Zajonc's fruitful use of cognitive paradigms led him to conclude that cognition and affect were categorically different. Among the distinctions Zajonc noted were that: (a) affective reactions are primary in that the first level response to the environment is affective; (b) affect is basic in that, unlike cognition and language, affect is universal among the animal species and it forms the first link in the evolution of complex adaptive functions that eventually differentiated animals from plants; (c) affective reactions are inescapable in that it may not be voluntarily controlled, and that when emotional regulation is achieved it comes at the expense of considerable cognitive resources and effort; (d) affective judgements tend to be irrevocable in that such judgements feel valid and are beyond rational counter-argumentation ("A passion must be accompanied with some false judgement, in order to its being unreasonable; and even then 'tis not the passion properly speaking, which is unreasonable, but the judgement", Hume, 1898, cited by Zajonc, 1980, p. 157); (e) affective judgements implicate the self in that they represent the state of the individual in relation to the object; (f) affective reactions are difficult to verbalise and, therefore, rely more on nonverbal channels for communication, in contrast to a mathematic expression—a quintessentially cognitive entity—which is difficult to impossible to convey through nonverbal channels; (g) affective judgements need not depend on cognition, which he argued based on the weak correlation between what he termed discriminanda and preferenda but which is perhaps better supported by research on decorticate animals (Panksepp, in press); and (h) affective reactions may become separated from content.

A key finding for this latter point was Zajonc's work showing that participants showed exposure-related increases in liking for the stimulus (the mere exposure effect) even though they were not cognizant that the stimuli had been presented (cf. Rotteveel & Phaf, 2007 this issue). Whether or not this was sufficient evidence to conclude affect and cognition were distinct has been debated for the past quarter century. Eder, Hommel, and De Houwer (2007 this issue) and Storbeck and Clore (2007 this issue) each critique the evidence and reasoning upon which Zajonc reached his conclusion that affect and cognition derive from independent psychological systems. For instance, processing ease, which increases with exposure frequency, is sufficient to promote positive affect (Winkielman & Cacioppo, 2001).

As compelling as might be the case, one is left with the questions of whether affect can be studied using cognitive theories and methods is strong evidence that affective processes fall within the dominion of cognitive processes, and, if not, whether cognitive methods and theories are the appropriate means to examine the non-cognitive, unique parts of affective processing. The choice of research paradigm determines the scope of the research findings, so it should not be surprising that cognitive paradigms tap into the cognitive processes. We are reminded that, prior to the cognitive revolution, the methods and theories of behaviourism were fruitfully employed to investigate affect and behaviour (e.g., Miller, 1948). That is, behavioural theories and methods proved useful in understanding affective behaviour, but in retrospect this did not prove to be especially strong evidence that a behavioural explanation for affect was correct or best. One wonders what will be said in 100 years about the current hegemony of cognition over affect.

Question 2

If affect involves information processing, then is it not by definition a special form of cognition? Behaviourists treated the mind as a black box. Cognitive scientists replaced the black box with a computer box, and the operations of the mind were modelled using the language of information processing theory (Miller, Galanter, & Pribram, 1960). According to this perspective, thinking is information processing, including but not limited to perception, encoding, representation, storage, retrieval, response selection, and response execution. Information processing covers a very broad waterfront indeed. Information processing has been variously defined but a common definition for it is the manipulation of data so that new data appear in a useful form. That is, information processing is any operation on a datum that changes its form or function. Such a definition includes but is not limited to the coding, retrieval, and combination of information in perceptual recognition, learning, remembering, thinking, problem solving, and performance of sensorimotor acts (see, also, Moors, 2007 this issue, or Marr, 1982, for discussions of what constitutes cognition).

The difficult question is not whether all cognition is information processing but whether all information processing is cognition. If the former is true, it tells us what cognition is not, but this alone does not provide clear guidance about what might be a fundamental distinction between cognition and affect, where and on what basis is the line drawn between cognition and affect, and when is it useful to do so. If the latter is true, then by definition affect falls within the domain of cognition. The definitive nature of the latter is inviting if only because it would end a long-standing debate but there are some unintended side effects if we accept this argument. If we accept that all information processing is cognition, then a spinal cord reflex is a cognitive act even when the spinal cord has been dissected from the brain. According to the topological account of cognition (see Moors, 2007 this issue), cognition is limited to the brain. But if cognition is equated with information processing in the brain, synaptic transmissions and intracellular processes become cognitive processes, as do DNA to RNA transcriptions that occur within the brain. In fact, the simplest biochemical reaction is an operation on data that changes their form and function, and therefore it meets the definition of information processing. Does this event also fall under the dominion of cognition as long as it occurs in the brain even when it has nothing to do with behaviour?

Marr (1982) distinguished between computational, algorithmic, and implementational levels of analysis, and cognition could be limited to the transformation and construction of mental representations (i.e., the algorithmic level) and not to information processing in general (e.g., implementational level). The ability to specify an algorithm for a series of information processing operations that correspond to the physical implementation of affective processing does not render it as cognitive, however, any more than the ability to specify an aperiodic time series in terms of a periodic time series using a Fourier Transform renders the aperiodic time series periodic.

Finally, restricting cognition to the more limited definition of information processing to include perception, encoding, representation, storage, retrieval, response selection, response execution, and related constructs from computer science may still provide sufficient explanatory scope to subsume all aspects of affect, especially when the absence of the conscious perception of a stimulus can be characterised in terms of preattentive or nonconscious cognitive processes. But this begs the question of whether the activation of a smile or disgust display in an anencephalic infant (Steiner, 1973) represents a nonconscious cognition. If so, then what besides location separates these reflexive actions from spinal cord reflexes? If the answer rests with the underlying neurobiology, then does affect fall within the domain of cognition or the domain of the neurosciences?

Question 3

Is a similarity in neural substrates sufficient evidence to conclude that cognition and affect are the same? William James (1884) suggested this as a litmus test for the question of whether cognition and affect represented different aspects of the same process. Evidence that the *entirety* of the neural substrates for two outcomes is identical can be strong evidence against the hypothesis that these outcomes are the result of different mechanisms. However, is evidence that cognition and affect share *some* neural underpinnings to be interpreted to mean that cognition and affect reflect the operation of the same general mechanism? All behaviours rely on lower motor neurons as the final common pathway, but such shared neural structures does not mean all behavioural outcomes are the product of the same underlying mechanism (see Eder & Klauer, 2007 this issue, for a similar argument). The upper motor neurons innervating the cell bodies of the final common pathway, for instance, represent at least two very different central motor systems (Solodkin, Hlustik, & Buccino, 2007).

The sharing of neural substrates indicates that some component processes (e.g., sensory, autonomic, somatomotor) may be shared, or that the function in which an overlapping area is involved may be the same. Well-defined localisation of sensory and motor functions poses as a hypothesis but does not prove that more complex integrative processing by the brain is similarly compartmentalised. As Uttal (2001) pointedly noted:

> We need to distinguish between a nonhomogenous brain in which different regions can influence different mental or behavioral processes, on the one hand, and the hypothesized role of these regions as unique locations of the mechanisms underlying these processes, on the other. It is the failure to make this distinction that fuels many of the more imaginative theories of cognitive localization in the brain. (Uttal, 2001, p. 11)

Duncan and Barrett (2007 this issue) review evidence that affective processes include areas of the brain involved in classic forms of cognition, and Storbeck and Clore (2007 this issue) review evidence that the amygdala—an area known to be involved in emotion—is also involved in cognition. Investigators differ in their interpretation of the significance of such findings, however. Passingham, Stephan, and Kötter (2002) have argued that each cortical region has unique patterns of cortico-cortical connections, and that it is these more distributed subsystems of brain regions that produce the observed (more localised) differences in neural activity during different tasks. Uttal (2001) extends this argument to include cortico-limbic connections. The more general point is that what appears to one investigator to be a minor difference in neural circuits may represent qualitatively different functional mechanisms to another (Davis & Shi, 1999). Theoretical advances are promoted more by competing theoretical hypotheses than by empirical observation of a partial overlap in neural substrates.

The specific methods that are used to identify "overlapping" areas are also critical to interpretation. For instance, functional magnetic resonance imaging (fMRI) studies of the amygdala have found it to be activated by positive and negative stimuli (Wager, Phan, Liberzon, & Taylor, 2003). Given the spatial insensitivity of fMRI to specific regions within the amygdala, however, the simple activation of the amygdala in response to positive and negative stimuli says nothing about whether the same neuronal sets or circuits within the amygdala are shared. Moreover, the basolateral amygdala receives inputs whether appetitive or aversive stimuli are presented, but the projections from the basolateral amygdala appear to travel to the central nucleus of the amygdala in the case of aversive stimuli whereas they are more likely to travel to the ventral striatum in the case of appetitive stimuli (Davis & Shi, 1999; M. Davis, personal communication, 14 May 2007). Contemporary fMRI studies cannot distinguish between these circuits when imaging the amygdala.

It is also the case that showing that cognition and affect *differ* in some neural underpinning is not strong evidence that cognition and affect do *not* represent the operation of the same general mechanism. The region of the sensory cortex that represents the left and right hand are easily distinguishable by spatial location, even using fMRI, but this does not imply that they represent different central or psychological systems. Again we see that the interpretation of the neurobiological substrates of affect cannot be divorced from the extant theoretical formulation(s) regarding the role of these substrates in affect and cognition.

Finally, we need to remain cognizant of the possibility of the category error in investigations of the neural substrates of cognition and affect. The categorical error in cognitive neuroscience refers to the intuitively appealing notion that the organisation of cognitive (or affective) phenomena maps in a one-to-one fashion into the organisation of the underlying neural substrates. Memories, emotions, and beliefs, for instance, were each once thought to be localised in a single site in the brain. We now know that most complex psychological or behavioural concepts (e.g., think more complex than motion perception) do not map into a single "centre" in the brain but rather each is associated with several different neural mechanisms. What appears at one point in time to be a singular construct (e.g., memory), when examined in conjunction with evidence from the brain (e.g., lesions), often reveals a more complex and interesting organisation at both levels (e.g., declarative vs. procedural memory processes). The last of these revisions we suspect is far from having been written.

Question 4

How much of the central nervous system would need to be eliminated to reject the hypothesis that affective reactions are necessarily cognitive? In the *Expression of Emotions in Man and Animals*, Charles Darwin (1872) observed that:

> I put my face close to the thick glass-plate in front of a puff-adder in the Zoological Gardens, with the firm determination of not starting back if the snake struck at me; but, as soon as the blow was struck, my resolution went for nothing, and I jumped backwards with astonishing rapidity. My will and reason were powerless against the imagination of a danger which had never been experienced. (p. 38)

In this comment, Darwin illustrated the distinct although interacting, and sometimes conflicting, dispositions that can arise from affective and cognitive processes. Darwin (1872) did not suggest that all emotions were irrational, rapid, and mandatory, but he was struck by those that were and he posited that these emotions were similar to the emotional responses he observed in nonhuman animals.

Affective processes are early evolutionary developments that serve important adaptive and survival functions. As such, they are observable not only in nonhuman animals but at lower levels of the neuraxis in humans, including levels such as the brainstem and spinal cord, where cognitive operations—as conceived by most people—are minimally represented. Infants are born with simple affective reflexes (Steiner, 1973), and lesion studies in animals point to a surprisingly adaptive and organised behavioural repertoire under affectively evocative circumstances.

Following up on an observation of Walter Cannon on "sham rage" in decorticate cats, the notable physiologist, Philip Bard pursued his dissertation on the brain mechanisms of this rage-like reaction, which was easily triggered in animals after removal of the cerebral cortex (Bard, 1928; see Dror, 2001, for review). These early studies noted striking signs of rage and aggression in response to stimuli that would yield pain in intact animals. This research ultimately lead to the Cannon–Bard "thalamic-theory" of emotions (see Cannon, 1927), proposed as an alternative to the James and Lange afference model of emotion that was popular at that time. The rage-like reaction was termed sham rage because of the assumption that, in the absence of the cortex, the animal could feel no pain. This was an important political consideration in the face of early 20th century antivivisectionism (Dror, 2001). Although the hierarchical evolutionary model of John Hughlings Jackson (1884/1958) would suggest some level of awareness might exist at subcortical levels, the phenomenological features of the sham-rage syndrome are not of paramount importance for our consideration. What is more important is that decortication would be expected to degrade cognitive operations of any significance. Nevertheless, there remains in the decorticate clear evidence of an enhancement of affective expression, manifest not only in behaviour but in autonomic and neuroendocrine activation. One need not stop at the cortex—surgically decererbated animals and tragic cases of developmental decerebrate states in humans document considerable affective organisation within the brainstem (e.g., Berntson & Micco, 1976; Grill & Kaplan, 2002; Steiner, 1973), at a level of the neuraxis where cognitive operations, at least as traditionally conceived, are minimal. Moreover, as noted above, even spinal networks evidence affective organisations in the form of flexor (or pain) withdrawal reflexes that parallel Darwin's avoidance response from the puff-adder. One perhaps could define cognition broadly enough to include even spinal reflexes, but would the construct of cognition at that point be so broad as to lack meaning and invite equivocation?

Storbeck and Clore (2007 this issue) review LeDoux's (1995) proposal that the amygdala can elicit emotion in the absence of the cortex and conclude that "the low route does not play a role in processing the complex stimuli typically used in social and emotional research ... [and] the amygdala, and emotion in general, does not function independently of perceptual and cognitive processes". Barnard et al. (2007 this issue) take a very different approach to this literature, arguing that phylogenetically older neurobehavioural organisations for adaptive action constitute specifiable subsystems the ascending influences of which impact perception and cognition (see, also, Berntson, Cacioppo, & Sarter, 2003). The value of decorticate studies would not seem to be to suggest that these mechanisms in isolation explain complex forms of human behaviour but rather to determine the different neurobehavioural organisations across the neuraxis, investigate whether these organisations operate serially or in parallel, and examine the nature of both descending and ascending influences among these neurobehavioural organisations.

Question 5

Are feelings a necessary condition for affect or emotion? If feelings, which are conscious and communicable through language, are a criterial attribute of affect, then the lesion work reviewed above may be viewed as irrelevant to our understanding of core issues in affect and emotion. Many believe that nonhuman (or at least nonprimate) animals do not have feelings, which would render comparative studies of affect pointless. Yet comparative studies have revealed general principles underlying affect and emotion that have been found to hold for the human animal, as well (e.g., Darwin, 1872; LeDoux, 2000; Panksepp, in press). For instance, the existence of adaptive reflexes that are modulated by more recently evolved descending cortical mechanisms (e.g., the inhibition of the flexor withdrawal reflex when receiving a life-saving injection; e.g., Berntson & Cacioppo, in press) and the existence of neural mechanisms that originally evolved to serve one purpose that are later co-opted to serve another purpose (e.g., Eisenberger, Lieberman, & Williams, 2003) are well known in animal and human research.

The modulation of the operation of lower neurobehavioural organisations by cognition may not constitute evidence that these lower neurobehavioural organisations are "cognitive." Cognition can strongly influence respiration, but one needs neither cognition nor a cortex to respire. Hypoxia, which is associated with the activation of the anterior insula, including spindle neurons, and the anterior cingulate in humanoid primates, produces a feeling of oxygen hunger and a strong urge to breathe. Craig (in press) reviews evidence that these neural structures are necessary for the *feelings* of oxygen hunger, and he further argues that feelings of emotion are also bodily readouts and rely on these neural structures (see Duncan & Barrett, 2007 this issue). These structures are not required for normal respiration or for a respiratory response to hypoxia, however. The evidence from decorticate studies indicates that these neural structures are not required for orchestrated affective behaviour either.

LeDoux (2000) has perhaps argued most strongly in recent years that advancing our understanding of affect and emotion may be slowed if subjective feelings are used as the defining feature:

> It is widely recognized that most cognitive processes occur unconsciously, with only the end products reaching awareness, and then only sometimes. Emotion researchers, though, did not make this conceptual leap. They remained focused on subjective emotional experience. The main lesson to be learned is that emotion researchers need to figure out how to escape from the shackles of subjectivity if emotion research is to thrive. (LeDoux, 2000, p. 156).

CONCLUSION

Reverse engineering observable behaviours using the notation of cognitive science has led to a rapid expansion of theories and methods in the behavioural sciences, and the contributions of this special issue underscore the power and importance of cognitive theories and methods for understanding affect and emotion. As was the case in the magic trick involving "transportation" with which we began, however, the ability to reverse engineer a feat does not necessarily mean the underlying mechanism has been duplicated. This uncertainty is inherent in scientific inquiry and the reason theories are just that. Scientific theories represent intellectual structures that provide adequate predictions of what is observed, and useful frameworks for answering questions and solving problems in a given domain. It is parsimony that favours the interpretation that the ability to reverse engineer a feat also implies the underlying mechanism has been duplicated. The hazards of letting parsimony off its leash are important to recognise, as well, for parsimony can promote the status quo at the expense of imaginative theorising and hypothesis testing. As Albert Einstein opined:

> The mere formulation of a problem is far more essential than its solution, which may be merely a matter of mathematical or experimental skills. To raise new questions, new possibilities, to regard old problems from a new angle requires creative imagination and marks real advances in science. (http://quotes.zaadz.com/quotes/topics/science?page = 7)

We look to the current special issue not as the final word but as an important step toward addressing a new set of questions that are of fundamental importance in research on affect. Yes, there is much yet to be gleaned about affect from the perspective of cognitive science, but can all aspects of affect be subsumed within cognition, and if not what is the fundamental distinction between affect and cognition, where and on what basis might the line be drawn between affect and cognition, what is the nature of the interactions between affect and cognition, and how are these processes implemented in the human nervous system? As long as we remain open minded enough to raise new questions and possibilities and to regard old problems from a new angle, the 21st century science of affect and emotion should indeed be an exciting period of inquiry.

REFERENCES

Bard, P. (1928). A diencephalic mechanism for the expression of rage with special reference to the sympathetic nervous system. *American Journal of Physiology, 84*, 490–515.

Barnard, P. J., Duke, D. J., Byrne, R. W., & Davidson, I. (2007). Differentiation in cognitive and emotional meanings: An evolutionary analysis. *Cognition and Emotion, 21*, 1155–1183.

Berntson, G. G., & Cacioppo, J. T. (in press). The neuroevolution of motivation. In J. Shah & W. Gardner (Eds.), *Handbook of motivation science*. New York: Guilford Press.

Berntson, G. G., Cacioppo, J. T., & Sarter, M. (2003). Bottom-up: Implications for neurobehavioral models of anxiety and autonomic regulation. In R. J. Davidson, K. R. Sherer, & H. H. Goldsmith (Eds.), *Handbook of affective sciences* (pp. 1105–1116). New York: Oxford University Press.

Berntson, G. G., & Micco, D. J. (1976). Organization of brainstem behavioral systems. *Brain Research Bulletin, 1*, 471–483.

Cacioppo, J. T., & Berntson, G. G. (1994). Relationship between attitudes and evaluative space: A critical review, with emphasis on the separability of positive and negative substrates. *Psychological Bulletin, 115*, 401–423.

Cannon, W. B. (1927). The James–Lange theory of emotions: A critical examination and an alternative theory. *The American Journal of Psychology, 39*, 106–124.

Chomsky, N. (1959). A review of B. F. Skinner's Verbal Behavior. *Language, 35*, 26–58.

Craig, A. D. (in press). Interception and emotion: A neuroanatomical perspective. In R. Lewis, J. M. Haviland-Jones, & L. F. Barrett (Eds.), *The handbook of emotions* (3rd ed.). New York: Guilford Press.

Darwin, C. (1872). *Expression of the emotions in man and animals*. New York: Appleton.

Davis, M., & Shi, C. (1999). The extended amygdala: Are the central nucleus of the amygdala and the bed nucleus of the stria terminalis differentially involved in fear versus anxiety? In J. F. McGinty (Ed.), *Advancing from the ventral striatum to the extended amygdala: Implications for neuropsychiatry and drug use. In honor of Lennart Heimer* (pp. 281–291). New York: New York Academy of Sciences.

Dror, O. E. (2001). Techniques of the brain and the paradox of emotions, 1880–1930. *Science in Context, 14*, 643–660.

Duncan, S., & Barrett, L. F. (2007). Affect is a form of cognition: A neurobiological analysis. *Cognition and Emotion, 21*, 1184–1211.

Eder, A. B., Hommel, B., & De Houwer, J. (2007). How distinctive is affective processing? On the implications of using cognitive paradigms to study affect and emotion. *Cognition and Emotion, 21*, 1137–1154.

Eder, A. B., & Klauer, K. (2007). Common valence coding in action and evaluation: Affective blindness towards response-compatible stimuli. *Cognition and Emotion, 21*, 1297–1322.

Eisenberger, N. I., Lieberman, M. D., & Williams, K. D. (2003). Does rejection hurt? An fMRI study of social exclusion. *Science, 302*(5643; Oct. 10), 290–292.

Grill, H. J., & Kaplan, J. M. (2002). The neuroanatomical axis for control of energy balance. *Frontiers in Neuroendocrinology, 23*, 2–40.

Jackson, J. H. (1958). Evolution and dissolution of the nervous system. In J. Taylor (Ed.), *Selected writings of John Hughlings Jackson* (Vol. 2). New York: Basic Books. (Reprinted from 1884 Croonian lecture at the Royal College of Physicians, *Lancet, i*, 739–744)

James, W. (1884). What is an emotion? *Mind, 9*, 188–205.

Lavender, T., & Hommel, B. (2007). Affect and action: Towards an event-coding account. *Cognition and Emotion, 21*, 1270–1296.

LeDoux, J. E. (1995). Emotion: Clues from the brain. *Annual Review of Psychology, 46*, 209–235.

LeDoux, J. E. (2000). Emotion circuits in the brain. *Annual Review of Neuroscience, 23*, 155–184.

Marr, D. (1982). *Vision: A computational investigation into the human representation and processing of visual information*. New York: W. H. Freeman.

Miller, G. A., Galanter, E., & Pribram, K. H. (1960). *Plans and the structure of behavior*. New York: Holt, Rinehart, & Winston.

Miller, N. E. (1948). Fear as an acquirable drive. *Journal of Experimental Psychology, 38*, 89–100.

Moors, A. (2007). Can cognitive methods be used to study the unique aspect of emotion: An appraisal theorist's answer. *Cognition and Emotion, 21*, 1238–1269.

Panksepp, J. (in press). Neurologizing the psychology of affects: How appraisal-based constructivism and basic emotion theory can co-exist. *Perspectives on Psychological Science.*

Passingham, R. E., Stephan, K. E., & Kötter, R. (2002). The anatomical basis of functional localization in the cortex. *Nature Reviews: Neuroscience, 3*, 1–11.

Rotteveel, M., & Phaf, R. H. (2007). Mere exposure in reverse: Mood and motion modulate memory bias. *Cognition and Emotion, 21*, 1323–1346.

Solodkin, A., Hlustik, P., & Buccino, G. (2007). The anatomy and physiology of the motor system in humans. In J. T. Cacioppo, L. G. Tassinary, & G. G. Berntson (Eds.), *Handbook of psychophysiology* (3rd ed) (pp. 507–539). New York: Cambridge University Press.

Steiner, J. E. (1973). The gustofacial response: Observations on normal and anencephalic infants. In J. F. Bosma (Ed.), *Fourth symposium on development in the human infant: Oral sensation and perception* (pp. 254–278). Bethesda, MD: National Institutes of Health.

Storbeck, J., & Clore, G. L. (2007). On the interdependence of cognition and emotion. *Cognition and Emotion, 21*, 1212–1237.

Uttal, W. R. (2001). *The new phrenology: The limits of localizing cognitive processes in the brain.* Cambridge, MA: MIT Press.

Wager, T. D., Phan, K. L., Liberzon, I., & Taylor, S. F. (2003). Valence, gender, and lateralization of functional brain anatomy in emotion: A meta-analysis of findings from neuroimaging. *NeuroImage, 19*, 513–531.

Winkielman, P., & Cacioppo, J. T. (2001). Mind at ease puts a smile on your face: Psychophysiological evidence that processing facilitation elicits positive affect. *Journal of Personality and Social Psychology, 81*, 989–1000.

Zajonc, R. B. (1980). Feeling and thinking: Preferences need no inferences. *American Psychologist, 35*, 151–175.

Subject index

www.ingramcontent.com/pod-product-compliance
Ingram Content Group UK Ltd.
Pitfield, Milton Keynes, MK11 3LW, UK
UKHW020354010325
455677UK00021B/451